FROM NIGERIA TO CRACKING WALNUTS

From Nigeria to Cracking Walnuts

The Itinerant Ecologist Series

MALCOLM MARKS

Coeur de Rose Publishing

This book is dedicated to all the people we knew in Calabar: students, colleagues and friends who together made our life so enjoyable, challenging and special. Our life has been enriched by learning from and exchanging with so many people of so many nationalities.

Our dear Aunt, Henriette (*Canou*) Pervilhac, finally succumbed to her cancer in May 2021, aged 80, and went to re-join her family in Heaven. Her passing occurred on the day that I was making the final edits to the text. Thank you, dear Canou, for giving me the idea and the impetus to write my first book.

Coeur de Rose Publishing

162 Chemin de la Touvière,

Rix, 01680, France

This book is part of a four-part autobiography series, The Itinerant Ecologist, by Malcolm Marks. The description of events has been honestly portrayed to the best of the author's memory.

This is the first edition of *From Nigeria to Cracking Walnuts*.

Copyright © 2023 by Malcolm Marks

All rights reserved. No part of this book may be reproduced in any manner whatsoever without written permission except in the case of brief quotations embodied in critical articles and reviews.

For information, contact:

Malcolm Marks, 162 Chemin de la Touvière,

Rix, 01680, France.

Coeur de Rose Publishing paperback edition August 2023

Designed by Melanie Marks Purnode

Edited by Melanie Marks Purnode and Emma Pomfret

Manufactured in Europe

~ 1 ~

NOSTALGIA AIN'T WHAT IT USED TO BE

The café table is covered with a plastic tablecloth that has seen better days. The remains of dried ketchup (at least it looks like ketchup) shines dully from the far corner and something brown and murky lies at the bottom of the discarded cup that sits in front of me. The tin ashtray overflows with the short remains of roll-up cigarettes and the saucer has served to stub out yet more.

"Two teas and a coffee, please" my supervisor asks of the waitress who wipes ineffectually at the table with a cloth that seems even more unsavoury than its target. At least the murky mix in the cup and the smelly ashtray disappear from their dominating positions in front of us.

Our waitress, a pretty, rather plump, middle-aged lady, has the most stunning appearance: her skin tone is black and shiny, her hair is braided with each strand sporting a red bead at its end and her smile helps to melt some of the nerves that are twisting in my stomach. Behind her the café is already busy but more and more customers are crowding in out of the rain while the volume of their chatter goes up in unison. As an accompaniment to the café's clamour, the road outside, separated from us by thin glass windows and a pavement, has a continuous stream of traffic; each vehicle seeming to honk a greeting as it goes by. In the background sirens are welcoming the mid-afternoon bustle.

Are we already in Nigeria? Perhaps central Lagos or my ultimate destination of Calabar? Not in the least, I have only managed to get as far as the Mile End Road in East London, in a café that sits across from the tube station's entrance. We are in June 1979, a few days from my 26th birthday, and the most important day of my academic life.

At the table with me is the bearded and bespectacled shape of my supervisor, himself only a decade older than me and just as nervous. But he is already an accomplished academic with a growing reputation in plant eco-physiology that will later lead him to join the brain drain to the U.S. and a professorship at the University of Maryland. Making up our trio in such an insalubrious setting is a renowned professor of plant physiology from another college of the University of London. The professor is a British national of German origin who came to the UK in the late 1930s, just before the outbreak of the Second World War. While speaking a most impeccable English in a soft, almost whispering voice, he retains his heavy, native accent. Because of the café's bustle and his quiet tone of voice, he is practically impossible to hear despite sitting right next to me.

While both my supervisor and I are in a high state of nerves, mine are off the scale and I am almost petrified. That is because today is the day that three-and-a-half years of effort, sacrifice and student poverty *should* be coming to an end. Today I am defending my doctorate thesis that looks at the physiological ecology of wild lettuce. My research has attempted, pretty successfully we believe, to explain the role of several physiological reactions, that I have uncovered and investigated during laboratory work, in helping the species to survive and thrive in the wild. Real Darwinism in action. Yes, I do realise that it does not sound as sexy as researching a cure for a terrible disease or even as glamorous as finding a saline-resistant strain of rice to feed the developing world but well ... it was a topic that the Science Research Council was prepared to support with a grant and one of the few available at my *alma mater* London University's Queen Mary College. Anyway, in comparison to one of my buddies who spends his time counting the heartbeats of snails, or of the lady in the lab next door to him who counts the number of rings on fish scales – to what end I never learnt – I think my topic is not too bad. And so is that of my lab mate who is also researching wild lettuce but his work seems to be mostly measuring plants along the motorways of middle England.

But more seriously, the primary aim of PhD work is to train the student in a variety of disciplines rather than adding enormously to the scientific knowledge of humanity. Should discoveries occur, that is an added bonus; and a potential career boost to both the lucky student and his supporting supervisor.

I am my supervisor's second PhD student but, for various reasons, I am the first to reach the stage of writing, submitting and now defending my thesis. In fact, a difficult first few months aside, I found my research increasingly fascinating as results were collected in both the laboratory and the field. As an experienced naturalist, especially in botany and ornithology, I loved the fieldwork aspects that took me on a biweekly basis to the Queen Mary research station near Brentwood, where I had established a colony of wild lettuces in an abandoned field. But while fieldwork is the perfect way to get the London smoke out of my lungs, it is the analyses of results from field and laboratory work that proves both the most challenging and the most stimulating.

Rather like an artist who starts by facing an empty canvas and gradually turns it into a wonderful landscape, slowly but surely the secrets of the wild ancestor of the humble lettuce started to be revealed to us. And, as time passed and more and more of the plant's secrets were revealed, the stimulation of my work grew exponentially until I found I was spending almost every waking hour reflecting just what the newest set of results might mean and how they would fit into the wider botanical puzzle. Anyone who has not experienced such a 'data rush' will not have the faintest idea of the sentiment I am talking about! My lovely and patient wife, Véronique, loves to tell the story of us sitting down to lunch during one such eureka moment (as she prefers to call them) when I suddenly put down my knife and fork, without a word, leaving (coincidentally or was it the catalyst of fate?) a lettuce salad sitting on my plate and ran to our bedroom where my writing desk stood cramped in the corner next to the window. While Véronique continued her leisurely lunch, I started to scribble rapidly and the words that I automatically wrote revealed one of the great secrets of not only the wild lettuce but also of many other similar plant species. That secret, perhaps of little interest to the vast majority of the population, was to my supervisor and I, and the rest of our laboratory, a very exciting discovery.

Just about every thesis worth looking at will contain some new information, new techniques or new theories. Mine, offers the first published proof that cold stimulation of flowering can be reversed not only in the laboratory (which was hypothesised for one or two species) but, interestingly (for plant physiologists and ecologists of course) that it can also be reversed in nature. Further, it shows why wild lettuce, in common with a few hundred other UK species, need to undergo a period of cold stimulation in order for flowering and seed production to occur within the period of our relatively short growing season in the UK.

My thesis was completed just after Christmas 1978, peer reviewed and proof-read internally at Queen Mary College, typed up (yes, no computers at that time), all graphs drawn by hand with pen, ink and stencils, and the finished item taken off to be leather-bound. Our bank manager kindly allowed a few hundred pounds of overdraft to cover the printing and binding process.

In early 1979, with bound copies in hand, my University requested the eminent professor, sitting in the café with us, to expert-review the thesis and to conduct the traditional *viva* or oral exam which precedes the award of a doctorate. Unfortunately, for his own reasons, he was not available to conduct the viva for the next several months; meaning lost time before I could begin working and earning any reasonable income. But at least I had a job offer ...

In mid-1978, when the end of my research was in sight, I started to search out future work opportunities. My ambition was to be an ecology lecturer and, to this end, I began the thankless task of job applications. Mostly this involved a mad scramble each week to be the first in the staff common room to grab the latest editions of New Scientist, Nature and the Times Higher Education supplement. Just very occasionally, a vacant post was advertised but most of those adverts were clearly written for a targeted person and not an unknown, yet to graduate, postgraduate student specialising in wild lettuce. This was an incredibly hard time to get a decent job that merited the efforts and level of education while paying a reasonable salary. That period in the late 70s saw cutbacks in budgets of universities and the easiest cuts could be made by simply not replacing staff. Many of my research colleagues sadly drifted out of the sciences and into jobs for which they were over-qualified or not qualified at all: pharmaceutical reps, schoolteachers, estate agents, and so forth.

On many occasions in the more recent past, my kids have told me: "you had it so much easier than us Dad" but as I write this sentence, I am doing a Google search based on 'International Job Vacancies' and get 177 million hits. However, in the computer dark ages of the late 70s, no internet meant, of course, no Devex delivered to email boxes each week. Job searching was a very tough proposition and required real flexibility, and just about all the best possibilities came via word of mouth.

I am lucky in having a French wife who is not over-attached to either London or the UK. So when my undergraduate mycology (fungus to you) lecturer told me that he had just been appointed Head of the Department of Biology at the University of Papua New Guinea and that there were some more junior vacancies to be filled, we said "why not?".

Murphy's Law of course states very clearly that when you have waited long enough for a bus, three are sure to arrive at the same time. Similarly, for jobs, because not only was there the opportunity in PNG, but the weekly scramble for the New Scientist turned up an advert from the University of Juba, South Sudan. This university was founded just a few years earlier and was now looking to expand. And finally, while chatting over coffee with Peter Wanstall, a smashing person and a real old-fashioned botanist, I told him about my hopes for a job in Papua New Guinea or South Sudan. He asked if I might not be interested in a job at a Nigerian University. Well, why not keep my options open?

It turns out that Peter had spent time in Nigeria during pre-Independence days and had enjoyed the experience and thought that I might too. He had recently heard that the military junta who had been in power in Nigeria since 1966 had drawn up a new constitution, based on the Westminster format, and elections were being held as we were speaking. The new constitution stipulates that each state of Nigeria shall be represented by a minister and, importantly, each state shall have at least one university. Since there are currently 19 states, and prior to the signing of the new constitution, there were only eight universities (in the towns of Benin, Ibadan, Ile-Ife, Kaduna, Jos, Lagos, Nsukka and Zaria) there is a rush to get new universities formed as has occurred recently in Kano and Calabar. But on what basis? The new universities, starting from scratch, are initially cannibalising staff from existing universities by, for example, offering them promotions. But all this has achieved is to create vacancies across the entire Nigerian university sector. However, since there is a government promise to keep, and Nigeria is fast becoming a pretty rich country having the majority of its economy based on oil, university recruiters have gone global. Just to give an idea, the international oil price doubled between 1978 and 1980, and 1980 was the year that oil reached its highest ever inflation adjusted level of almost $120 per barrel in today's money. To cope with the rising demand for university staff, the Nigerian government set up recruitment offices in cities such as Delhi, London and Washington DC with the aim of attracting young as well as experienced expatriates to move to Nigerian universities.

The application form I recently completed had a list of all universities looking for new staff. Applicants were asked to tick the boxes of those universities they were interested in. I ticked the lot and within a week received a call from the Universities' office inviting me for an interview in central London for the University of Calabar. I have few recollections of the interview process, so it cannot have been too horrendous, but I do remember three things from that day. First, the polite interviewers asking me to describe the areas I would like to teach (plant ecology and physiology); second, whether I could start in October 1979 (yes, most certainly), and third whether I had any questions to ask them.

Of course, what all job-seekers are *really* interested in is the salary, but I thought better to leave that until later, and so instead I asked which aspects of my application had interested the University of Calabar the most. Was it my research interests? My publication history or perhaps my teaching interests?

The answer was none of the above. The lead interviewer instead told me in all seriousness "Your application stood out because we heard that the University of Kano were going to make you an offer."

So the cut-throat competition for staff had left Nigeria and was strong and thriving in W10!

A few days later I received my acceptance letter and an offer of a Lecturer II position at the grand salary of Naira 400 per month, plus 25% expatriate allowance (15% of which was to be retained until the end of contract). Not a fortune clearly, but it was based on the Nigerian Universities' salary scale. In 1979 with the Nigerian economy floating on a sea of oil, the Naira was almost equivalent to the UK pound. Today 500 Naira will only buy you a single pound coin. And that is not because the UK economy has boomed during the last 40 years, far from it but rather because the Nigerian economy has failed to profit from all its massive oil income.

So with a completed thesis, a job in my pocket, and a lovely wife happy to leave Blighty with me for distant shores; I was set to meet with the eminent professor for the viva. In early 1979, my university sent a package to the professor containing not only a copy of the bound thesis but also two peer-reviewed scientific papers that my supervisor and I had already written from the lettuce research and had published in the highly reputable *New Phytologist* journal. At that time, perhaps it still is, it was relatively rare for a student at the end of his doctorate research to have already published two high-level papers and we had three further ones from my thesis in development; reasons to be confident.

My supervisor had suggested this particular professor because he was working on vernalization and devernalization and, 20 years previously, had suggested – but not proven – that Chrysanthemums are likely to undergo natural vernalization and devernalization, just as I have proven with wild lettuce. Although lettuce and chrysanthemums belong to the same botanical family they do have different life cycles.

Anyway, after a long wait, we finally hear back from the professor setting a date for the viva in June; what frustration to have to wait almost six months when all we want to do is get on with our new life. Despite patience never being one of my greatest virtues, I settle down to wait for the big day and am lucky enough to have some teaching assignments proposed by the university to fill my time and help pay my way.

Finally, the big day arrives and at a few minutes to 2 pm, my supervisor and I pick up our copies of the thesis and notepads and start our trip to the meeting. On leaving our laboratory, best wishes ring out from my two fellow PhD students and our laboratory technician.

"See you in the student bar at 6 pm Mr Marks" they shout in chorus with the emphasis firmly on the Mister.

On the walk down from our sixth floor in the university, my supervisor makes all the right sounds, knowing that before any serious event like conference presentations, I get nervous: "relax, you have an interesting and good thesis. Don't forget that several people have checked through it for you. Many of your findings are original and supported by strong statistics. The professor will be really interested in what you have found." Thank goodness I do not have any forewarning of what is soon to occur.

My supervisor opens the door to the designated room within the Mile End Road campus and stands back to let me enter before him. Since students usually only go through a PhD viva once in a lifetime, this is obviously a unique occurrence for me and only a second for my supervisor who had previously only attended his own viva around ten years previously at the University of Lancaster – so I am unsure what to expect. But what I am not expecting is the cold reception from such an eminent professor. He remains seated behind the interview table, grudgingly shakes our hands, and curtly says "sit".

My supervisor and I exchange glances. What has happened here? So, of course, we sit!

My supervisor opens the interview. "Prof. may I present my PhD student Malcolm Marks? He has been working in my laboratory since 1975 and has produced what we consider to be a very strong and interesting thesis."

To which I add "thank you for giving your valuable time to review my thesis and for having agreed to be my external examiner for this viva."

"Yes, my time is valuable so let's get on with this interview as I have a train to catch back to my College" retorts the eminent professor doing absolutely nothing to settle my poor nerves and certainly starting the butterflies flapping in my supervisor.

"So, starting at page 1" and he reads out the text in his heavily Germanic English accent. Getting to the third sentence he announces "I would like to see this sentence split in two. Then you need to put a comma after the fifth word of the sentence ..." And so he drones on. For fully fifteen minutes he reads down the first three pages commenting on every word and every punctuation mark.

If the situation was not so serious for me, I would have happily nodded off. I assume that my supervisor is feeling the same. To relieve the boredom, I do some rapid mental arithmetic. If he is taking fifteen minutes to go through the grammar of the first three pages, then it will take him more than seventy times fifteen minutes to process all 220 pages of my thesis. That should see us finish up the interview sometime tomorrow lunchtime; providing we work right through the night. Oh my God!

My supervisor tries to interpose in the monologue of punctuation marks by asking "Prof. did you enjoy reading the thesis, do you have questions specific to the context of the findings, for example the vernalization and devernalization aspects in which we believe you are likely to be the most interested?"

"We will get to all that in due course, if you will let me continue. Now on page 4 ..."

On and on until at 2.45 pm the fire alarm starts ringing and stops his slow deliberate reading of the text. My supervisor suggests that we wait a couple of minutes to see if the ringing stops as this is likely only a practice. But a few moments later there is heavy knocking and one of my fellow PhD student's embarrassed face appears around the door.

"The IRA have issued a bomb warning for the university and the police are evacuating everyone, sorry but you have to leave the building. The police will provide an all-clear when it is safe to come back in."

During the 70s, the IRA were very active in England with many bombs placed and several exploding in the centre of London, killing and maiming innocent bystanders. Areas that were particularly targeted were where the public gathered *en masse*. So train stations and the Underground were frequently targeted, including Stepney Green which is only a short walk from the university.

So we troop outside, but rather than waiting to see if we might soon be allowed back into the building, the respectable professor simply announces "right, that's it then, I'm off to Mile End Station," and indeed off he strides.

Luckily it is almost a mile from the university to the station and so we have enough time to catch him up and literally beg him to find a different solution. Having required almost six months to get him to this meeting, there is no way that he is going to escape us so easily; hence my supervisor's quick-witted suggestion of taking a cup of tea in the transport café.

Here we are then, back at the table with the plastic tablecloth. Our teas and the coffee are now cold on the table in front of us and the general pandemonium on the main road is dying down along with the police sirens. Five pm has already passed so the café is thinning out as people start making their way home. We have managed to get to the end of the main body of the thesis and are now looking through the appendices.

Then suddenly "OK, fine" says the eminent professor looking at his watch. "I am interested in what you have said about osmotically distended seeds but feel that you did not research the biochemical causes sufficiently well."

Osmotic distension is an unusual reaction of lettuce seeds in waterlogged conditions in which the seeds become distended (bloated) and lose viability (die). I had theorised that this reaction to wet conditions might help, at least partially, to explain why the wild lettuce is not found in waterlogged or marshy conditions. I provide some experimental evidence of conditions in the laboratory that cause such distension but have not gone into the biochemical changes that occur within the seeds during and after distension. We considered that this is outside the scope of my research – and frankly there was enough work to do without going down a blind alley.

"But," my supervisor attempts to interject, "that aspect is only of passing interest to the body of the thesis and really I am surprised that you have said nothing about the excellent work in the laboratory on inducing flowering by low temperatures and the reversal of that process, and especially the fact that Malcolm shows not only that the phenomenon also occurs in the field, and this is already a first, but its ecological importance to the survival of the species. Are you not interested in those aspects?"

"Hrumpf, I will only pass this thesis when I have received some additional research on the biochemical causes of osmotic distension. Gentlemen goodbye."

He stands up, walks out the door and strides across the road disappearing into the mouth of the tube station. This is the last time I ever see the eminent professor.

My supervisor's eyes are full of sympathy. I believe he takes this reaction almost as badly as me. After all, we have worked together closely for almost four years and the efforts I have made have been pretty much under his guidance and support.

"Malcolm, I want you to look on the positives, OK? It's annoying that you will have to do a little extra work but the whole department will support you and you should be able to complete this in a month or so."

But I think he is missing the biggest deception, or perhaps he is just trying to show his sympathy and friendship. What really gnaws at me is that all the new findings that are reported in the thesis – especially the time and effort spent unravelling the role of vernalization and devernalization in the field; aspects that really impact the survival of the species – have been totally ignored during a four-hour stint bickering over whether this sentence is too long or that sentence lacks a comma. I feel hurt that three years and more of my life, where I have certainly worked as hard as I ever have, can be summed up in a handful of punctuation marks. Surely this is not what serious research is about and especially this is not the role of distinguished professors?

As we walk the mile back from the tube station to the university, I begin to calm down and start to plan the needs of the next few months: which aspects of the distended seeds do I need to look at? Who do I need to talk too about analysing the biochemical aspects (a relatively new area for me)? Practically, what do I need to do to my leather-bound thesis in order to add in all those wretched commas? But the hardest part for me is how to break what I consider terrible and humiliating news to Véronique. She has been so supportive and patient with me during our four years together, and I am certainly not worried about any reflections from her side but simply how to deal with the disappointment she will feel for me, and the shock that she will know has been delivered to my pride.

Véronique and I had met literally a week before the start of my final BSc exams. Back in late-May 1975, my then flat mates, Rob and Robert, both economics students at QMC, and two of the nicest people that I have ever known, were also gearing up for their finals. So we had decided to let our hair down for one last time and spend the evening on the town before concentrating one hundred percent on revision. Although Rob is English, he grew up in Paris where his father works at a fashion house, and so is fluent in French both orally and in his behaviour. He is a great influence on me because, as a true friend, he has been able to chip away at my English stiff upper lip – read shyness – at least as far as the ladies are concerned! Robert, on the other hand, is seven or eight years older than us and so brings a level of sophistication to our behaviour that is lacking in two 22-year olds. The fact that he is very handsome and owns a Morgan motorcar adds to his air of sophistication and popularity.

Where to go tonight? "La Poubelle of course," says Rob.

La Poubelle (or The Dustbin to us English) is a night club – actually a disco in 70s jargon – in Piccadilly. Us lads have been there a couple of times in the past but it is a fair distance from our flat near to Turnpike Lane tube station and is expensive on a student budget. However, for this one last night out before the exam crunch, why not?

So off we go to the club and after buying our pints and finding a seat, Rob notices two girls dancing around their handbags, as is the habit of many women at this time.

"I know your taste in ladies, so you dance with the slim one and I'll ask her friend." And as they say, 'the rest is history'. Véronique and I were together from that evening on. Véro proves to be a completely different character to me. While I have a tendency to be a bit shy and reserved and do not like rapid change nor to stand out in a crowd, she is an extrovert with a capital E and loves, in fact seeks out, change. I had never known anyone quite like her and laugh when I think of the 'polar bear' coat that she loves to wear as she goes across London on the Underground to her work. This coat is quite unique being so large, hairy and pure white that she almost disappears inside it. She is also a very caring lady, always thinking of others before herself. She is a far better linguist than me, having studied Italian and Spanish at *lycée* and has picked up a reasonable level of English during her one year in London as an *au pair* to Sue, a top notch, freelance caterer based in Ealing. No matter our many differences, we click immediately and get married two years later in a beautiful summer ceremony in France. In 1982, after seven years to the exact day since we met in the dustbin, she gives me as an anniversary gift, a beautiful baby girl, Mélanie. A few years later our handsome son, David, joins the family.

So, a vicious circle of emotions is going round and round in my thoughts. I am sad for Véronique because I know that she will be even sadder for me.

Finally, our walk back from the tube station is complete and the university has reopened after its terrorist scare that proved a false alarm. I have only a single thought on my mind for today: get home and relax. However, after walking up to our laboratory to drop off books and notepads, I read a message, from my fellow students, propped up on a pile of petri dishes on my desk "Come down to the bar, everyone is here for you."

Is a drink really what I want? Perhaps not, however, it is what I need. Just to be on the safe side, I call home, explain events briefly to Véro and am told "see you later but go and get a drink at the bar first."

So with approval from the Minister of the Interior, off I go promising myself a quick pint before leaving. I traipse back down the stairs, past the squash courts, conveniently placed a few flights below my room, and into the QMC Student Bar. Oh My God, how can I face this crowd of friends and colleagues: postgraduate students, laboratory technicians and some of the younger lecturers who have all come to celebrate 'my success'.

As I walk across the bar towards my well-wishers, a beaming Geoff, the chief barman who has been pouring my pints for the last seven years, hands me a pint of Double Diamond and says "on the house *Dr Marks*." That single sweet gesture almost caused me to crack but, keeping my *sang-froid*, I slowly tell my friends that I have not quite made it and my supervisor weighs in with the frustrating details.

These are met with gasps of 'it's not possible!' 'I have never heard of that' and one or two of the more senior lecturers present tell me gently 'leave it with us.'

As always happens in student bars, sympathy leads to kindness and kindness leads from one pint to the next so that by 8.30 pm the entire contingent of forlorn souls is beginning to warm and brighten up. With the downing of the pints also comes the tightening of the bladder and trips downstairs to the toilets. While standing at the urinal and looking up (I know, it's better to watch your shoes), I reread for the umpteenth time the graffiti on the wall:

'Nostalgia ain't what it used to be'

How true I think, laughing so loud that I surprise one of my mates as he makes his way out of the loo. By the time I get back to the bar, the word has gone around that 'Dr Marks has re-found his spark' and it is therefore time for people to start drifting home. Boy, what a day this has been!

The trip home on the bus to Culford Road in Dalston goes in a flash as I read through my notes from the interview. I do not even notice our progress through Hackney and past the Dalston railway station. But as I get off the bus on the Balls Pond Road, I notice that the Greek butcher, right next to the bus stop, is still displaying sheep's testicles in a metal tray in his shop window. Despite seeing them every day that I pass his window, I have never plucked up the courage to ask him if this is Greek humour due to the name of the road or a great Greek delicacy. Given his blood-stained apron, large biceps, shaven head, chest hairs sprouting over the top of his vest, and his permanent 5 o'clock shadow, I am never likely to ask.

Turning left into Culford Road, the pub-theatre is advertising its next event for the coming weekend; we will go, it's always fun even if not always very professional. Although the paper shop opposite the pub brought down its shutters several hours ago, my friend Gino who runs an amazing Italian delicatessen on the corner of Warburton Close, is only just now closing up. A relatively new immigrant to the UK, he works his socks off to succeed; no forty-hour week for him. I have nothing but respect for Gino and his wife. He turns as I call out my goodnight and says that his son, Paulo, cannot wait for me to take him to the Gunners' next home game. Despite being only nine, Paulo is one of the Arsenal's most dedicated supporters and since Gino works such long hours 'uncle Malcolm' takes him frequently to matches. Even when we cannot make a match, the cheers and groans of the Highbury crowd carries easily to Culford Road and tells us which team has just scored. But I have never told Paulo two important facts: first, I am a rugby player and have rarely played football, and second, if pressed for my favourite team, it is Leeds United.

A hundred metres further down the road I turn into the gate of our little garden apartment and Véro is already at the door to greet me. There is no visible sign of a rolling pin or heavy skillet, so I know that I have not stayed out too long. Joking aside, she is of course so sympathetic that I feel that she is the one suffering and not me. A few expletives and we decide to put the interview on to the backburner.

The combination of a few pints of Double Diamond in the bar, a good meal at home and a lot of love and kindness means that I sleep like a log and awake fresh to the clamour of the alarm clock. After a quick shower and shave, I am back to the bus stop on the Balls Pond Road to see what this new day will bring.

As soon as I walk into my room, the internal phone rings and the departmental secretary says "Hi Malcolm, Prof asks if you are free to meet with him now." The face behind the 'Prof' is none other than the Head of the School of Biology at Queen

Mary College and a most eminent geneticist in his own right. He is also a thoroughly nice man to all his students and I have had excellent relations with him throughout my time at QMC. Thus to be requested to a meeting with him so soon after the turmoil of yesterday causes me no additional worries.

His suite of offices are two floors down; conveniently opposite the staff coffee room. The outer office is the domain of his two secretaries. The more senior of the ladies is the Guardian of Access to the inner sanctum of the professor. Although she may seem to unannounced visitors a bit scary, she is in fact a lovely, caring lady. Her more junior colleague is the lady who kindly typed out my thesis; she is not much older than me and a real sweetheart to the postgraduate community and known for her kindness and patience.

"Sorry to hear about yesterday, Malcolm. Prof. is waiting for you now." So bad news travels quickly.

I knock and enter Prof's room. I am a relatively frequent visitor here as for the last couple of years I have served as the postgraduate representative on the School of Biology's board as well as being the organiser of the School's Christmas parties. I suspect that I am probably better known in that role.

"Good morning boyo", the Prof's voice rings out in its appealing Welsh accent, "come and sit down and tell me what happened yesterday."

My eyes flash across the second door in his office that is marked 'REM Room'. REM stands for Rapid Eye Movement and was apparently an academic prank played by the three biology professors when the architects had been drawing up the plans for this new biology building into which we moved in late 1975; near to the start of my PhD research. REM occurs when we are asleep and so this room was to be where the professor could take a nap after lunch. I never saw across the threshold and so do not know to this day what actually goes on behind that door. It is probably only a convenient toilet. But then I digress.

I give him a rapid resume of the events starting with a broad outline of the way that the interview proceeded with the emphasis on punctuation rather than the contents of the thesis, and the news that I must do some extra research if I am to be awarded my PhD. I drop in the facts of the bomb scare, emergency evacuation of the university, and the hours spent in the transport café as factors that I believe may have caused my interview not to have proceeded in the usual manner.

But the Professor is not only a very intelligent man but also a wily candidate; and he was not going to be bluffed by me.

"Come on now, a bit earlier I heard from your supervisor and he was not quite as accommodating as you. Frankly he was flabbergasted at the way the interview passed and we are thinking of putting in an official protest. What's more, I got waylaid by a zoology lecturer during my walk from the station, and even he is angry on your behalf. I even heard the words 'unprofessional conduct' from a third party. So please tell me, in confidence if you like, what happened yesterday."

"OK sir, it would be easy to say that my interview went badly because of academic jealousy. After all I am only a student but was able to prove a physiological reaction in the field that the examiner had suggested twenty-odd years ago *might* occur but he had never proven it."

"Ah, now you are starting to tell me the same thing as the others!"

"But Prof. I don't believe that this was the case." He begins to interrupt but I politely raise my hand so that he will let me finish. "What I believe is that for one reason or another he forgot to read my thesis before the interview and so probably only started reading it during the 30-minute ride on public transport to QMC. His emphasis on reading the more than 220 pages of thesis, line-by-line, and critiquing punctuation rather than content seems to indicate to me that we were dealing with one very embarrassed professor who did not know the thesis contents."

"I appreciate the slant you are putting on this Malcolm first because I know how upset you must be and so it would be understandable if you were feeling resentful but second because it will help save me from having to make a complaint to another London University's college. So what to do next? You probably know that I wanted to get an Oxford Don in as your external examiner?"

Before becoming Professor of Biology at QMC, he had been an eminent Don at Oxford and still had very strong ties with his old university.

Taking a breath, he continues "but your supervisor wanted this professor with relevant research to yours but there is nothing to stop us now going my preferred route and you passing the viva exam another time. I can arrange someone to come quickly too. Wouldn't that be preferable?"

And of course he is right. For the sake of simplicity, we could get someone else in and I could be awarded my PhD more rapidly than undertaking yet more research and that in a relatively unfamiliar area of biology to me.

However, I surprise myself by replying "Prof. you have always looked out for me and I appreciate immensely all that you have done in the past but you know my pride took a bashing yesterday and in the very near future I am off to start a new job as a lecturer and I want to know in my heart that I earnt my PhD."

He chuckles and says "we all thought that would be your response! So a bit earlier I spoke to Viv Moses about the extra work you must do and he is waiting for you to drop by and will help you as much as possible. Let me know if there is any more I can do. Goodbye now."

With that we shake hands, I express my thanks and walk out past the two secretaries who both give me radiant and knowing smiles. There are few secrets at university.

It is moments like these, I mean the time I just spent with the professor, that I recognise the love of a person for his work. He really cares for his students and always treats them as equals even though, like me, we are light years apart in academic and intellectual achievements. This is one of the many kindnesses that he has shown me. I remember back to the third year of my undergraduate days when he insisted in meeting individually with all graduating students to chat through their ambitions for the future and also to suggest possible career avenues, even to help if needed. Why could the university career officers not have been so useful?

When it was my turn to meet with him in 1975, he already knew that Peter Wanstall had spoken to me about doing PhD research on chestnut woodlands, just north of London, while my future supervisor, in the neighbouring laboratory, had suggested joining his group to work on wild lettuce.

His opening statement was therefore a little bit of a shock to this nervous undergraduate "why the hell do you want to stay here for your PhD? You should go to Oxford."

"I would love that sir but I have neither a place nor the funds to undertake research there."

"Oh, is that all? If I find you a place would you be interested?"

"Of course I would Prof!"

With that he picks up his phone, dials a number and says "Give me Harley". Just by way of introduction, Harley or Professor John Harley is the Head of the Department of Forestry Science at Oxford University and just about the top in his field.

"John? Alan. I'm with my best ecology undergraduate and he wants to do a PhD in forestry at Oxford. What do you have for him? Ah-ha, OK, so you have a new lecturer with a grant available to look at shrub colonisation of chalk-lands in the Downs. Does my boy have a chance? No problem, he'll get it? Great. OK, give me his telephone number and I'll get my lad to give him a call. Thanks John, bye, you too."

The Prof. hands me a slip of paper with a name and an Oxford area phone number and says "get on with it then." A few minutes later, I am in a public phone kiosk in the quiet basement of the old QMC building discussing meeting up in Oxford the following week. To cut a long story short, I go, we meet, we chat, he offers me the position and I accept. Job done, Oxford here I come. This is May 1975.

A few weeks after that I meet Véro for the first time in *La Poubelle* and, while dancing (still around the handbag, of course) I proudly tell her that I am to be a postgraduate student at the University of Oxford. We begin discussing life in Oxford and those discussions go on into August. Everything in my world looks really great. I am in love, I have achieved a good degree result in biology, I have a research post at Oxford.

Véro goes back to her parents' home in the medieval village of Crémieu for the summer. They live about an hour's drive from Lyon in the countryside and she needs to tell them that she has met an Englishman.

"*Sacré bleu, tu dis un anglais ma bichette*", I hear her father say while her mum will clear her throat, in her very own way of showing disapproval.

Never one to be put off from the course she has decided, Véro then states "and I am going back to England in September to be with him."

In my turn, I go off with a rather heavy heart for a vacation in Crete with a university buddy. We reserved and paid for the trip several months previously but I would far rather be in Crémieu, of course.

A week into the Crete holiday we wander along a clifftop path and spot below us an isolated beach with a few dozen tourists and locals. An idyllic location with clean sand and bright turquoise water.

Suddenly, there is much screaming and shouting from further along the beach and we see a child, a young girl of around eight or ten, we believe, holding on to a lilo that is getting blown out to sea. The lilo turns over and over but the young girl holds on tenaciously. At the same time, we see a man jump into the sea, start swimming and try to catch up with her. But with the speed of the wind, he is falling further and further behind. About a mile offshore is an island and the child sees it. She lets go of the lilo and swims the hundred metres or so to the island. The man however, being so much lower down than us, can only see the lilo's progression as it flips over in the wind and goes further and further out to sea. He cannot see that the girl has dropped off the lilo nor that she is now safe on the island. What eventually happened to her frantic dad that we see continuing to swim out to sea? We never learn. That scene haunts me to this day.

Back in UK after the vacation in Crete, I am staying at my parent's home in Coxheath, a village outside of Maidstone. The phone rings. "It's for you Malc" says my mum "someone from your university."

"Hello, Malcolm Marks here."

"Malcolm, it's Prof. at QMC. I have some dreadful news to share with you. The lecturer at Oxford with whom you were to do your PhD has died. I do not know the details but it seems he died on vacation .... I believe trying to save his child."

Chill fingers wrap around my heart. Could it have been? To this day, I have never learnt the truth. And the last thing on my mind was a thought for my own future that was now being thrown into turmoil.

Breaking through my thoughts the professor continues "we want you to know that we are all feeling for you and that the department has a grant available from the Science Research Council and it's for you if you want it. But sorry, I need a response straight away because if you are not interested we will offer it to the next person on our list."

What to say at such a time? "Thanks sir, I would be honoured to be a PhD student in your department."

"Good, that's settled then. Give your supervisor a ring and chat details with him."

My daydreaming is arrested as I arrive at Viv Moses' office door at the other end of the corridor. To be honest, Professor Vivian Moses is rather a hero of mine although I have not interacted with him to the same extent as with the head of department. Viv is world famous having been part of the US-based team that unravelled the biochemical processes of photosynthesis; the so-called Krebs Cycle. But despite this global reputation, he is a rather unassuming person and always kind and available to students. I get to see him immediately and he tells me that one of his research assistants will be helping me get to grips with the additional research I must perform. He first proposes that I should do a crash course in paper chromatography – "here's an article on it" – and also that there is a piece of sophisticated machinery in the neighbouring Chemistry Department that has been blocked for me to use. Within two hours of arriving this morning it appears that the entire department has mobilised for me.

The extra research takes me about four weeks to complete, then write-up and get typed out. The beautiful bound copies of my original thesis are back with the Binders who open them up, insert the new section and close everything up again. I then undertake the task of adding in all the additional commas, breaking sentences and rewriting small sections; which rather spoils the appearance of my thesis. But when completed, the finished product goes back to my examiner, and I wait with fingers crossed. A few weeks later a simple letter is returned stating that I have cleared the last hurdle. Degree awarded.

I make a quick round of the department to thank all those great friends and colleagues who have gone out of their way to help me, and we are ready to get on with the move to Nigeria, now timed for September 1979.

~ 2 ~

IN NIGERIA, ANYTHING IS POSSIBLE

Preparations, preparations, preparations. It's all very well deciding to go off to work and live in a foreign country; many people do it, but to Africa, especially to Nigeria and in 1979 too? *Complètement fou* as the French say and indeed did say to us, and on several different occasions! Luckily we are young, naïve, energetic and, importantly, do not have children at this time.

But in reality, once push comes to shove, we do start to have some serious doubts. The furthest away from UK and France that we have both been is Greece and then only for short vacations. We start making separate lists and then compare notes before combining them into a single to-do list, and here we go:

Véronique: needs to give notice for her job and to start working out what we need to take with us and have the space to pack.

Me: to start the process of getting our apartment rented out, get our air tickets and miscellaneous charge orders (for additional baggage) from the Nigerian University Office, ensure that the University of Calabar is still expecting us! And fix appointments for the required jabs; there seem an awful lot of them that are being recommended: cholera, typhoid, smallpox, yellow fever, gamma (ouch my butt) globulin, and on goes the list.

Both of us: pack and send as much baggage in advance as possible to Nigeria, and say goodbye to parents and friends in the UK and France.

All that sounds relatively easy, some of it is, but remember we are living in the land of the dinosaur with no internet/emails to do our work for us nor even mobile phones since they did not start being used in the UK until about 1985.

Véro gets on with her chores in her usual efficient manner that seems to involve a lot of chatting with a lot of people but always bears positive results. So, by the end of her day at work, she has given notice to the *Compagnie Française de Pétrole* in Cavendish Square that had recently been swallowed by Total Oil & Marine; a date and venue set for her going away evening and been asked by the head of office what she would like as a leaving present ('a travel trunk please'). That travel trunk will come in very useful, as you will see. We will worry about packing over the coming weekends.

I start on the details of renting out our little garden apartment in Culford Road but first I have to contact the Halifax Building Society for approval to proceed with the rental before we contact potential rental agencies.

I am well known at our local Halifax branch, on Holloway Road, because back in 1975 when Véro and I first set up home together we had rented a grotty, with a capital G, apartment in Tabley Road in the shadow of the Holloway Ladies (*sic*) Prison. That flat had two major advantages. First, it was cheap – so we could save – and second, it was so grotty that it challenged us to get out as quickly as possible.

Without wishing to put my readers off their appetites for the next week, we shared a toilet on the landing of our floor with an Irish *'gentleman'* who was fond of Guinness and had a terrible aim. Our bathroom was also shared with the two apartments on the floor below and we put coins into the meter to get hot water for an eventual bath, providing no-one else stole the water before we arrived. On the ground floor were a friendly, middle-aged couple from Barbados who loved cooking dried fish and home-prepared fermented yam; no more said.

Soon after arriving at the apartment that I had found while Véro was still in France, Véro asked "why do we not buy a flat ourselves?"

For me, this was foreign territory. My parents have always lived in a council house and buying was something that rich people did. So after an initial list of objections against the proposal which included "we will never get a mortgage with me on a student grant and you on an entry-level salary." But as often happens, when I am faced with a new idea, I mull it over with stubborn logic for a few days and then get excited over possibilities.

So, on the following Saturday, we traipse into the local Halifax and ask what we need to do to get a mortgage.

"Do you have an account with us sir?" asks the smart young man behind the counter.

"Actually, no", I admit.

"OK, then the first move is to open an account." A few moments later the account is open and now contains fifty pounds. "Next" he asks "what sort of price are you thinking about paying for a property?"

"Wow", I say, "I have no idea at the moment."

"OK sir you will need to save at least 10% of the purchase price and be with us for a minimum of twelve months. So can I suggest that you do that, find a property and have the 10% in your account and then come back to talk with us?"

"Sounds like a plan, thank you." We leave the office feeling very pleased to have taken this first, important step.

Fast forward twelve months. We have been with the Halifax for a year, saving around one hundred pounds per month and so have some twelve hundred pounds in our account. We find a newly converted, small garden apartment in the upper class sounding area of de Beauvoir Town (sadly pronounced as Beaver by the older residents) priced at £11,000 (yes, really). A bit of quick negotiations via the estate agents and we get the price down to £10,000. If the younger generation of readers are already getting jealous, let me add that our would-be apartment is in the N1 postcode, yes really!

OK, ready to roll, and back to the Holloway branch of the Halifax.

Sadly, our smart young man has been promoted to another branch and we are faced with an older gentleman who looks like a used-car salesman; in fact, he is a cracking image of Dick Dastardly, waxed moustache and all.

"We have had an account with the Halifax for a year now and have saved enough to put a 10% deposit on a £10,000 apartment in de Beauvoir Town, can we now look to obtain a mortgage for £9,000 from the Halifax please?"

"OK", says Dick Dastardly (and I swear), twirls his moustache, "what are your professions?"

"Well my girlfriend is a secretary with a French oil company and I am a postgraduate student at London University." He gives a slight snigger after the word 'student' so I knew what was coming.

"And your annual incomes are? First the higher earner then the lower earner."

"Well Véronique earns £3,500 per annum and my grant is around £2,000."

"Oh dear" he says with a smirk, "we can only allow two times the highest earner and half the second income; and by my calculation that makes a maximum loan of £8,000. Better you come back when you have a proper job sir. Goodbye!"

What a let-down and what a nasty manner the creep has to shatter our dreams. So off we go to our grotty little flat in the shadows of Holloway Prison and I get out my best pen.

"What are you doing *mon chéri?*" asks Véro.

"Writing to the ruddy building society to complain" I reply. I sit and, after a couple of false starts, draft a polite letter addressed to the Chief General Manager of the Halifax Building Society, address: Halifax, Yorkshire. I tell him of our deception to be refused so nastily, asking him to check our account with the building society, to note that each month we have been saving more than the monthly repayments on the loan would be – despite paying rent – and ask him to project my earning capacity into the future, not to consider me today as a doctoral student. Well, wonders of wonders, within three days, not only do I receive a letter back from the Chief General Manager himself but he also says that he was impressed by our letter and so has spoken to the manager of a City-based branch. Kindly call and set up an appointment. I did and, a couple of days later, we are shown into a very plush office by a very smart gentleman wearing a suit that must have cost more than my annual grant.

Crazy to think back on this, but we spend an hour with him over tea and biscuits. He has a list of reasons why we would not be able to reimburse the loan; and we have sincere answers for all those issues.

By the end of the hour, he stands up and announces "I am as impressed with such a lovely young couple as my Chief General Manager, and so we have great pleasure in according your loan.

We will send approval through to your local branch and ask that you go there next week to sign the paperwork."

Wow! And am I looking forward to going back in to see Dick Dastardly!

We manage to buy our little love nest with the contract going through just in time for our wedding in 1977. We come back from our honeymoon in France and move into Culford Road the next day. Perfect timing.

But now is the moment, two years later, to start the rental process. First, we need the approval of the building society, and so return to speak to Dick Dastardly. This time, we are received with utmost politeness and a rapid approval with the sole proviso being that the rental amount must cover the mortgage. It does fivefold; such are rental costs in London. Once approval in place, Véro signs us up with a rental agency near to her office and the next day is couriered a list of appointments for Saturday starting at 9 am and continuing every fifteen minutes until 1 pm. Since we like the first couple who visit, we accept them and cancel the rest of the appointments.

A few days later our tickets and charge orders arrive from Nigerian Airways which stimulates a quick trip to The Army and Navy Store, the purchase of sailor duffel bags (you know, those sausage-shaped bags that you see wartime sailors carrying over their shoulders) and some padlocks to close them securely. We stuff our duffel bags with sheets, blankets, pillows and whatever else will go in and padlock them closed. The travel trunk, kindly provided by Véro's company as her going away present, receives not only my books and teaching papers but also cutlery, crockery, pots, pans and anything else that we can fit in including a French-style pharmacy bag. The French as a nation are rampant hypochondriacs and most carry around an unbelievable collection of out-of-date prescription drugs, creams and remedies;

Véro is no different. I drive over to Heathrow Cargo and drop off the luggage for onward transmission to Calabar via Lagos, being told that customs' clearance is at the airport in Lagos.

A week later we arrive at Heathrow Airport in the late evening, board our Nigerian Airways plane and off we go, destination Lagos. The adventure is starting.

The plane is only around a third full in economy so plenty of room to spread out. But, of course, I am too excited to sleep despite the overnight flight and so try reading a book. Around midnight I notice a couple of air hostesses come into the cabin so I switch on my 'attention' light, so I may ask for some water and ... am totally ignored. Instead the ladies go to an overhead locker, take out blankets and pillows and make themselves comfortable beds across the central seats. Service is cancelled until the cabin staff have had their night's sleep. Welcome to Nigeria.

After a scant and rapidly served breakfast, the pilot announces that we are making our descent to Murtala Muhammed International Airport where the outside temperature is 29C. We touch down, on time, at just before 6 am and the stairs are rapidly put in place. Because of the lack of passengers, we are soon heading towards the exit and exchange nervous smiles wondering what our day holds for us. As we exit the plane and stand at the top of the aircraft stairs carrying our small cabin bags, we are not anticipating the sensation that we have just stepped in front of the open door of an oven. Despite spending the next thirty years working and living in very hot tropical countries, that first feeling of shock, almost suffocation, has never left me. How can a temperature of 29C be so hot? Answer, when the humidity is close to 100%.

As we descend the stairs, to my left I can vaguely make out the special rounded-shape of palm tree shadows on the far side of the runway but, apart from that, all else in that direction is shrouded in darkness.

In stark contrast, to the right of the stairway, we are almost blinded by the bright lights of the entrance to the terminal building. We have little time to take in our surroundings as passengers are eager to get through the airport formalities and back on with their lives. We are swept along with travellers, certainly more experienced than us, and into the terminal building where we are awaited by several lines of uniformed police. Our turn comes soon enough and I place our two passports on the counter. A cursory glance at our temporary six-month visas, a smile and a "first time to Nigeria?" leads to a whole page in our passports being obliterated by an entry stamp. We are through the first part of our arrival and it was nowhere near as frightening as some of the stories we have heard about passing through Lagos Airport.

We follow other passengers from our flight into the baggage hall and while waiting I start a conversation with a Nigerian gentleman and tell him that we now have to take a flight to Calabar that leaves close to midday. I learn from him that we should leave this terminal building and take a taxi to the Domestic Airport which is a couple of kilometres around the airport ring-road.

Our new acquaintance adds "you will need to bargain the taxi price hard before entering the car and, no matter what the taxi driver tells you, the price should not be more than two Naira."

Our cases arrive and we pass unhindered through customs, indeed the two officers on early morning duty seem to be having fun making a very rotund lady empty her two trolleys full of bags tied up with string, and battered suitcases on to the counter.

Another passenger sees me hesitate and says "keep walking so you do not draw their attention. That lady must be a trader returning from overseas. They will reach an amicable agreement on the amount of customs duty to be paid! Everyone wins, except the Nigerian state."

We find ourselves outside on the airport pavement and straightaway a very battered yellow taxi draws up. "You won' go where?" he asks sticking his head through the open window.

"Domestic Airport" I reply.

"Ten Naira, OK?"

I make a chuckle and remember the earlier advice "No, my friend. We are not newcomers. The price is two Naira; you know that."

A return chuckle and he steps out of the car, unties the length of rope that holds the car boot closed, kindly lifts our suitcases in and ties the rope back in place. Five minutes later we draw up outside the domestic airport, our driver goes through the process of untying the car boot, retrieving the suitcases and then, when offered a five Naira note, searches through all his pockets and comes up empty.

"Sorry sir, I no get change. You go be first ride today."

Nigeria lesson number one: always have the right money with you when paying.

We walk into a domestic terminal bereft of other passengers but find a check-in counter already open. "Can we check in for Calabar, we know the flight is not until midday?" I ask the smiling hostess.

"No problem sir."

That opportunity to obtain our boarding passes and check-in our suitcases proves a very lucky move for us. What to do for the next four hours or so? We notice at the entrance to the terminal is a sign that reads 'Cargo Section' so, why not see if our forwarded luggage has arrived from Heathrow? We follow the sign, go through a door that leads outside, across a sandy yard with rubbish strewn around and up to a small single storey building. Outside are three young men chatting and smoking.

"Where do we go for baggage clearance please?" I ask of the men. One nods to the door. We knock, enter and receive welcoming smiles from two middle-aged officials wearing uniforms with very impressive epaulettes.

"We sent luggage last week from London Heathrow and would like to see if it has arrived please."

One officer says "Good morning" and nothing more. They go back to discussing with each other in Yoruba.

Nigeria lesson number two: take your time and remember to greet people politely.

Remembering my manners, I start again "I am so sorry sir, good morning to you both. Please excuse me." Immediately, the smiles come back and the tone changes.

"Do you have your paperwork with you, sir?" says one of the officials. The other gets up from his chair and leaves by a second door.

We hand over our paperwork that includes our final destination of Calabar and the inventory list. The officer checks his file and says "yes, your cargo arrived the day before yesterday. If you want to clear it through customs here and now you will need a Customs Clearance Officer. Do you have one?"

"Well, no, we only arrived on the London flight this morning. How may I find a Customs Clearance Officer?"

"Very easy. Just ask one of the young men outside." So I do. We have three volunteers, each proffering a different dog-eared company card stating that he represents a different clearance company, headquartered in Murtala Muhammed, Ikeja; which is exactly where we are standing. No problem, so I ask the gentleman who had nodded us into the office at our arrival if he can clear our baggage through customs and he replies in the affirmative.

We go back with him into the customs office and the other two clearance officers from different companies follow in closely behind.

"Why are the other two coming in?" I ask.

"No problem-O, they go help."

So my Clearance Officer speaks with the Customs Official in Yoruba and, after at least thirty minutes, comes back with a pile of forms to be filled, in triplicate.

"Can I not fill in one example and then use the photocopier over there to copy them?" I ask with my UK logic.

"Photocopier no work today" is the response in Nigerian logic.

I later learn that a small donation to the family pot can always and magically make any broken machine work – but then I am new to Nigeria just this morning. I work away at the forms gradually filling them in with the most tedious part being to re-copy our inventory on to the proffered plain paper when I have several very presentable copies in the folder I have brought with me. But in true civil service fashion the world over, UK included, clear reasoning is one thing, how one MUST do it is rather another. Being in a position of weakness, I keep quiet and keep filling. As form filling proceeds, I notice that the hands of the clock appear to be going around rather too fast and I start to become concerned about clearing the luggage in time to make our flight. After all, once clearance is finished we will need to go back to the terminal counter, check in this unaccompanied baggage to our flight, and proceeds through formalities.

I ask my helper how long the process will take and he replies very simply "all OK sir."

Finally, the Customs Officer takes out a big stamp and his pad of royal blue ink and makes a big display of stamping all the forms. He then turns to me and says "please sign here that you have received everything correctly."

"But how can I? I have not seen my luggage yet!"

"Quickly sign and then you can take your luggage" he says.

Oh my goodness, what to do now. I turn to my clearance officer and prejudging my question he says in a soft voice "best you go sign now sir." Understanding that any delay on my side will likely cause problems and since I was not signing away a fortune, I sign. The Customs Officer shakes my hand and indicates that we should leave through the second door. I note the time: 11.45 am and so only about 15 minutes until take-off. We are going to miss our flight.

Once outside we see why we had to sign before seeing our luggage. Our three duffel bags have each been slit below the padlock and bits and pieces of material, sheets and clothes are hanging out. One of the suitcases is lying open and looks half empty. Luckily the travel trunk appears to have held up.

Seeing my look of horror, the other Customs Official whom we had seen go through the same door soon after our arrival, says with an angelic smile "Oh sir, Heathrow Airport is full of thieves. Do you see what they have done to your luggage? They are so bad that we call that airport 'Thief Row!'"

Before I can reply the silence is broken by aeroplane engines revving. My Clearance Officer says "Oh sir there is the Calabar flight, we go quick-quick."

"But we will miss it, how can we go back into the terminal in time?"

"No problem-O", he turns to his helpers and says "load carts, we go-go."

And that's precisely what happens. All our luggage is placed on two airport trolleys and we race across the tarmac towards the plane that must be at least 300 metres away. My helpers are pushing the trolleys as fast as they will go which is not as fast as my Clearance Officer and I can run.

We notice that an airhostess on the plane is just about to close the door and so we shout out as loudly as we can "wait, wait, wait for us" and she does. Magic.

Finally, we arrive at the foot of the plane and, since the cargo doors are already closed, my erstwhile helpers go charging up the stairs carrying duffel bags, suitcases and then the now famous travel trunk. These are piled into Business Class since there are no passengers there.

I ask my Clearance Officer how much I owe him and he replies "You go give me all your money sir that will be enough."

Luckily the maximum amount of Naira that we were allowed to purchase in UK was only fifty Naira each and I had deliberately kept the two bundles apart. So I pull out the bundle where I had already paid the taxi and remove twenty-five Naira from it. This I hand over to the clearance officer.

"And the other money sir?" he asks looking at the notes still in my hand.

"Oh that is to pay our taxi in Calabar" I reply. He gives me his broadest grin, shakes my hand and leisurely walks off the plane to his friends waiting below. I watch them split the money and off they walk across the tarmac to wait for the next Oyibo (or foreigner) to appear at the Customs Office. But their day's pay is already earnt and we are eternally grateful, if not puffed, to them for their help.

An airhostess tells us that we are welcome and to fasten our seatbelts for take-off. Seeing youngsters like us running across the runway from the wrong direction is likely an everyday affair. I apologise for any problems we created for her and the other passengers and said how surprised I am that they waited for us to run across the tarmac.

Her response lives with me until today: "In Nigeria anything is possible, sir." And off we go towards Calabar. The flight is even on time despite our best efforts to delay it.

Once we have relaxed a little, Véro and I look at each other and our smiles slowly grow broader until we both burst out laughing and give each other an enormous hug. What on earth has just happened to us?

Our airhostess serves us synthetic fruit juice and a snack. Today we learn that the standard food on Nigeria Airways internal flights is the humble sardine-filled roll. We also learn that it is generally not a good idea to eat them on the Lagos to Calabar route because about thirty minutes after take-off, from either Lagos or Calabar, the flight always hits turbulence. Not the type of turbulence that you and I have experienced going through thunderheads in Europe, but the one where the plane drops vertically for up to ten seconds; quite enough time for those sardine-filled rolls to tell you that it was a bad idea to eat them!

~ 3 ~

WELCOME TO CALABAR

The two-hour flight to Calabar proceeds due East and is spent with both of us taking turns to be glued to the window. What magnificent views of the southern Nigerian countryside we witness as we fly across Africa for the first time in daylight: small villages composed of thatched huts, mile upon mile of beautiful forest interspersed by riverine swamp and marshland. As we get closer to Calabar so the amount of wetlands increases dramatically and we also get occasional glimpses of the sea fringed by yellow sand. This is to be our new home, our new scenery.

Somewhere down there, as we fly across Eastern Nigeria, is the land of the Ibo people who, in the decade before, led an unsuccessful attempt by a large part of southern Nigeria to cede from the rest of the country, and especially from the Hausa-controlled North. Sadly, the cessation attempt led to the terrible Biafra War that lasted from 1967 until 1970, and became front-page news almost every day in the UK such were the horrors of the war and the famine in the south that it caused. Up to two million people are thought to have died in those three short years. While the breakaway was led by the Ibo people, the tribes of the Calabar region, the Efik and the Ibibio, were also involved and, pre-departure, we had been concerned about what traces of the war still exist in Calabar less than a decade after its end.

Should anyone be interested in learning more about this terrible period in southern Nigerian history, it is worth mentioning that the renowned fiction novelist, Frederick Forsyth, wrote his most famous non-fiction work entitled 'The Biafra Story' and also based his fiction novel 'The Dogs of War' on his experience in the south of the country during the civil war.

Our imminent arrival shows that Calabar airport is even smaller than we had anticipated. It appears as a streak of black tarmac surrounded by lush green grasslands and bordered by palm plantations on two sides and tall forests on the two others. Our pilot makes his approach, descending rapidly at an angle across a wide expanse of river and then across an array of rusted tin roofs. But instead of continuing his descent to the runway, he takes us back higher, circles around and comes in for another landing attempt ten minutes later. A hostess tells passengers near to us that the pilot had to wait for a small herd of cattle to be cleared off the runway.

Finally, we touch down and taxi right up to a small brick building standing just off the runway; Calabar's one and only terminal building. Soon airplane steps are put in place and the thirty or so passengers descend to the tarmac and continue into the building. As this is an internal flight, there is no passport or customs check, indeed no nothing, the building appears empty.

After a fifteen-minute wait, the baggage starts to arrive and we quickly reclaim our two suitcases that had accompanied us from London but none of our luggage that had flown business class inside the plane.

"Blast" I exclaim to Véro "I bet no-one told the baggage handlers about our luggage inside the plane."

I go back outside the building and find three men putting the last of the hold baggage on to the conveyor belt. I try to tell them about our luggage but one worker tells me "No English boss." Luckily, at just the right moment, our air hostess comes down the aeroplane steps and speaks to the workers in Efik, the local language of Calabar. Two workers break off from loading the conveyor belt and make their way up the aircraft steps and into the aeroplane. They descend with our luggage and place it on the conveyor belt. By the time I walk back inside and grab a second baggage trolley, our second batch of luggage is about to arrive.

We walk outside in the early afternoon, wondering if we will need two taxis for all our bags, cases and the travel trunk, when a scrawny young white guy with an unruly black beard wearing a floppy denim hat that tries but does not succeed in covering his lank and curly black hair comes up and, in a true Stanley-Livingstone mimic, says "Dr Marks, I presume? Welcome to Calabar."

We introduce ourselves to our new colleague, a biochemist at the University who has been here already one year and is in Calabar with his wife. Luckily he has come with his car, a soft-top Suzuki Jeep, and we load all our baggage in the back. Now it is all in one place, we realise that we have four suitcases, three duffel bags and the travel trunk, also not forgetting our little carry-on suitcases. It's a squeeze to fit everything into the back of the Jeep but we manage. The tiny cab at the front means that Véro will have to sit on my knees as I cannot fit in the back with the bags.

When the car is loaded, our new colleague stands back and says "how did you manage to get all that on the flight from London? The excess baggage charges must have cost a fortune."

"Not at all, we sent most of it on ahead and picked it up in Lagos."

"Let me shake the hand of one who has just broken the university record for efficiency. Did no-one tell you that the university will pay you to go back to Lagos for several days to clear your luggage and get it flown to Calabar? I took almost a week to get mine out of customs. So when did you arrive in Nigeria that gave you enough time to go through all the customs formalities?"

I explain that we came in on this morning's flight and cleared the bags ourselves at the domestic airport in Lagos. Such is the manner that Urban Myths are created. Even before I had set foot out of Calabar Airport, one myth was already in the making! Me, efficient? That's a good one.

We are kindly driven straight to the university campus which is only a couple of miles away from the airport. As we bump along (is there any car more uncomfortable than a 1978 Suzuki Jeep?) with Véro's head occasionally knocking on the roof struts, we ask question after question during the short ride such as "where is the town centre?" and "are there supermarkets?"

The first draws the response of "we are just passing through it." Since all we see on the roadside are a few homemade tables with tins of sardines (yes, those must be the sardines for filling Nigerian Airway's delicious rolls!) his reply is a bit worrying but we later find that he was speaking with a marginal tongue-in-cheek.

To the latter, he answers more honestly "well, there are few shops that have 'supermarket' in their shop names but ..."

We later find the Children's Shop on the estate where our colleague lives. It is run by an English lady who is married to a Nigerian national. Her shop proves the only source in town for Mateus Rose wine, HP baked beans and, very occasionally, tinned, processed cheese.

Soon we arrive at the campus. The university has only existed in name since late-1975 and is housed on a former high school campus. At first glance it looks attractive with several late colonial style buildings surrounding a large area of green, the university football ground. As we drive through the main gates, our colleague indicates the post office in a small isolated building on the left, with the Registrar's offices in the larger building next to it.

I am told that first thing on Monday I need to go and meet the Registrar and get myself on the payroll or, as he puts it, "nought as sure as brass to make Nigeria liveable!"

We proceed right, around the football pitch, passing rows of trees that I later identify as *Casuarina equisitifolia*, or the 'Australian Pine' which is a misnomer as it does not belong to the same family as the pines. Like Eucalyptus, Casuarina has been transported around the world, especially in the tropics.

Finally, we pull up in front of a scruffy-looking building next to the Geography Department where we pass piles of discarded and rusting fridges and air conditioners and enter through a door marked 'Works Department'.

I am told "you will either be put into the town's one and only hotel and it is brand new (so keep your fingers crossed) or be condemned to the university's guesthouse."

We draw the short straw and are assigned to the guesthouse which, had we known that this was to be our home for almost the next year, we may well have gone straight back to the airport!

Back in the jeep, back along the bumpy road, direction the airport but, at the airport junction, we make a left and head south around the airport perimeter fence. The buildings we pass as we continue our journey are local constructions of dried mud bricks with thatched or the ubiquitous tin roofs interspersed with small cultivated areas planted with straggly bushes that we are told are cassava. We soon come across an imposing building; the only one with a second floor.

"The Guesthouse" announces my new colleague who had himself stayed there for a short while when he first arrived.

We knock and enter and are immediately met by a tiny bundle of mischief and energy called Anna, quickly followed by a pretty bespectacled young lady called Marian and then a handsome beach-boy (is the only word I can use), grasping a bottle of beer for dear life. This is Andy and these are the Kemps, a wonderful British couple, destined to be our close and dear friends throughout our stay and for many years thereafter.

Marian and Andy arrived ten days before us, coming directly from Barbados where Andy had been lecturing at the University of the West Indies before now moving to Calabar. He is a couple of years older than me, a Geologist, and slightly more senior; being a Lecturer I (both my new colleague and I are Lecturer II). My colleague of the floppy hat takes his leave but invites us for Sunday lunch, which is tomorrow, and an opportunity to meet his wife and some of his neighbours who also teach at the university.

Two minutes after arriving, I am clutching a very cold and excellent local beer called 'Champion' while Véro goes with a Coke. We are soon chatting rapidly with the Kemps while Anna hops from lap to lap with her new friends. As with all new introductions, we initially stay on the safe ground of our trip over and we laugh about getting our luggage out of customs while we waited for the Calabar flight. In contrast, Andy tells us that they arrived with only a couple of suitcases and Anna's pushchair because they have a full container arriving from Barbados and a car coming in from Germany both into the Port of Calabar. Calabar Port is a new installation for the town being built by a Dutch company with many of the senior workers hailing from Southern Ireland. Marian is very nervous about their container and explains that it contains all their worldly goods including wedding presents, Anna's toys, kitchen equipment and everything else they possess.

Having the rest of the afternoon and evening with Andy is a perfect way to settle in and catch-up quickly. He explains the workings of the university for newcomers like me, and he speaks from very recent experience. He also talks about life in Calabar for an expatriate. He tells me that banking is the biggest laugh in the world and it would be best if I go with someone who knows someone working there. That sounds ominous! He tells us that taking town taxis is, err, unusual. They stop next to you at the side of the road – whether you want one or not – and that the usual way of getting attention is to make the noise 'ppsstt'. Taxis have a standard fare of 30 kobo (about 25p at the time) no matter where you want to go in town, and they pick up and drop off everyone who needs a ride. So, a ten-minute trip can turn into a thirty-minute nightmare if the taxi driver decides that you are not the priority on his route planning. Cheating during shopping is rife, so be prepared to haggle and bargain for everything, even a kilo of onions. Since you are foreigners, expect to pay much more than the locals. It is assumed that you are rich and so can afford the extra. People are generally very friendly but never lose your temper and stay away from confrontation. The many lessons we learn on that first day are stored away for future reference.

As evening approaches, Marian makes a meal for the five of us. Being a guesthouse we had assumed that there would be a cook; but no. It is a guesthouse in name only and so first thing tomorrow morning the two ladies will be off in a taxi to explore the town together and make the necessary purchases for future meals. At lunchtime Trevor is to pick us up for Sunday lunch at his house; our diary is already starting to fill up.

Sunday morning passes without too many hitches except that the ladies manage to attract the besotted attentions of a naked man during their trip around a very muddy Calabar market. While the naked man does not try to touch them or do anything threatening, just to be followed from stall to stall by a very dirty man in his birthday suit is a little off-putting on Véro's first day in Calabar. The other men in the market find it hilarious to see the two white ladies (M'bakarah as white people are called in Efik) trying to escape their resident naturist's attention. In contrast, the market women come to their defense, shouting in Efik at their menfolk – which brings roars of laughter from the men – until one lady emerges with a broomstick. All the men, clothed or otherwise, beat a hasty retreat!

Our wives arrive back laden with exotic vegetables, which Marian knows well from Barbados while we recognise the yams and cassava from Gino's shop in Culford Road, plus more mundane items like potatoes, onions and corn-on-the-cob. They also come back with some slightly smelly fish making us all tease Véro about buying the fish in order to support the French economy.

In case my avid readers are scratching their heads about how this could help France, let me give you a clue: 'Asterix' – still no? Is it possible that there are people out there who have never read about the hero of the magic potion? Well, if you want to understand the teasing, you must first start by reading some of these important historical documents. Then look out for 'Ordralfabétix' in French versions or more logically 'Unhygienix' in the English translations. All will be revealed if you follow this sage advice.

Just time for a quick shower in the permanently hot water (the black water tank sits on the roof in the blazing sun showing just how simple green energy can be) and then my new colleague's arrival is announced by the pop-pop-pop of his Suzuki and the rattle-rattle-rattle of newly filled crates of Champion beer and various soft drinks.

Let me diverge and tell you about buying bottled drinks in Calabar; indeed, we subsequently find this to be true for many countries of Africa. There is always a shortage of bottles because people use them to store other liquids like car oil, petrol, paraffin and even crop sprays. This is possibly the cause of the strange taste of some bottles of beer and certainly (so we tell our wives) for the frequent headaches after evening drinking sessions with Andy. Because of the shortage, one must first buy a wooden case containing the requisite number of empty bottles. Once these are paid for and in your possession, the drinks' trader then checks every bottle that he has just sold you and should any be found with chips around the rim, they are refused.

"... but you just sold me these!" and you must repurchase unchipped ones from him.

Only once do you make the mistake of not checking the bottles before handing over your money! Next, the empty cases and bottles are exchanged for full bottles and the price paid for the contents. We often wonder what the eventual arrival of cans does for this money-generating venture.

We leave the guesthouse in the pop-pop-mobile with the accompanying chink-chink-chink of the bottles, direction my colleague's home. Our arrival in Nigeria yesterday was hectic, to say the least, and so I had not taken in much of the surroundings. But today as we head towards his house, I am able to relax and look more seriously at our new surroundings. The first thing I notice is that all of the tarmacked roads are boarded by deep culverts, some being over a metre deep and just as wide. I am told that during the frequent rains – that we have so far been spared during our twenty hours or so in Calabar – these culverts become full to overflowing in a matter of minutes, and are a real risk to vehicles and pedestrians alike.

After about eight miles, we turn off of the metalled road and on to the unmade tracks inside the housing estate where he lives. Some of these tracks are incredibly bumpy and very, very dusty. Since the tracks have been surfaced with laterite, we drive through clouds of red dust that makes visibility at times very difficult, especially when a car comes from the opposite direction. On the occasions when the dust thins sufficiently, I marvel at the vegetation growing on areas of wasteland still awaiting housing development. The vegetation in these areas is dominated by a very tall and striking grass with bright red flower spikes, called *Pennisetum*, which belongs to the millet family. In contrast, the edges of the many earthen drainage ditches are full of *Phragmites* or reed, a species that grows commonly in Europe too. The mosaic is completed by most gardens being composed of either bare soil or cassava plants. Apparently, one needs only to cut a short piece of stem off a cassava bush, stick it in the soil and wait two years. Heh presto, dig your own cassava.

Most houses are, of course, occupied by Nigerian families and, on this late Sunday morning, there are lots of children of all ages playing outside and steadily changing colour to red as they scamper and roll in the dust. It seems that the university possesses around twenty percent of the houses on the estate and provides these at a very nominal rent to its staff.

Finally, we arrive at our host's house and carefully climb out of the jeep since it has now taken on an orange hue and we are told that the dust cannot be simply brushed off clothes. We are met at the door by our friend's wife and follow her into their sparsely furnished home. But it is not the sparsity of furniture that first strikes us but the incredible number of local artefacts that they have amassed since they arrived last year: giant masks, strange shaped chairs, decorated calabashes and so the list goes on. Shipping that lot home at the end of his tour will not be easy, I think.

They have been living here for almost a year and his near neighbour is the Head of the Department of Biology and Dean of the Faculty of Science; in other words, my new boss. As soon as lunch is over, I am taken to make a courtesy visit to the Professor's house. The professor appears to have so many children that I lose count of how many I have seen but in response to my compliment that he has a lovely big family, he tells me that he actually has only four children of his own and the rest belong to miscellaneous relatives living in villages 'in the bush'. Nonetheless, he is responsible for their upbringing, schooling, clothing and so forth. This is my first proper introduction to the realities of an African Extended Family.

The following morning arrives and I have no need of the alarm clock. After a quick breakfast, Andy and I go out the gates and after practicing my 'ppsstt' a taxi pulls up. Four minutes later and thirty kobo each we are inside the university gates. Andy stops off in the Geology Department that neighbours geography and I continue a hundred metres further along the university road until I see the sign for Biology. A kindly secretary shows me to my new office on the first floor and I meet my room-mate, Maurice. Maurice is a few years older than me and teaches entomology (insects). He is from the Ibibio tribe, hails from the Cross River State, and turns out to be both a political activist – more of that later – and a thoroughly nice man.

On my desk is a file of internal departmental papers with my name misspelt as Dr Marques on the front. Maurice explains that he is on the timetable panel and that I will see when and in which subjects I am expected to teach when university starts back in three weeks' time. Aside from several advanced ecology courses for third and fourth year students, I am also down to teach introductory courses in general biology, plant physiology and plant ecology plus a little genetics. All fine by me. Maurice also explains that as I am the first Ecologist to grace the university, the advanced courses are not only new but for me to design and lead. Apparently they were added to the department's curriculum following my interview in London! Nice to be entrusted with this role on my first morning in post, but a little daunting nonetheless.

Soon after my arrival, I receive a visit from a rather elderly Sri Lankan gentleman who introduces himself as Professor Tambiah. He kindly says that I may go to meet him on any occasion that I experience any difficulties with the university or with settling into Calabar generally. With that he leaves and Maurice explains that Tambiah and the head of department are at permanent war and that each tries to bring staff to their side. Forewarned is forearmed; I will try to be diplomatic!

I then tell Maurice that I believe I should go to meet the Registrar to settle administrative details such as getting on the payroll and obtaining a statement from the university that I have arrived so that I may chase my visa.

Instead Maurice says "leave it to me." He picks up the internal phone and asks for the Registrar. He speaks rapidly in Ibibio and two minutes later says "that's all settled. A messenger will bring a few papers for you to sign this afternoon."

Maurice then laughs, because he can read my mind, and says "oh, the Registrar comes from the same village as me which means that we are considered brothers!"

Nigeria lesson number three: Take care in what you say to people because everyone, no matter how humble, will be related to someone important.

Since it is still the long vacation at the university, there are few staff members around the department and those that are in the office have no teaching to concern them. For the majority, therefore, time is spent rather too leisurely, I find, in doing a little research or writing up lecture notes a couple of hours a day. I settle down at my desk, for this first morning in my new job and start sketching out possible contents for the new courses I must design. Every fifteen minutes or so there are knocks at our door either by staff who want to say hi to me or yet more relatives who want to greet Maurice. After one burly character departs, Maurice tells me that he is the chief laboratory technician in Chemistry and his brother-in-law. The reason for his visit was to ask Maurice to pay for the production and binding of his son's MSc thesis. Obviously curious, and knowing that Maurice and his brother-in-law must be on similar university paygrades, I ask, to my mind, a quite logical question.

"Why does he not pay for his own son's thesis?"

Maurice tells me that it is all down to tribal, and therefore, family hierarchy. Since Maurice is higher in *perceived* hierarchy within the tribe, he will always be asked to pay whether or not the request comes from someone who earns more salary than he.

"Not quite how we function in the UK" I reply.

But I notice from the tone of his voice that the encounter has rather upset Maurice and so, a few minutes later, I am not surprised when he speaks out and shows his annoyance with the request from the brother-in-law.

"He expects me to hand over my salary to him but when I need help he will always find an excuse. He annoys me, so let's go and get some lunch." It's already past twelve and I have not seen the time pass.

Maurice takes me in his beaten-up Peugeot 504 to a quaint hillside bar/restaurant a couple of miles away from the university. There is an inside seating area with plain tables and plastic chairs but we go straight through the room, out the backdoor and into a cute garden area. This has been separated into different shapes, squares, rectangles and circles, of different sizes by the judicious planting of shrubs to form hedges including hibiscus which today are covered in bright red flowers. The hedges afford a degree of privacy to customers sitting within their chosen shape. He tells me that the bar is popular in the evenings with young and not-so-young lovers!

A young waitress arrives and Maurice orders two beers. She quickly returns with our order on a plastic tray and I notice that there are two glasses and two 75 cl bottles of Champion beer. And the bottles still retain their metal capsules. Next the young lady removes the tops, pours a small amount of beer, really only an egg-cupful, into each glass, swills it around and then pours it on the ground.

My new friend sees my look and says "this will always happen and it is to show you that the glass does not contain poison! And if you are ever given an already open bottle, refuse to accept it." He went on to add "but often you will see people do this" and he gently pours a small amount of beer from his bottle on to the soil "that was an offering to our ancestors and we call it libation."

Maurice will prove a godsend as he guides me during the next few months, in such a friendly manner too, to pick my way through Nigerian culture generally, and university and Calabar society and politics in particular.

Next, Maurice asks "would you like something to eat?" and this is a most welcome suggestion as I can feel the Champion going rather rapidly to my head. Several days of living on adrenaline before we left UK and now the heat and humidity of Calabar, not forgetting the alcohol content of the beer, are combining to make me feel rather woozy! So with a well-practiced 'ppsstt', Maurice gets the attention of the young waitress and orders for us in Efik.

The young girl responds by asking something about 'M'bakarah' to which Maurice nods his head. Ten minutes pass and the waitress comes back with her plastic tray holding two bowls, two dessert spoons and some pieces of bread. I was wondering if she might taste each to prove that there is no poison but, no, she simply places a bowl in front of each of us. They contain a thin gravy with five chunks of meat submerged inside. Without going into the finer details, the meat looks rather like the poor animal was massacred with a machete with little regard to prior skinning or taking out the internal organs. Maurice informs me that this is a favourite Calabar dish called 'Goat Meat Pepper Soup'. The waitress is instructed to bring two more bottles of beer ... just in case. Ominous!

My friend sits back in his chair, looks at me and says "go on try it". I tentatively sip a spoonful of gravy covered with little oil slicks containing small pieces of red (tomato?) floating on top and ...

"Oh my God" I now know why the extra beers have been ordered – indeed half of my bottle follows very closely behind the spoonful of volcanic lava that burns and then numbs my tongue and continues burning down my throat and into the nether regions below. My eyes water, my nose pours liquid and my entire face goes bright red with sweat pouring down my face. Naively, I thought that the pepper part of the dish's name referred to peppercorns not to Montezuma's hottest chilies!

Maurice begins to laugh and soon tears are running down his face too. "Welcome to Calabar my new friend. You have passed your first test!"

Now I know what to expect, the rest of the pepper soup is dispatched into a hungry stomach but I am keeping that ice cold beer very close to hand. As an eventual outcome to this story, pepper soup becomes one of my favourite dishes and, many years after I leave Calabar, the very thought of a pepper soup would make me salivate in anticipation.

Finally, it is time to go back to the office and so I pull out my wallet and 'ppsstt' the waitress over. But Maurice intervenes and says "no, this is taken care of". He then asks "so what do you think of the bar?"

I reply "it's lovely and I will certainly bring Véro and my guesthouse friends here."

"Great" says Maurice "because this is actually my bar and my wife runs it for us."

My reply is honest because the setting is quaint, the multitude of flowering hibiscus plants beautiful and the service quick but discrete, and I had really enjoyed the experience. But to this day I do wonder how he would have reacted if I had been critical.

As we leave to get into his car, I notice the sign above the door reads 'Green Onion Bar and Restaurant'. "Why green onion Maurice?"

"A funny story really" he replies, "when we bought the place and had finished the renovations, I had fluorescent lights wrapped in a blue plastic filter installed for the opening night.

When we looked at the onions that we had purchased to go in the goat meat pepper soup, we noticed that they appeared green. And the name stuck."

We drive back to the campus and as we are about to turn right into the university gate, I notice a bar on the opposite side of the road with a sign above the door reading 'Green Onion Annex.' Yes, Maurice is a real entrepreneur and the Annex being so handily placed becomes the local drinking hole of the 'M'bakarah contingent' of UniCal.

I quickly learn two things. First that Nigerians, as a nation, adore chilies and it does not matter if the person comes from Calabar, Kano or Port Harcourt; the hotter the better. The second item I learn (and those of a sensitive nature please look away) is when invited to eat at a Nigerian home, best to realise in advance that all the best chilies really do burn twice (I am serious). Step up Peter and Sandra to prove my two points. Peter is from the UK, an engineer and part of the team building the new Calabar port. He is married to Sandra, originally from Lagos. Sandra has become good friends with Véronique and so has invited us around to their home for an evening meal. Sandra asked Véro in advance if we do not mind a little chili in our food to which she replies, only a little for herself and I am OK with chili. Fast forward to the evening which starts with cold Champions and peanuts on the veranda and a bluish-violet light on the wall in front of us. This makes a zinging and a zapping noise every ten seconds as it fries mosquitos – and every other insect sufficiently careless to get drawn to the luminous equivalent of the Siren's song.

We settle down to a meal that starts with a small salad and freshwater shrimps. Delicious and light. The next course is pounded yam, fast becoming one of my favourites and rather like a creamy mashed potato, served with a slow-cooked beef stew, Jos-origin green beans cooked with morning glory. I can feel that everyone around the table is silently drooling at the anticipation aroused by the delicious odour generated by the stew. Sandra passes the different dishes around the table and Véro helps herself to modest amounts of pounded yam and beef stew, looking after her figure as all young French ladies do, and rather more of the green beans and morning glory. I dish myself out rather more of the first two and less of the veggies, as most working class kids do. We wait for Peter and Sandra to finish serving themselves and then everyone tucks in. My first reaction is that the stew is delicious but I have to admit, rather spicy. But not quite as spicy as Maurice's pepper stew. Véro tries some stew and her face rapidly goes through most of the colours of the rainbow and then she starts to cough and then to swallow her glass of Champion as though her life depends on it – which to her it probably feels that it does.

Once Véro's shock of swallowing liquid metal starts to subside and she has wiped away most of the optical cascade that still streams down her face, Peter turns to Sandra and asks "why did you put so much chili in the stew?"

"I only put a fifth of what I would normally put" she replies in some embarrassment.

No one dies at the table that night and the mango ice cream that we eat for dessert does cool those areas of taste buds and parts of the tongue that appear to be particular targets of capsaicin. Later, on the drive home to the guesthouse, I confess that the stew was a little spicy and that Véro should be ready for a warm greeting when she goes to the loo the next day!

Nigeria lesson number four: Do not forget to put the toilet roll in the freezer if you are going to eat Nigerian food.

As Maurice and I walk into the Biology Department after our Green Onion lunch, a young man hands me an envelope and informs me that it comes from the Registrar's office. This contains various forms to complete, sign and return. By the end of my first day I am an official staff member and on the University's payroll. One of the forms still remains to be completed as it asks for details of my bank account where my salary should be paid. I ask Maurice how I go about opening an account and where the banks are.

Remembering what Andy had warned me, he responds to my secret hope by saying "let's go together tomorrow morning to take care of the details."

True to his word, the following morning we get into his 504 and head in a new direction for me that takes us into an area of Calabar called Duke Town. There are two banks on the road, the only two banks in town, and Maurice recommends Standard Bank as the other bank, the Mercantile, is new and untested. We head through the door of Standard Bank and I am immediately lost for words. The room we enter is enormous and there are literally hundreds of people milling around inside and no obvious queues to join. Everyone seems to be talking at the same time and the cacophony of dozens of different voices is deafening. In the centre of the room is a semi-circular counter, fully twenty metres long, with around a dozen clerks walking backwards and forwards trying to deal with the commotion of customers. Hands gripping cheques and pieces of paper are being proffered over the counter and the air is full of 'ppsstt'.

Maurice tells me not to worry as he knows someone to help. So he takes my hand, I notice already that hand-holding by men is very common in Calabar, and he pushes through the throng and gets right up to the counter. "Femi ppsstt" he calls and a harassed young man comes across immediately with a broad smile on his face.

"Uncle, hello." Yes, another of Maurice's relatives. I am introduced and Femi brings me forms to fill. "Fill them now Doctor and I can get your account open." All around I can hear ppsstt but not with the same success as we have just had. With the account opened, Femi kindly calls all the other clerks across, introduces me, and proudly claims that Dr M'bakarah is his friend and that they should help me in the future when I come to the bank.

That single act of kindness not only saved me hours of future queuing but also was essential in getting our bimonthly remittance cheques signed and handed over without needing to provide 'dash' (or small bribes when translated into English) as many people, local and international, are obliged to pay in Nigeria. Indeed, my one achievement throughout our time in Nigeria was that on no single occasion did I ever pay or receive dash. Sometimes life would have been far easier had I paid but as time went past, it became a question of pride and then a challenge always to resist the temptation.

The days pass quickly during this first week in Calabar and we settle into a routine of work at the university for Andy and me while Véro stays with Marian looking after little Anna and doing the market runs for provisions. The women discover a small market just around the back of our guesthouse which means that shopping takes less time and effort, although the supplies are very basic. In Calabar, bread is becoming an issue because we can only find sweetened bread in the market. It tastes more like cake, and it grows impressive mould in less than a day. The final straw that broke these loaves back was when I saw a bread seller blowing into the plastic bread bags to open them so that he could put the loaves inside. Yuk! From that day the ladies begin to make their own bread and we all dream that one day a French Master Baker will ride into old Calabar Town and set up a bakery. But be careful what you wish for.

One evening towards the end of this first week, I arrive at the guesthouse and Véro tells me that a government official came to the house to meet with me and said that I should report to the Chief Inspector of Immigration as soon as possible. By chance the Immigration Office is only a few hundred metres further down our road. The following day, a Friday close to the start of October, I enter the immigration office and ask to speak with the Chief Inspector. A few moments later, I am shown into the office of a chubby, late middle-aged gentleman with impressive insignia on his uniform (with a similar design to my old friends, the customs inspectors, in Lagos).

"Hello doctor. Please give me your passports, immigration forms and employment papers" he asked in a very severe manner.

I remember to reply to his greeting and then hand over the official documents and our two passports. The officer takes mine and puts everything into an envelope and that into a bright red file but pushes Véro's passport and immigration forms back over to me.

"She is an alien" he says in a very serious tone of voice.

"Really sir?" I query, "I can understand your confusion but she really is from Earth, from France in fact." That flippancy seems to break the tense atmosphere and he laughs aloud.

"That's a good one doctor. Here, in Nigeria, we consider any foreigner not from the United Kingdom and the Commonwealth as an Alien, so your wife is officially an Alien, like it or not! To get her registered you have to go to the Alien Branch of Immigration" and he explains where that office is located. "Now"' he says "your temporary work visa is good for six months but must be extended in good time or else you will be expelled from the country. Getting an extension is very hard and time-consuming work for me so I would ask that you make a small contribution to help get the work completed. Do you understand the urgency?"

Well I understand perfectly that he has just found a convenient way to say 'dash me buddy' but I play the foolish newcomer by replying that I have just arrived and that he should understand that I work for the university and that I am on a local salary, and blah-blah-blah.

"Come back this time next week doctor." The meeting ends abruptly.

And we play out that scenario every week for the next six months. In fact, I become so well-known at the Immigration Office that I no longer have to present myself at the desk but just walk straight into his office. But finally, the crunch. I have reached Expulsion Day minus one. Tomorrow, I am to be kicked out of the country.

On entering his office, the Chief Inspector says very bluntly "your visa expires tomorrow and we will expel you from the country. However, you know that you can still have my help, if you want it."

I sense a bit of exasperation in his voice and so I reply "I understand perfectly the situation sir. Tomorrow I will report to you with my suitcase ready for expulsion." And I leave his office without another word.

Next day I am back, carrying my (empty) suitcase but pretending it is heavy. "OK sir, I am ready to be expelled from Nigeria."

He looks at me and a slow smile begins to spread across his face "you are a very stubborn fellow; do you know that?". He opens his drawer, pulls out my dark blue passport and slides it across the counter. "Your permanent work visa is in there, doctor."

I check the date of my visa and note that it was stamped on the very first day I had visited his office back in September the previous year. We had spent six months playing a game but my refusal to pay dash made me feel that it had all been worthwhile.

"Doctor, you know something, I enjoy English novels very much. Do you happen to have any you can give me?"

Therefore, and considering that I have just won the dash competition, I check inside my briefcase and come out with a tattered version of Graham Greene's 'The Human Factor' and, on handing it over, I warn him that once he has read the book he will never touch peanuts again.

His last words to me are "Really? But I love peanuts, doctor."

Meanwhile, getting back to our first weekend in Nigeria. We have just eaten lunch and cleared away the dishes, Anna has gone for her nap, Andy is finishing a cold beer while Marian, Véro and I are relaxing over various novels. We hear a car drive across our culvert and into the guesthouse garden. Car doors open and close and then the front door opens and two people walk in carrying suitcases. Welcome to Simon and Rosalind, freshly arrived from the University of Ibadan, and part of the growing brain-drain from the established universities to the new ones. They are also to be staying at the guesthouse. Our contingent is growing. Simon is from France and a Senior Lecturer in Semantics in the French Department. His younger partner is an Associate Lecturer and is here for her first teaching post in the Department of Religious Studies.

Both Véro and I take immediately to Simon, a very gentle and obviously highly intelligent gentleman who must be around fifty years old. Rosalind is about our age and seems rather a reserved character. During chats with Simon, I mention that he is now the second Alien to descend into the guesthouse and explain what the immigration officer had told me yesterday. Having already spent several years in Nigeria, he knows the ropes and will take us to the Calabar Aliens Office next week.

As always happens, the weekend passes too quickly and we are now back in the University preparing for the students to arrive. I am starting to give thought to which avenues of research I will follow. I know that I want to continue on my broad PhD theme of physiological ecology but have to confess this is rather daunting in the southern Nigerian context since the entire rainforest and riverine forest environments are totally new to me. I know so few of the tropical families, let alone their species, that it is hard to make a start. So I consider the best thing to do is to think through interesting areas to research and then focus down on the species and their ecologies.

I decide that, since I am in a country that still has so much poverty and many problems to solve, I wish to follow an arm of research that could be of benefit to the country. However, I still want to follow my own Darwinian logic that says that any character possessed by a species should have a reason to exist. I really do not consider that anything is 'vestigial' but believe rather that Nature is highly selective (by that I mean ruthless) so if a character does evolve and proves of no use, natural selection should quickly weed it out of the genepool. Walking around the campus, I notice that there are several common species of *Compositae*, the same family that includes my old friend the wild lettuce. Some of these species are pretty little herbs and others are large bushes. Perhaps there is something interesting to study here. I also notice that many areas of wasteland within the campus have been turned into small farming areas but there seems to be little attempt to keep the crops weed-free. The blue-flowered shrubby composite I have already noticed seems to be particularly common.

As I am looking at the plants, a young Indian gentleman comes up and introduces himself and asks me to call him Nanu. He is a new arrival at both the university and to Africa and is here to teach botany, so a new colleague. He quickly identifies all the plants I am looking at by their Latin names and, in response to my surprised look, tells me that the same species grow in his part of India. Nanu is a godsend for me in these early days in Calabar.

Returning to my office, I ask Maurice why so many cultivated areas seem to be left to the weeds and he replies threefold: first the climate is so hot and sticky that it makes long periods of labour in the fields very difficult; second, farmers do try to clear the weeds but they seem stubbornly to grow back; and third the poverty of most farmers precludes the purchase and use of pesticides. Studies on farmland weeds seems to be a promising area where a better knowledge of the species may help control the incidence of weeds without raising the workload on farmers or requiring pesticides. Quite a few points to think about.

I believe my preparations for the imminent arrival of the students is going well and I have written up my lectures for all subjects going forward several weeks. What I need to concentrate on is the development of practical work for my early laboratory sessions with the first year students. I am warned that there will be a lot of them, so keep it simple. I go to see my new biochemist friend, who had collected us at the airport, for some botanical samples because he not only teaches biochemistry but is also the Director of the Botanical Gardens and Research Sites. I find him as friendly as always but he seems strangely hassled.

"What's happening You seem worried," I say.

"Yes, I have a big job on at the botanical gardens and there are problems. Do you fancy coming to see?" he replies.

So we go to his jeep, turn right out of the biology carpark to drive the 200 m or so to the botanical gardens but, instead of stopping there, as I had supposed, he keeps driving on to the dirt track that leads to the Students' Halls of Residence, straight past them and towards the forest that I presume eventually must end at tributaries of the Calabar River. Four or five hundred metres past the student halls I can see a gang of workers with shovels, pickaxes and wheelbarrows and beside them are a pile of 100-millimetre diameter steel pipes that must be fully six or seven metres long. We pull up and immediately a slim, muscular man with a shaven head of about forty comes over and greets us. I am introduced to Chief Eko who is the senior worker in the Botanical Gardens. With him are Iyamba, a smaller, brawnier character, two ladies, one of them obviously very pregnant plus two temporary workers.

I learn that the botanical gardens include not only the hectare or so of gardens we have just driven past and with which I am familiar but also an area of unknown size, in fact thousands of hectares, of tropical and riverine forests. These forests are, in effect, a massive but unmanaged nature reserve. They begin a few hundred metres further down the track, and what the team is hoping to do is to bring water from the student residence to the nature reserve; stating that this will enable the botanical gardens to expand into the reserve. My ecologist hat slips a little on hearing this but since I have not yet visited the nature reserve, better I say nothing at the present time.

I am told with a certain amount of pride that the workers have been digging the trench by hand, linking the pipes as they go along and then covering them with soil. They have been working for several weeks to get this far and had hoped to finish in the not too distant future.

What is causing my colleague so much concern is that over the weekend, while the staff were away, a gang of thieves, obviously with a lorry, have dug up and stolen all the buried pipes. Even if he can clear the necessary budget to replace the pipes, the workers are becoming (very reasonably in my opinion) angry about having to do so much physical labour when they are supposed to be working in the botanical gardens.

I ask three questions: why did he not hire a small mechanical digger and so get the work done more rapidly? I have to accept a one-word response spat out with some venom 'budget'. Second, how will he prevent future thefts of such expensive material and third, I ask why he needs such massive diameter pipes which would be sufficient to bring water to a large village. But he is in such a state of irritation that I do not push for answers. The fact that each pipe cost around 40 Naira and some sixty have been stolen, means that the poor guy must provide the department with some very difficult explanations.

Over the next weeks, I notice that my friend is getting more and more depressed by the theft and, I believe, by the attitude of his team towards him. I also notice that around the department he is getting snappy with some of the support staff and that is not a good sign. I am not surprised therefore to get a call one morning from the head of department who tells me that he has resigned as Director of the Botanical Gardens and that it is proposed that I should replace him. I see the job as an additional challenge, on top of my teaching and research duties, but a challenge I am happy to take on. For this additional job, I am to receive the grand sum of 25 Naira per month (before tax of course!).

Soon after my appointment as Director, I do a round of the Botanical gardens – the very large Nature Reserve will have to wait. At the former, most of the gardens are laid out to square beds approximately three by three metres and some straggly plants of various species are growing in a few of them. The most striking are the Hibiscus plants but they need pruning and shaping, while the air is full of a heavenly scent from a line of *Gardenia* plants whose white flowers exude an almost suffocating perfume. Towards the top end of the gardens are plots of various *Solanaceae* plants which I cannot recognise. They look like small aubergines but are green in colour 'bitter aubergine' I am informed by the Chief. Apparently they are the research project of someone in geography who comes by every few days to pick the ripening fruits! The gardens are surrounded by tall and spindly Casuarina trees, except for the path leading into the gardens which has a row of six trees from which hang large green fruits covered in blunt spikes, These, I am told, are soursop trees and the ripe fruit are delicious. I am promised the next one to ripen, provided that Iyamba does not take it first. Iyamba is proving a very strange character and spends his days cracking palm oil nuts with his teeth – never try that.

The sole infrastructure at the gardens is a medium-sized shed covered on the sides and roof by corrugated sheeting. Chief leaves his motorbike locked inside along with the other workers' bicycles and this also serves as their shelter on the many rainy days. Stacked up against the outside of the shed are a number of shallow earthenware dishes piled higgledy-piggledy, some broken, others with the soil and the dead remains of plants still in them. I ask why they have not been sorted and cleaned ready for reusing and I am told that no-one has ever told them to do so.

With my future research in mind, I ask how many flowerpots we possess.

There is a look of astonishment on Chief's face "but doctor you have seen them in the piles over there" he says indicating the earthenware dishes.

When I explain what I mean by flowerpots, he tells me that they do not exist in the Calabar market; and he is right because I spend hours searching for them and never find a single one. We manage to compromise by buying every plastic drinking mug we can lay our hands on. These are conveniently four inches across (just like 4-inch flowerpots) and approximately the same depth.

I show the botanical garden ladies how to make four holes in the bottom of each of the mugs with a thin metal strengthening rod I scavenge from behind the recently completed university theatre. This brings shy giggles from the ladies who whisper to each other in Efik – I imagine saying how crazy this guy is to spoil perfectly good drinking cups – until I explain that we will grow plants in the mugs and the holes will serve for drainage.

"M'bakarah!" they say in kind mockery.

The other essential element that is missing is a shade-house. This is to serve the opposite function to a greenhouse by cutting down the sun's rays so that seedlings and young plants may have a chance to get established and grow without being roasted in the sun or battered down by heavy rain. But this needs better planning and designing before I can think about buying the material and getting carpenters in to help with the building.

I walk back to my office, nod a greeting to Maurice as he works diligently at the opposite desk, and settle down to work on the design of the shade-house. Half-an-hour later my thoughts are disturbed by a loud knocking on the door and in walks a smiling gentleman carrying a brand new briefcase.

"Good morning doctor, the head of department sent me to speak with you."

"OK, do come in. What can I help you with?" I ask.

He opens his briefcase and pulls out a glossy brochure. "I represent a company selling Hydroponic Greenhouses and the professor says that the department has sufficient funds to purchase one but that you must first give your approval."

I look through the brochure but the contents are not quite what I am considering for the gardens, at least yet, given the lack of even flowerpots! Out of interest I ask how much the greenhouses cost.

In response he tells me "they start at Naira 50,000 and if you order one, you will be OK."

I am a little baffled, so ask "what do you mean, I will be OK?"

To which he replies in all seriousness "give me your bank account details here or in England, as you wish, and I can transfer funds in for you. It's OK, this is quite normal."

I look across the room to Maurice and he grins back at me. How do I deal with this without being offensive?

So I simply reply "thank you very much but currently the department is looking to purchase only some basic equipment and materials. But if I may keep your brochure, we can contact you in the future. It was kind of you to visit, goodbye."

He leaves the office insisting that I hold on to his business card where his Lagos address and phone number are underlined in red ink.

Allowing him time to walk down the corridor, Maurice and I burst out laughing. Maurice tells me "well-handled and it really is that easy to receive dash." We roar with laughter again.

Nigeria lesson number five: It really is easy to receive dash.

Back to the guesthouse in the evening, I find Andy and Marian in a high state of excitement. Véro whispers to me that a messenger brought a note earlier in the afternoon saying that the ships with their container and car on board both arrived in Calabar Port a week or so ago. Tomorrow Andy must go to start the clearance process. Marian is so happy to be reunited with her worldly goods, Anna with her toys and Andy finally to get his car. Taking taxis is proving tiresome for all of us, not just the overcrowding we endure but also the frequent tropical downpours that catch us outside waiting for a taxi to pull up.

The next morning Andy comes down dressed in slacks, an ironed shirt and wearing black shoes. Everyone says "wow" because up to this morning we have never seen him wear anything other than cut-off jeans, t-shirts and flip-flops. He leaves early and we are not to see him again until late evening. When he does arrive, he is downcast and says nothing to us. Instead he asks if we can look after Anna while he chats with Marian. Thirty minutes later they come back into the common sitting room and Andy explains.

When he arrived at the port and asked for his container, no-one would talk to him. He was told that the senior officials were too busy and that he should wait. After a couple of hours with no news, he had nosed around the port area and came across a container covered in mud. On closer inspection of the container number, he identified the container as his. He went back to the officials' office, loudly insisting that he would be seen. Finally, one officer came to him and said that while the crane was unloading his container from the ship, the chain had broken and the container had fallen into the Cross River. This had apparently occurred almost a week ago and thus the contents had been soaked and allowed to fester inside the container for almost a week. Given that the container had been sitting in the full sun, temperatures inside must have reached very high levels. There was no way to console poor Marian.

At noon the following day, while I am at the university, a lorry arrives at the guesthouse with the container still full of the dripping contents. To make matters worse, as it crosses the cement bridge that spans the metre-wide culvert into the guesthouse, the bridge breaks and the front end of the lorry goes down into the culvert, stuck fast. The first job is to empty the lorry of its contents – there is never a shortage of labourers in Nigeria – and the second is to try to extricate the lorry from its cement prison. Step forward Andy who takes on the role of Archimedes by producing two very stout metal bars from the guesthouse shed and, with some of the muscle present, levers one front wheel of the lorry up. Stout wood is then placed across the culvert and under that wheel. This is repeated on the other side, and heh presto Andy also enters the realms of an urban myth. The biggest surprise was that the workmen were so shocked by this superhuman M'bakarah feat that they left without asking for dash.

Meanwhile poor Marian is unpacking cardboard boxes soaked in very muddy and salty river water. She pulls out more and more of her treasured possessions: embroidered sheets; featherdown pillows; blankets; towels; different items of clothes and all sort of other things still dripping wet.

Making the situation ten times worse is the black mould that has started to take hold on every surface. As she unpacks, so the tears roll faster and faster down her face. Little Anna stands back and says "don't cry mummy" with tears rolling down her face too. Véro joins the tear's party with hers falling in sympathy as she tries to help by organising the contents as they appear from boxes.

Clothes that can be saved are put into one pile and the guesthouse cleaner, present for the day, is enrolled to fill a bath and wash everything she can. No washing machines in Calabar, so everything has to be washed by hand. Books and papers are spread out around the room to try to dry them; some of Anna's toys simply need a rinse but others require careful cleaning and drying. Many of the kitchen electrical utensils have given up the ghost during their dunking in the river and can only be sold to the scrap man in the market.

I come back in the evening to find this catastrophic scene and think that the best thing I can do is to make everyone some stiff gin and tonics. After the third G&T, spirits are rising (while in the gin bottle they are falling) and I am then packed off to the kitchen to explore and practice my English cooking talents.

Later as we sit back and try to relax, I ask Andy about his car. "Oh f*ck! I was so angry about the container that I forgot the car entirely." He will be back in the port tomorrow then.

The next evening when I arrive home (is this wretched guesthouse really home?) I find Andy down in the dumps because he has not managed to get his car out of customs. What happened is that when he bought the car from Volkswagen Germany, he also ordered many spare parts, universal joints, a spare carburettor, different filters, and the like. The Customs Officers have jumped on these extras and require customs duty to be paid in advance. They told Andy that Nigeria possesses a VW factory and that he should buy parts locally. This was not the advice given by Germany! The problem for Andy is that the duty is expensive, more money than they have in country, and the car will not be released until the duty for the spare parts is paid.

Luckily, and just in case of such emergencies, we have brought a Cashier's Cheque drawn on Barclays with us. I hand this over to Andy and Marian to be paid back when they can.

Problem solved. Early the following week, Andy drives up in his brand new "Volkswagen Thing" that closely resembles a World War II German staff car.

For the coming weekend, Andy has suggested that we go out for a drive to explore the countryside. So on the Saturday morning we load a cool-box with food and beers, throw in our rain gear, just in case, and set off with Andy and Marian in the front and Anna perched between Véro and me in the back. Andy has little idea of the direction he is going and I have even less, but after a few hours' drive along bumpy dirt roads we see small buildings in the distance which we soon pass. We continue into relatively unpopulated countryside and decide to stop by a small river to eat our lunch. The rain has held off for most of the morning but as soon as we put the blanket on the ground, down comes a torrent – so everyone back in the car. Lunch in the German Staff Car is a little cramped, to say the least, but everyone is hungry so few complaints. Lunch complete the sun comes out smiling again. Anna starts to get a little cranky, as any two-year old cramped in a car would do; so Andy suggests that it might be an idea to start driving back to Calabar. We do a U-turn and head back towards the group of small buildings. As we draw level, a uniformed man walks in front of the car with his arm raised "vos passeports si vous plait" (passports please). We look at each other and laugh nervously because why should we need passports and why is the officer speaking to us in French?

Véro steps up to the plate and says "Bonjour Monsieur l'officier" which rather sets him back because he had forgotten to greet us. "Pourquoi voulez-vous nos passeports et pourquoi vous nous parlez en Français ? Nous sommes des professeurs de l'Université de Calabar." (why do you want our passports and why are you speaking to us in French? We are lecturers at the University of Calabar).

To which he replies, failing in his efforts to contain his laughter, "parce-que nous parlons en français au Cameroun et vous venez de traverser notre frontière !" (because we speak French in the Cameroons and you have just crossed our border!).

What to do? We apologise profusely telling him that we have not been in Calabar very long and that we must have gotten lost. Then Andy, as he does when stressed (and, come to think of it, does when not stressed either) goes to the cool box in the back of the car, pulls out a cold bottle of Champion beer and flicks off the capsule. "Do you want one?" he asks our frontier policeman in English. A nod, a smile, a beer in hand and a 'bonne journée'. Off we drive back into Nigeria and a diplomatic incident avoided thanks to ice cold Champion beer!

Nigeria lesson number six: Champion Beer is a great problem solver.

Later the following week some good luck awaits both the Kemps and Simon as they hear that the latest Housing Committee Meeting has assigned them houses. Simon's is on the housing estate and Andy and Marian are assigned a newly finished house on Calabar University land about a kilometre from the teaching campus. Both move out of the guesthouse as soon as they have keys and an allocation of university furniture. We are sad to see them go but so happy, especially for the Kemps, that they have a place to call home and Anna will have a garden to play in. Our name did not come out of the hat on this occasion because being a more junior lecturer and having no children, our points do not yet warrant one of the available houses. But then month follows month and we are still not allocated a house, and always with the same reason – the lack of points.

In desperation, I tell Maurice about our lack of housing and ask "what can I do?"

His reply was very logical; I must be a slow learner. "Come on Malcolm, you must do what everyone else does: invent a few kids! Just send a letter to Dr John in Languages who is head of the committee and say that your two children are arriving soon. He will understand perfectly what you mean but, to help, I will go and have a word with him just to make sure."

"But Maurice, that would be dishonest and means I jump the queue ahead of other people."

"I tell you everyone does it, so if you want to get out of the guesthouse, stop being so bloody British!" At that moment he sounds just like my old flatmate Rob! "Also, in a few months' time, there will be a new batch of lecturers arriving and you will slip down the list again. The time to act is now."

So I write a letter to Dr John and follow up with a personal visit to his office. As I knock and enter his room, I find Maurice with him. "So Malcolm, good news about your children arriving, Maurice has already informed me. We are allocating you a house in Road-10 on the Housing Estate. Once you get the official letter, go to the Works Department for the keys and to choose some furniture. Then go to the house to check if any refurbishment work is required. They will handle that."

Could it really have been so easy? Yes, it is, but it has taken me eight months to play the system and I do not feel very proud about having done so.

~ 4 ~

WATCH OUT FOR THE TERMITES

It is November 1979, and finally, the students are arriving back *en masse*. The campus has changed overnight from being a quiet, almost empty village to a bustling town. Big, dented coaches arrive one after the other on campus and disgorge a mass of young, noisy people. Old friends meet with hugs, followed by handshakes, followed by the clicking of fingers as they pull their hands apart (I must practice that). The students, as everywhere in the world, come in all shapes and sizes ... and ages. It is easy to spot the 'townies' from those from the countryside, especially among the women. I see a few ladies walking in bright red high heels wobbling as they try to navigate the irregular pavements around the campus and pulling wheeled suitcases. However, most students, men and women alike wear the ubiquitous flip-flops and carry holdall bags. I also notice a divergence in shape. While most are squat and muscular, a few are tall and slim, almost regal in appearance. I learn later that the majority of the intake is from the southern states bordering Cross River and so are predominantly Ibo, Efik or Benin with a few Yoruba – originally forest tribes – but a small minority, the taller, thinner individuals, come from the more northerly states and are Hausa or tribes linked to that ethnic group. The Hausa are an interesting people since they belong to a large family of tribes that has spread right across dryland Africa from the Peul or Fulani in Sahelian Senegal to the Maasi in Kenya. They are traditionally the cattle-rearing nomadic tribes that transhumant with their herds in search of grazing. Of course, most have now settled in urban areas.

With the students also comes an influx of returning staff. The Nigerians have mostly been away to spend time in their birth villages with elderly family members while the expatriates are returning from overseas vacations. I notice one rather scruffy and skinny individual climbing out of a beaten-up green Volkswagen Beetle and heading towards me as I watch the milling students from the doorway of the Biology Department.

"Hi," he says, "I'm John Reid and you must be Malcolm. I am so pleased you have arrived, as the head of department was threatening to make me teach botany if you had not turned up!"

John is a Zoologist with a capital Z. He is not very fond of teaching as it stops him from traipsing off into the forest, getting lost and involved in all sorts of crazy adventures. He turns out to be one big and lovable character and, if he had been discovered by a TV channel, could easily have been serious competition for the likes of Steve Irwin. At this early stage in my career at UniCal, I am just making his acquaintance but he will crop up many times, usually in dangerous but hilarious situations, in the pages that follow. He is also destined to be my close neighbour and even closer friend.

My first lecture finally arrives. I have prepared so hard for this maiden outing in the lecture theatre that I could probably recite my first hour-long lecture blindfolded. Fifteen minutes before the start on a Monday morning, I tell Maurice that I have first-year students for Biology 101 (yes, introductory courses really are called 101). This is not only my first lecture at UniCal but theirs too. I ask him where the lecture room is located and he says "oh that is the large lecture theatre on the ground floor of the Finance and Administration Building."

I make my way over and arrive in plenty of time but the students are obviously more nervous than me for their first lecture and it appears that everyone is already inside. What I am not expecting is the sheer number of students that awaits me. I walk into the room and there is a thunderclap as everyone gets to their feet and says, "Good Morning Doctor". I cannot believe that I am being faced with some three hundred students and, on this first day, everyone looks alike with very few exceptions. The room itself is enormous – well, it has to be to contain so many students – and must previously have been a chemistry laboratory or something similar with rows of laboratory benches and hundreds of stools. At least it is light with rows of windows all along the walls both to the left and to the right.

It takes me about two months to make out the different features, that of course do exist, to distinguish one Nigerian from the other, but in those two months, I make so many mistakes with student identity and names that they laugh at my many errors. I feel less guilty when some of those same students that were teasing me about my identity confusions start to call me Dr Dale or Dr Reid.

As I was jokingly told on many occasions by them, "all white people look alike!"

I begin my lecture in the same style as my old lecturers at QMC; that is, to stand at the front and develop the topic with explanations and examples. However, it only takes me a few minutes to realise that very few students seem to be following and or even fewer are taking notes. So I slow down and walk around the packed lecture room trying to make eye contact as I go. What I see are eyes that clearly have not the faintest idea what I am talking about; a little off-putting, to say the least.

During my student days in London, as a way of earning some extra income, I had given some private tuition support to school students struggling with their A levels. The look I see in the eyes of my current batch of students tells me that they are also struggling. So I stop the course – we are now perhaps fifteen minutes into the hour – sit on my desktop and look out on the student hoard in front of me.

"How many of you understand me easily when I speak?" Only a few hands are raised, just perhaps twenty out of the three hundred students, including one hand from a pale-skinned young man sitting right in front of me. "OK, can you please tell me the problem?"

"Sorry, doctor but it's your accent," the young man replies.

"But I do not have an accent", I reply indignantly "I come from southern England and went to school and university in the south. I have an accent just like the Queen and the BBC news readers!"

"Yes, sir, that's the problem for these students. If you go to their village or town schools, you will find that their teachers hardly speak English and many will only speak pidgin English."

"So, how come you speak such good English and understand me?"

"My mum is from the UK." That explains a lot!

"And if I write much more on the blackboard as most teachers do in schools, do you think that will help?" He answers in the affirmative and so that is what I will start to do. I also get him to speak to the students and say in Efik and then in pidgin that the doctor is here to help them learn about biology but they have to listen carefully, take notes and stop me when a concept is too difficult. We proceed by trial and error for the next twenty minutes but after that, my eye contacts see far fewer blank looks and I feel that we managed to make a fair amount of progress. My first hour is coming rapidly to an end and so I tell the students that I wish them to look through today's notes before our next lecture in two days' time and let me know then if anything is unclear. "Thank you for today, you can go."

There then follows a rush of the three hundred, not towards the door but towards me! "Dr sign my form", "Dr mine first", "please, doctor."

"Hold on everyone, what are these forms?" I learn that they are class enrolment forms that have to be signed by the lecturer for every student and for every class. So I say, "those of you that do not have a class next, stand back and only those who need to get to their next class come forward." In that manner, I eventually get all the forms signed. This is also the moment my signature is curtailed to a squiggly M.

I share the teaching of this class with two other lecturers. In total, we each have two hours per week for blocks of four weeks. My four weeks pass quickly and I see real progress in my students (as they get use to my accent, of course!) and get a feeling that many of them will eventually do very well in their four-year degrees. Finally, I arrive at the end of my last lecture and so tell the students that the following week they will get a new lecturer called Dr Jahn. He is an Indian gentleman who has been at the university already for two or three years and so knows the ropes and also knows, I presume anyway, how to teach these newcomers. During this four-week period, I have learnt some real lessons in how to structure a lecture to different skill levels. This will be an experience that will serve me well during my future career.

I leave the classroom feeling pleased with my first month of teaching in Calabar and set off to my new office that was assigned to me a couple of days previously. This office is in a single storey building standing next to the main Biology Department and sits beside the UniCal Theatre that belongs to the Department of Theatre Studies under the leadership of Professor Frank Speed.

I have already started to set up a few research experiments looking at the germination characteristics of several of the *Compositae* species that occur on the campus. On the Monday following the end of my teaching block to the first-year students, I walk around some disturbed areas near to the university campus roads and collect seeds of half a dozen species into envelopes. As I go about my seed collection in silence, not needing to move around too much, I notice a six-or seven-inch lizard slowly appear from within a drainage pipe and walk along the edge of the concrete culvert lining the road. Once he, for he is surely the male of the species, moves out of the shade and into the full sun, he starts to bob up and down, flashing the most stunning colours of red, purple and yellow that I have ever seen on a reptile. This is a rainbow lizard, and he is very aptly named. After five minutes of display, I notice two sandy brown lizards slowly approaching him through the short grass. His dance has borne fruit in the form of two females of the same species. Time for me to let nature go about its marvellous work. The rainbow lizard is perhaps the most obvious but he is not the only lizard member of the reptile family that we commonly encounter in Calabar. Look around damp areas, under rocks, for example, and a small white-striped skink is sure to be hiding there while in every house or hut in Nigeria, there is sure to be a population of the mosquito and fly-eating gecko. The gecko is a popular inhabitant of our house, given his dietary preferences, although he does have the unfortunate habit of leaving his droppings in hard-to-reach places!

I sit down with packets of newly collected seeds and begin to sort through them for each species. I have noticed that one species, called *Emilia sonchifolia,* has two types of seeds in its pretty composite flowers of yellow and pink, some of the seeds are white and some are brown. Another species, *Tridax procumbens,* which has yellow flowers produces some seeds that are fat with only a tiny parachute (called a pappus) as well as smaller seeds with well-developed parachutes while a third species, *Syndrella nodiflora,* with blue flowers has seeds of different shapes, again in the same flower head. As I subdivide the seeds for each species into their different forms, my mind wanders to my first students. I wonder how they have got on with their new lecturer. I do not have to wait long to find out because, as if in response to my thoughts, I immediately hear a knock on my door.

"Come in", I shout and am told "best if you come out doc."

Going outside, I see a crowd of my old students from which a small delegation comes forward "please doc, you have to come back to teach us." I look puzzled and so they shout in unison and in all seriousness, "we cannot understand Dr Jahn's Indian accent!"

While I have fun teaching this enormous class of newcomers, my real pleasure is teaching the more advanced students, starting in their second year, to understand and grasp the importance of ecology. And, while we can lecture about ecology in the classroom, the real understanding of ecology, and Darwin's place in teasing out the way that species are adapted to the environments in which they live, can only be grasped by doing fieldwork. Now, despite my second and third-year classes being significantly smaller than those in the first year since students begin to specialise, these classes still range from fifty up to around eighty students. How to organise field classes with so many students to keep an eye on? In the UK, lecturers use their postgraduate students as teaching assistants and usually with a ratio of one postgraduate to twenty students but the department here has only a single postgraduate – and he is researching animal parasites with the head of department. I ask John Reid how he handles his large classes and he tells me very frankly that he is able to do almost no work outside the classroom with his students. I need to mull over this issue because there is no way that I will not use the incredible nature that lies just down the road to train my students to be real ecologists and of future value to their country.

I decide that the only solution is to develop and hand out teaching sheets to the students well in advance of our fieldwork. So, after developing and Xeroxing them, I take time during a theory class to hand out folders and discuss the work we will be doing in the field in future weeks. Although I assume that the students will be more bush-savvy by a mile than me, I do say that they should dress appropriately, look carefully as they walk, stick to the trails that I have been marking out and not wander off into long grass just in case there are snakes. Of course, there are plenty of snakes in Calabar, and many are venomous in this part of the world. However, the noise of eighty enthusiastic students is perhaps our best defense against anyone getting bitten. Indeed, in the two months since my arrival, I have only seen one snake, a rather rare and unusual creature called a Calabar Python, and sadly he was dead. What I understand about Calabar Pythons is that they feed on earthworms and ingest them rather like you and I would suck in a string of spaghetti.

For the first field class, we meet up at 2 pm sharp at the Student Halls, where 95 per cent of my students live in extremely cramped conditions, even taking it in turns to sleep and study. Everyone is in high spirits to escape the classroom; many tell me this is the first time they have done any fieldwork. We chat as we walk down the dirt road, parallel to the trail of Trevor's ditch, empty of pipes and caving in from the rain. I notice a few of the girls in our group are dressed as though they are off to meet their boyfriends with brightly coloured miniskirts, halter tops and the full array of make-up. Bees around a honeypot may be an old adage but it is a just description of the magnetic appeal of these ladies in a university where boys outnumber girls by at least ten to one. For safety or simply to chat, the ladies stick together as we approach the forest entrance. While I may digress from the line of my story, it is important that I have set THIS scene in the readers' mind.

As we get to the forest entrance, I remind the students to be careful how and where they walk, especially as most only have their usual flip-flops but one young man laughingly tells me that "Doctor M'bakarah you should not be afraid as you have Nigerians, to look after you."

I can see that he is playing to the female audience but they ignore him and get on with reading the notes I provided. I have given my students a very simple challenge to start with: investigate obvious adaptations that enable species to live precisely where they do in the forest. We wander around the various trails making sure that no one strays too far. Most students, rather shyly at first, start to handle the plants and a few insects, then begin to really look at them, standing back and seeing where they are growing or feeding, and then start to scribble down field notes. After an hour or so has passed, I call everyone together and they form a loose group around me so that we can speak without shouting.

I have chosen a naturally clear area around an old termite mound that almost looks like it has been swept clean of leaves and debris, so generally a good place to stand and discuss. Also, there is a species of shrub that I cannot identify, growing up through and out of the top of the mound – I have noticed the same shrub growing out of neighbouring mounds too, and seemingly nowhere else. I wonder if any of the students have also noticed this.

As we start to talk through our adaptation discoveries, such as the thorns on the vine that enables it to grip as it grows up through the lower levels of vegetation, or the elongated tips of leaves that allow rainwater to drip off or the brightly coloured beetles that are most certainly poisonous, I notice two of our mini-skirted ladies and three of our better-dressed men sit down on the different earthy protuberances on the termite mound.

One student whispers in my ear, "Prof., you should say something to them." My winked eye brings a smile to his face.

Our discussions continue for a further ten minutes and then, one after the other, our five seated students yelp, stand up and smack themselves with their hands. Nothing more for me to say than:

Nigeria lesson number seven: 'Watch out for the Termites'

A lot of good-humoured teasing then begins with exchanged insults of 'townies' from the standing audience and 'bushmen' from the bitten few. But yes, termites do nip and they hurt!

At 5 pm we make our way back to the Student Halls and several of the youngsters say to me "Doc. we have all really enjoyed our afternoon with you. Would you like to drink wine with us?"

Well, there is nothing that an adopted Frenchman like me enjoys more than drinking wine, so I accept gratefully but wonder where they get the wine from.

They take me for my first visit to the campus of the student residence and across to some very rustic tables with even more rustic benches. We all sit down, apart from two students who go around the back of the building and reappear ten minutes later carrying trays covered in variously shaped and sized glasses containing a milky white substance.

"Palm wine", they announce, "we got uncut wine for you, Doc., because we think the wine collectors use stream water to dilute the wine, and we do not want you to get sick."

This was my first experience of drinking palm wine. For the record, it does not compare to a good Medoc or even a *piquette* from the Bugey but I am very flattered to be invited by my students and to show them that I am approachable, relaxed outside of the classroom, and happy to mix with them.

Part of the enjoyment of doing my Batchelor's degree and the stimulus to do better was the friendly relationships that many, but not all, of my old lecturers were happy to build with their students. Peter Wanstall and Bryn, my animal ecologist at QMC, were great at building relations with their students. I wanted to use the stimulating experience I had enjoyed with them to help my own students improve their work and gain confidence.

Time passes rapidly and I have entered a pleasant routine of work in the lecture theatre, with the botanical garden team and in the research laboratory. But I do try to spend as much time with Véro as possible, being worried that she might get bored now that Marian and little Anna have moved into their new home on the university campus. Now we are totally alone in the guesthouse apart from the daily visits of the cleaning lady and the occasional visit of a teenage boy who does some gardening and helps out the cleaning lady. However, I need not have worried because Véro always finds ways of keeping busy and meeting new people. So, I am not surprised when one evening I get back from the university to find a new couple sitting in the living room. This is Sami and Estelle. Sami works for an Israeli road construction company and is in charge of their mechanical workshop while Estelle is a full-time mum of two youngsters. Estelle and Véro met in a town shop earlier in the day when Véro heard Estelle speaking in French with her children. Estelle is originally from Morocco, hence the French, but her parents had emigrated to Israel with her as a child when tensions in North Africa built up against the Jewish community. Naturally, she speaks Hebrew and then French but little English. Sami, on the other hand, can speak no French but speaks excellent English. While Estelle is a tall, slim lady, Sami can best be described as the perfect shape to be a great prop forward in a rugby team and, indeed, was the Israeli heavyweight wrestling champion for every year that he did his military service. A bear of a man and a really gentle and loving character.

At the moment, the Israeli construction team has only some small ongoing roadbuilding and maintenance contracts and so the expatriate team is composed of just Sami in the workshop, a works foreman who spends most of his time in the field, and the local boss called Hymie. They occupy a village compound, about two kilometres away from us, composed of at least a dozen houses protected by a high, barbed wire fence with armed guards at the gate. Thus Estelle finds herself as the only woman living in a male-dominated compound with little to do but look after her children. So bumping into Véro is good news for both of them and they quickly become friends. Twice a week we are invited to watch films at the compound, and we learn just what film buffs the Israelis are!

By coincidence, a few days later we meet another expatriate couple, this time from Canada. Doug is a GP and has been working on a health programme in Cross River State for a couple of years. He lives in Calabar with his wife and their two young boys. Over a couple of cold beers, I happen to mention to Doug that I am looking to buy a car for use around Calabar and to escape from having to use Calabar taxis.

"My project has a ten-year-old VW Passat to sell at Naira 650 if you are interested," he replies.

At the next Israeli film night, I mention this to Sami and he tells me simply, "buy it."

"But I need to check it out first."

"Buy it, Malcolm and bring it to me at the workshop. I will do the rest."

At the next opportunity, I hand over the cash to Doug and receive the keys to a slightly battered sky-blue Passat in exchange. The car is rather dented and scratched and there is a click-click-click from the front end when I turn the steering wheel hard to the left. After taking Véro for a quick spin around Calabar, I bring the car to Sami at his workshop. Ten days later, he drives back into the guesthouse, hooting as he crosses the bridge. I go outside and discover that my bright blue Passat is now a bright red one! Sami also tells me that he has changed the universal joints of the drive shaft (no more click-click), changed the brakes, serviced the engine and a host of other things. As he reels off the list, I am a little worried about the bill or, rather, whether I have enough Naira in my bank account to pay the bill.

"Sami, thank you for all you have done. How much do I owe you?" I ask.

"Naira sixty-eight" is the answer. "I had all the parts in stock because we used to have several Passats in our car fleet but I did have to buy a few litres of paint to give the car a respray."

We now have a car, shining like new if already ten years old, and fully serviced for the grand price of less than seven hundred pounds. To add to the pleasure (and resale value), the car is already registered in Nigeria so no extra taxes to be paid now or when we eventually sell it on. We are both delighted to be independent and mobile at last.

~ 5 ~

MAMMY-WAGON MARRIAGE

As always seems to happen, when you meet one person you soon meet another and then another. During our first meeting with the Kittles, Doug's wife asks if we have yet discovered the Calcemco swimming pool. Since our response is no, she says that she will take us there on the following weekend to have a look. She mentions that the pool charges entry to swimmers but it is clean and uncrowded. On arrival at the pool we find a sole swimmer in attendance, a pretty, pleasantly rounded young lady of about thirty years old. She is the wife of the expatriate manager at the Cement Factory, and soon destined to be another new friend of Véronique.

We enter through the gate, pay a couple of Naira to the guard and jump into the soup-warm water. As we swim leisurely along, I hear 'plop' and a large avocado pear bobs up to the surface near my face. Looking up, I see that we are swimming under a very large tree and the ripe pears are falling every few minutes into the water without warning. Our lunch is being provided as we swim!

After a few lengths, Véro climbs out and strikes up a quick conversation with lady about her time in Calabar. We learn that she has gotten bored being a stay-at-home wife, especially since her husband's significant salary allows her to have cook, maid and any other worker she needs, and so she had looked for a job to keep her busy and found one at a private English primary school called 'Hillside International School' where she runs the administrative side of things.

After finding that Véro previously worked as a secretary, she says that the school is looking for a secretary "are you interested?"

First thing Monday morning, she arrives in her chauffeur-driven car and takes Véro to Hillside to meet the owner, a lady named Rosemary Uwemedimo. Rosemary is a most impressive lady, perhaps forty-five or fifty years old, mother of three highly intelligent and gifted teenage children. Rosemary is from the UK and married to Vincent Uwemedimo. She developed Hillside school from scratch before independence. The school enrols not only most of the expatriate children living in Calabar but also the children of any Nigerian who has sufficient income to pay the fees. Maurice's children are among her pupils.

After a few moments talking with Véro, Rosemary offers her a job "... and can you start straight away?"

So my wife is now a working lady, a secretary, with the grand salary of Naira 100 per month.

During the next few months we get to know Rosemary and Vincent very well. Rosemary married Vincent in Nigeria some twenty years previously and wrote about her early experiences in the country in a book entitled 'Mammy-Wagon Marriage'.

Vincent is a tribal chief of the Ibibio, the same tribe as Maurice, and soon to be elevated by the tribe to the rank of 'N'tisong' or 'Chief of Chiefs' of the Ibibio nation. Maurice has explained to me that it is important for the Ibibio to come together and create a unified political force because they are the fourth most populous tribe in Nigeria, after the Ibo, Yoruba and Hausa; each of which has its own political party and wishes to control the country politically. The Ibibios consider that while they may never govern the country themselves, they can become the 'king-makers' if only they can unite under a common flag. Hence the pomp and ceremony around Vincent's elevation.

While I always try to show Vincent the highest respect, he loves to tease me and put me into embarrassing situations. On one occasion, just after his coronation, I arrive with the car at Hillside, just after lunch, to collect Véro at the end of the school day. I pass through the entrance to the school and see that Vincent has moved his N'tisong throne to the end of the school path and is sitting in full robes on his throne.

"Hi Malcolm, come over here and drink a beer with me" he calls out.

I take off my shoes and walk towards him along the carpet that leads to his throne. He points to a slightly less grandiose chair, actually his earlier throne, beside him. As I approach, I wonder if I should bow or what and say the same to him. He laughs out loud and tells me that as I am now appointed an honorary Chief I can just sit down and enjoy the cold beer on a hot, sticky day.

We are chatting about nothing in particular when I see three individuals walk in. A rather rotund gentleman in expensive robes followed by two less well dressed attendants. The former sinks to his knees, lays his hands on the carpet in front of him and speaks in his tribal tongue to Vincent. Vincent replies in English saying that he should come back at a more convenient time, can he not see that he, N'tisong Vincent, has an audience with an important English diplomat? The visitor makes a quick apology and leaves, followed by his two attendants.

I begin to get up saying to Vincent that I can leave if he has someone to speak with.

"Not at all my friend, that was only the State Minister for Finance. He can come back when I am less busy! And do you know what will happen next? He will embroider the meeting today and tell everyone that his N'tisong received not just a diplomat but the British Ambassador and that the ambassador was obliged to sit on a lower throne than our N'tisong!" That was Vincent.

The term both at Hillside and at the University ends on the same day. Christmas is in a week or so and Marian says "I know there is a bungalow to rent at the Dunlop Estate, how about going there with us for Christmas?" Since this will be the first Christmas that either of us has spent away from our families, it sounds a lovely idea.

Outside of Calabar, on the main road leading eventually back to Lagos, there are several plantation businesses producing rubber and palm oil. The first is called 'Palm Oil' and is about a forty-kilometre drive from Calabar. The Palm Oil Estate is managed by a gruff Scotsman called Frank Fyffe and it has a small expatriate club with squash, badminton and tennis courts plus a nine-hole golf course. Now we are mobile, we have put in an application for membership both to get us out of Calabar and to start doing some real exercise; squash for me and badminton for Véro. The Dunlop Estate is a further fifty kilometres along the road to Lagos and has a swimming pool – a luxury in the context of Calabar where there are very few, and all private.

The first ten kilometres or so of the trip is on a recently built dual carriageway called the Murtala Mohammed Highway; almost a motorway but when that ends, the once metalled road has disintegrated to a bumpy track with large puddles of unknown depth. With the state of the road, the drive to Dunlop usually takes about two hours. As we drive in convoy with Andy and Marian, always a good idea both for security and in case of breakdowns, I note the encroachment of another plant I am studying called *Chromalaena odorata*. As with many of the other plants I have started to take an interest in, this species also belongs to the Compositae (or more correctly *Asteraceae)* family and is a rather attractive bush covered as it is with a host of sky-blue flowers. However, while the flowers are pretty to look at and provide vivid splashes of colour throughout wastelands, areas of forest regrowth and plantations – indeed wherever light can penetrate sufficiently – it is becoming a real menace in my area of Nigeria. The bush is native to the Americas but has been able to spread around the damper tropical regions of most of the world. It appears to have arrived in Nigeria, sometime around independence, in 1960. This led to it being given the name locally of 'Awolowo Weed' after the great Nigerian statesman, Obafemi Awolowo, a Yoruba. The shrub is colonising vast tracts of land and, as many introduced species, appears not to have many natural enemies apart from a beautiful large green and yellow grasshopper, called *Zonocerus variegatus* (the variegated grasshopper). This grasshopper is very large, locust-size, and a big pest to agriculture in its own right. Adults feed, for example, on cassava plants gnawing down from the growing tips and stripping off the bark thus killing the shoots, and probably providing an entry point for fungal infections too. I have noticed that their immature young or 'hoppers' or technically 'instars' seem to show a preference for chewing the *Chromolaena* flowers. Given my interest in turning my research towards improved weed control, these two species have attracted my attention.

We arrive safely at our bungalow on Christmas Eve which passes very pleasantly around the pool. One of the few saving graces of southern Nigeria is that it remains hot around the year and so swimming is possible every day; rain and storms allowing, of course. We plan to spend Christmas Day out on the river with a barbecue and cool boxes full of cold beers and soft drinks.

Christmas Day arrives and Anna ensures that we get up especially early just to check that Santa Claus managed to find us during the night at Dunlop. Luckily, he has, so we all gather in the sitting room while Anna gets on with ripping open presents from her mum and dad, from us, and also from 'Uncle Simon' back in Calabar who has miraculously also managed to get Anna's gifts delivered by Father Christmas.

After tidying up, a satisfying breakfast and a quick check that we have sun cream, insect repellent and all the food and drinks in the cool boxes, off we go to find a riverbank spot that had been recommended to us. What a beautiful sight awaits us all. A real sandy beach gently sloping down to shallow water moving leisurely over a sandy bottom. Andy and I jump straight in while the ladies plaster Anna with so much sun cream that she looks like a basted chicken ready to be roasted! The water is a marvellous temperature, warm but refreshing, and the sandy bottom really does only slope gently, so perfectly safe for Anna to play in. We walk out until the water is up to about waist high.

Andy asks "what's this?"

He bends down and comes up with a closed yellow shell, a bivalve or freshwater clam, about the size of his hand. I start feeling them under my feet too, and so we begin collecting and soon have commandeered Anna's sand bucket. These will be a part of our barbeque lunch and so to keep them fresh, we simply dig a hole in the shallows and tip them in. They cannot go far in the hour or so until we fire up the BBQ.

Until then, we leave Véro and Marian to sunbathe while we walk and swim down the river, espying a very elderly fisherman in a small dugout canoe who has in fact stopped fishing and has espied us too. Watching us is obviously far more interesting than trying to hook fish on his line. Our short conversation does not go far with his very, very limited English and our almost non-existent Efik. Nonetheless, he seems happy to have met M'bakarah and will, no doubt, embroider his story around the family campfire this coming evening!

We head back upstream to the ladies, light the charcoal in the BBQ and agree to put a sausage on for Anna – which happens to be her nickname – and start cooking some clams for us. We place half a dozen on the hot grill and at first they begin to sizzle as the wet shells touch the reddening grill, then they slowly open and we can see the white flesh inside from which steam starts to rise. I suggest that since the clams feed by filtering the water, it would be prudent to let them cook well and so kill off any bacteria that they may have ingested from the water. I am particularly concerned that there will be *E. coli* or tummy bug bacteria in the river as there are villages dotted upstream. We leave them sizzling for about ten minutes and Andy is elected, by a majority of votes of three to one, to be the first to try one. After fooling about, clutching his throat and pretending that he has ingested poison, he declares them tasty but full of large bits of sand. Since I do not believe it possible that the flesh can be full of sand, I open one and look in the flesh. What do we see? Pearls, real freshwater pearls! Of course, they are small and nothing like South Sea Island pearls, but pearls nonetheless.

A wonderful Christmas Day with lovely friends comes too quickly to an end back at the bungalow. None of us are late night people so after a few G&Ts with ice 'n' slice we head off to our bedrooms.

The next morning, we ask the ladies if they would like to go for a drive around the large Dunlop estate but they prefer to stay around the pool with Anna. Andy and I decide to see if we can do any fishing. His idea of fishing is with a snorkel and spear gun, as he loved to do in the West Indies, while mine is to sit on a riverbank waiting for a small float to start bopping up and down. However, the sum total of the fishing equipment I managed to bring from the UK is a small reel with line, a couple of floats, a few weights and various hooks but no fishing rod and, of course, no bait. When driving back from the river on Christmas Day, I had noticed a small stream running down through an area of rubber plantation and had suggested to Andy that it would be worth trying there – so we head in that direction. I have no idea what type of fish might be present in the stream but imagine small roach, rudd or bleak-sized fish.

We arrive at our stream and find that it is about three metres wide at the most and is running far faster than we had imagined; not quite a torrent but fast. Both of us have come dressed only in shorts, t-shirts and flip-flops; rather under-dressed we realise as we try to pick our way through the streamside vegetation. While I set up the line with float, weight and small hook, Andy is dispatched to find something for bait. He soon comes back with a centimetre-long cricket, a bit big for the size 14 hook I have tied to the line ... but let's see. I toss the float and weight out into the centre of the stream and as far upstream as I can. It touches the water and immediately 'zing' the line is broken close to the reel and so I have lost fish, float, weight and hook; all in two seconds.

"What the f*ck" is all I can say.

I tie on another and larger bullet weight and a triple hook that I would normally use for pike fishing but do not risk anymore of my precious floats. Andy hands over a larger grasshopper and we are ready to go. I throw the new set-up in and wait to see what will happen. Ten, twenty, thirty seconds pass and I see the line, despite the large weight, moving downstream with the current. Then a hard tug, to which I strike, then nothing; no movement at all. I give a tentative tug and it feels that the hook has caught on something, perhaps a sunken branch or a root. I give a harder tug, imagining already the loss of more of my precious equipment that had managed to escape the ravages of Customs and Excise in Lagos. Then a third and much harder tug but one I judge not sufficient to snap the line – remember I have no rod, the line is coming directly from the reel. Then I feel movement, there is a fish on the line. Nice too I think given the strength of the pull but then again, perhaps without a rod I am misjudging. The fish is pulling hard, trying to move further downstream with the current. I am letting line of the reel and at the same time keeping the line as taut as possible. I know that if I let it go slack I could easily lose the fish. I pull my handkerchief from my pocket with my free left hand and manoeuvre it across my palm and the middle finger of my right hand so that the line is no longer digging into my damp finger as the fish pulls. Andy wants to grab the line and help pull it in but I tell him to stay back. There is little space and there are too many bushes and branches in which the line could become entangled. Slowly, slowly I begin to pull the line in and I tell Andy to wind the slack on to the reel. After a full ten minutes of effort, a large tail breaks the surface of the muddy water, and then the fish takes its head again and plunges downwards. I have no idea of the depth of the stream nor of the state of the bottom. Is it sand and mud or is covered in broken branches and tree stumps? If the first, I can let the fish go deep and tire it further, but if the latter, it will certainly snag the line around a branch and the line will snap. So regretfully, I pull back against the fish, hoping that the triple hook is well set and that the line will hold. Not only do the hooks hold fast but the line does too. Slowly I pull the fish back towards our space on the bank, it comes inch by inch until I see its head with a whiskered mouth.

"A catfish", I tell Andy, but which sort I have no idea.

I ease the fish onto a flat part of the bank, bend down while keeping the line taut with my right hand and use the fingers of my left hand to go behind the gill flap or operculum and into the gills. One heave upwards, with Andy holding on to my right arm and tugging, and our first Calabar catfish plops up on to the bank. A lovely specimen with no skin abrasions from its fight or visible parasites; it must weigh at least four kilogrammes. Not bad for three kilogramme breaking strain line.

After dispatching the fish, placing it into a large plastic shopping bag and loading it into a cool box filled with ice packs, we decide that we will call it a day and go back for a swim and a Champion beer!

As we leave the shade of the streamside, Andy says to me "what are all those tiny bruises on your arms?" I look down and see what he means. I look at him and see the same also on his lower back, below his t-shirt line and above his shorts, it looks like he has lain on a bed of nails. Something has bitten us, and bitten us well. Thinking through my parasitology notes, I suggest that we have been ravaged by black flies. Several years later I find a memento of that fishing expedition by way of two subcutaneous lumps in my right arm that seem to migrate from the elbow to the armpit and back again. 'Calabar swellings', thank you so much.

We arrive back at the bungalow and use the kitchen scales to weigh the fish before I clean it. Four kilogrammes and three hundred grams. Very nice. I plop the cleaned fish, leaving on the head as the French are not as squeamish as the Brits, into the freezer. We will cook this as a celebratory meal in a few weeks' time and relive the enormous struggle of man against beast with friends, carefully selected to appreciate the courage that Andy and I displayed!

In mid-January we meet up with Samy and Estelle at the Israeli compound for a film evening. Véro speaks to Estelle about her and Samy coming round to the guesthouse to eat the large catfish with us. Estelle gently refuses, telling us that catfish are not considered kosher and so off their menu. Sad but we are so happy that we knew this in advance of placing a catfish complete with head on the table in front of them!

We have now been in Calabar for about six months and life has been relatively easy, apart from a few stomach upsets and a peculiar fungus infection that has taken a liking to my scalp causing lumps of hair to fall out, roots and all. Life, both in Calabar and the university, is proving interesting and we have made a number of new friends and Véro has a job that pleases her.

But all that changes one night.

We go to bed in the guesthouse and fall rapidly asleep. In the small hours of the morning, a faint noise stirs me from a deep sleep; in my stupor, or is it a dream, I imagine an object gently sliding down the wall and on to the floor. As one does in a half-sleep state, I turn over and gently drift down to sleep again except that some innate, primordial feeling keeps pushing my consciousness back to the surface. The effort to wake myself up is overwhelming and I remain in a dream-like state. Finally, and I have no idea how long since that small noise first woke me, I manage to get out of bed and go to the toilet in our *en-suite* bathroom. As I walk the few metres from my side of the bed, across our bedroom and to the door of the bathroom, still with my eyes closed in half-sleep, I kick a small object on the floor which should not be there. My brain starts to operate more effectively and I realise that something is amiss.

"Sorry my love but I need to turn the light on."

Scattered across the floor I see our clothes that we had lain carefully on a chair the night before. And strangely our bedroom door is open wide while I know that I had locked it with the key before sleeping. I go out on to the landing and see the contents of my briefcase scattered down the stairs with my briefcase itself several steps further down.

"We have been burgled" I say gently to Véro.

I run down the stairs, still in my 'birthday suit', and out through the front doors which stand wide open and on to the carport that covers the entrance to the door. I call for the night watchman who is usually sitting in his guard's chair gently snoring. Tonight, the first time since we arrived at the guesthouse, he is not at work.

By now Véro has put on a dressing robe and joins me in the sitting room, handing me my dressing gown. It is 4.30 in the morning and pitch black outside. Of course, further sleep is impossible so we begin to walk around the guesthouse to try to see what has been stolen and to fathom how the burglars got into the locked guesthouse and then managed to open our locked bedroom door.

The mystery of how they broke into the guesthouse is easy to fathom. The door is in two parts and made of strong metal and glass. The first part has been permanently closed since we arrived and is held in place by bolts at the top and bottom, like French windows. The door itself is locked by a key. The key is still in the lock and the latch bolt is still out. So there is no way that the doors could have been simply pushed open without breaking them and the glass; except, except ... I check the up and down bolts and see that the upper bolt is still out but the lower one is not. Someone, I am sure it must be someone on the inside of the guesthouse, has opened the lower bolt well in advance. All that our burglars needed to do was push hard at the lower side of the blocked door and the top bolt would have jumped out of the door frame. Once that was done, the two doors would simply have pushed open. Going to our bedroom, I see that the burglars appear to have first made an attempt to prise out louvre windows that connect the side of our bedroom to the large landing at the top of the stairs. They had managed to get one out but needed to remove more before anyone had a large enough space to climb through, that is our initial thought anyway. Their next effort was to unlock the door from the outside but since I had locked the door and always purposefully turn the key an extra 90 degrees, it could not simply be pushed out, and that had slowed their access. In the sitting room we find that they had taken the time to get thread from Véro's sewing box, removed two thin pieces of twig from the broom and tied them together forming a 'V-shape'. They must then have spent a considerable time trying to turn the key inside the lock and finally get it to fall to the floor (that is likely the noise that first started to wake me) and then used the tied twigs to fish the key out from under the door.

Our nocturnal visitors made off with everything that they could carry that had an overseas provenance: all our cutlery, plates, glassware; indeed, all we owned except a few items that we had left dirty and sitting in the sink from the previous evening's meal. All Véro's makeup and the pharmacy bag that lived in the fridge, all food items that were from overseas including a tin of baked beans and a jar of strawberry jam, and all the alcohol. Marian's typewriter that she had lent me to type up a scientific paper had also gone as did Véro's Elna sewing machine, a generous wedding present from her Godmother, Jacotte.

The burglars were kind enough to leave us a yam, some manioc and a tin of Scots Porridge Oats (made in Nigeria). From our bedroom, they had taken Véro's handbag and a necklace, both had been hanging on the bedhead right next to her face. I lost a small amount of cash from my briefcase along with a pen. Luckily, more valuable items remained locked in our infamous travel trunk that still stood at the foot of the bed.

When the morning is sufficiently light, I walk down to the Airport Police Station, which is close to the ill-reputed Immigration office, and report the theft. I am told to go back to the guesthouse and await the police. An hour later, three policemen arrive and the most senior introduces himself as a Detective Sergeant. He goes on to tell me that his brother also works at UniCal in the Biology Department and that he runs the chicken farm.

"I know your brother very well", I tell him, "and I hope you can quickly catch the thieves".

The facts are pretty clear, even to me: one of the two guesthouse workers (I guess the young man) had sprung the door bolt in advance, told the thieves where our bedroom was, and 'persuaded' the night watchman not to show up for work. I explain my theory to the policemen.

The DS rubs his chin in thought and then says "we lack the financial means to investigate, especially to buy petrol for the police car, and cigarettes and some beers for us. If you dash us some Naira, we can investigate!"

I am still sufficiently new in Nigeria to be horrified that a policeman could ask for a bribe to investigate a crime and so tell him in no uncertain terms to get out of my home. The case is never investigated and we never get any of our possessions back.

Although I am not initially frightened by the burglary, friends like Maurice and Simon tell me that we have had a very lucky break not to have woken up during the burglary. Apparently in Nigeria burglars are generally armed and often under the influence of drugs to provide them courage. So if challenged their response can be unpredictable and dangerous. Simon also tells me that his experience from Ibadan is that thieves will burn leaves under the door or through louvre windows which induce a drugged, deep sleep. Of course, that explains why only one louvre pane was removed and what the white ashes were on the floor – we had assumed that they were from a burnt mosquito coil – and also why I had so much trouble to wake myself up. From that day on, I sleep with a machete beside my bed and, for at least a year, never manage a full, uninterrupted night's sleep.

My response to the burglary is to tell the university that we have no further use either of the cleaner and her assistant or indeed of the night watchman. We hire our own and never have any further trouble. The first person to join us is a young Efik girl called Rose. She tells us that she is eighteen but we suspect that she is younger. However, despite her initial lack of English, she is a sweet young lady and she stays with us throughout our time in Nigeria. We are soon obliged to hire a second person to help Rose by doing the ironing. We had brought a rather sophisticated clothes iron from UK in the trunk and despite Véro's best efforts to show Rose how the temperature control and steam works, she manages to burn every item of clothing she tries to iron. We make a quick calculation that it will be cheaper to pay someone to do the ironing than to continually buy new shirts, trousers and dresses. As is frequent in Calabar, the person we find to do the ironing on a regular basis at a price we consider reasonable is a middle-aged man. He agrees to come each week for three hours, always on a Friday, and his name is …. Friday! So our Man Friday comes on a Friday and is called Friday. Impossible to forget any of those details!

As time goes on we find that some of the days of the week are commonly used in Calabar as first names. The most common is

Sunday, presumably for religious reasons, but we subsequently meet several Mondays, Tuesdays and of course we have our very own Man Friday.

Meanwhile, Andy and Marian have been discussing our burglary and they feel rather isolated and susceptible in their new home on the university campus, especially with little Anna sleeping in a separate room and the large areas of scrubland that encircles each of the newly-built houses; perfect hiding places for any wannabe crooks in the area.

Andy informs us over very large G&Ts that he wants to install a burglar alarm for added security. This brings forth lots of laughter and teasing from all of us listening to him because there are no alarm companies in Calabar and nowhere that he can buy the necessary equipment. However, there are lots of night watchmen looking for work and I tease him that he should hire a contingent of Fulani tribesmen from Niger who are considered ferocious and possess very sharp swords. Not liking to be teased too long, he disappears from the room and comes back with an old biscuit tin. This he has already painted black and added a red painted lightning strike across the middle and underneath he has carefully stencilled 'CalElectric'. The first item of his home-made security system.

I should add that because burglary is so prevalent and many burglars are dangerous if disturbed, all homes have iron grills at their windows while the doors are usually made of metal. Andy has had an idea but I am unsure if it is a good one. While he fixes the painted biscuit tin above the front door, he gets me to go around and fix electric cables on to the bars outside of the windows and drill small holes through the walls so that the cables can be passed inside the house. These we connect up to form an electric circuit, connect them to a house plug and switch on the electricity. All entrance points to the house are now carrying live electricity, and woe betide any foolish burglar who tries to break into *chez-Kemp*.

They were never burgled but this was certainly due more to luck than to CalElectric because Calabar had so many electricity cuts, load-shedding, brownouts, and system breakdowns, that any slightly intelligent burglar would only need to wait an hour or so for a cut and he could break in with no risk of electrocution. This is one of the enormous downsides of Calabar; lack of electricity, sometimes going on for days. The power company is called NEPA which theoretically stands for 'Nigerian Electricity Power Authority' but which is always known by locals and expatriates alike as 'Never Electric Power in Africa'.

The first semester is soon to end and so exam time will finally arrive. Many of my students have been to see me for some one-on-one or small group explanations of any concepts that they have not understood fully. I am sure that I am as nervous as they are as I watch them go past my office windows and into their different exams. All the lecturers help out with invigilating the university exams, collecting the papers at the end and ensuring that they get to the correct lecturers for marking. Each evening now I am loading my car with papers needing marking, and we have set a very tight schedule to get them finished before the start of the second semester. My biggest wodge of papers comes, of course, from Biology 101 with some three hundred students involved. I finish my marking and hand the papers to another lecturer (he of the Indian accent) and from there to the chicken farm manager. The same process is repeated for the more advanced ecology courses with much of the marking undertaken by myself and Dr Reid (he of the beaten up green Beetle).

Once I get all the marked papers back for the courses I am coordinating, I enter results into a results grid developed by the

Registry. These will eventually go back to the Registry but first they need to be reviewed, corrected and approved in a departmental meeting. The next step is to rank the students in order of their results from best to worst, then draw lines across the results to show the quality of the result from 'A' (what would be a First Class pass) at the top downwards across categories of 'B' (Upper Second), 'C' (Lower Second), 'D' (Third Class), 'E' (Pass) and fittingly 'F' for Fail.

As I complete the results' sheets for Biology 101, I note that there are around half-a-dozen students who have performed abysmally with percentage results in the teens and low twenties. Given that the pass mark is only 30% (too generous in my mind), these outliers are clearly very bad fails. I give my course lecturers the chance to review the results' sheets and then pass them into the departmental office. The following morning, I receive an internal phone call from the head of department in which he tells me to come down to his office.

I walk into his office and find that he has another senior colleague present. The colleague was once a student of the head of department at Ibadan University and has followed the professor from his old university to this one. This colleague is the overall exam supervisor.

"Dr Marks, why are there six students on 101 who have been given fails?"

How do I answer that without undue sarcasm?

"Prof. they have done so badly in their exams that they come nowhere near the pass mark at 30%. I never saw the student at the bottom of the list in my class and certainly did not sign a course admission form for him. Did he ever attend the university apart from taking the exams?"

"We want you", and he looks at our colleague who nods his head, "to go away and re-mark the questions for all failing students. Everyone should pass, OK?"

That order was a bit of a shock and not what I would anticipate from a university so I reply gently "Prof. I understand perfectly that it will be upsetting for the students concerned but I feel that it would be improper to pass students who are so far away from the 30% pass level. In fact, while I was marking the questions that they actually did attempt, I felt that I was being over-generous and so, yes, I will follow your orders and re-mark but, if I do so, they may end up with even lower scores. Is that preferable?"

"Oh, OK", he replied rather put out by my polite but frank refusal to cheat the results, "you can go doctor. I will talk to someone else about remarking."

Feeling rather shocked, my first port of call is to my friend Maurice whom I consider must have been through such a situation in previous years.

He asks to see the list of names of those that are failing and, after some scrutiny, says, "mmm as I thought, their names indicate that they are students from around the town of Oron and, you probably know, that is the professor's hometown. I hear that there is already a scandal brewing that Oron students were allowed into the university in preference to those from other areas. My suggestion is that you go and speak privately to Tambiah."

That suggestion comes as quite a shock because Prof. Tambiah is from Sri Lanka and he and the head seem to be permanently at loggerheads. This is the first occasion that a Nigerian colleague seems to be supporting the Tambiah camp. Until now I have tried hard to stay out of internal politics especially as it is apparent to me that there is a pretty clear split at the top of the

Biology Department between the Nigerians and the expatriate professors; I want no part in that. Many of my lecturer-level colleagues, both Nigerian and expatriate, agree with me that it is best not to get sucked into departmental politics and to leave well alone. Any rancour among staff can stay with the most senior members of the department.

However, I came to Calabar to help the university improve, I did not come to pull its standards down by passing students who have clearly failed. I find a quiet time the next morning to meet with Prof. Tambiah. As usual, he is charming and a good listener. After I explain the contents of the earlier meeting with the Head of Department, he suggests I do nothing.

Rather, he says "this afternoon we have the departmental meeting to confirm results before sending them officially to Registry, let's see if his instructions to pass the failing students are repeated in front of the entire department. I doubt they will be and, if they are, I will protest loudly!"

And that was exactly how the meeting passes. There was a short comment, in passing, by the Head that 101 had six failures but that their scores were so bad that the Exam Supervisor suggests that they are not worthy of remarking. Maurice nudges me and Tambiah flashes me a quick grin, and I feel good that my moral and academic standards have not been compromised at my first exam hurdle.

Nigeria lesson number eight: Do not allow your standards to drop under pressure.

While I may believe that the burglary has not impacted me in any significant way, our bodies have the habit of disagreeing with us and responding to suppressed stress. One morning in March, I wake up and my body feels like I have been run over by a train; my throat is sore, I have a raging fever and gushing diarrhoea. Véro takes me to the Health Centre at the University, where I am taken directly to a private ward and not into the usual doctor's waiting room. The nurse tells Véro that she is worried about me and tells me to get undressed and into bed – ominous.

An hour later, she reappears with a tray filled with drugs and tells me to take them all. Véro asks what they are for and the nurse reels off that this one is in case of malaria, these are for cholera, this for typhoid, and antibiotics in case of infection, …

We are both pretty much anti-drug, believing our bodies have most of the defences we need. And, anyway, I have already taken my anti-malarial prophylactic this morning, so do not want to double dose on that.

Véro thanks the nurse, telling her she will get me to take them in a moment and then waits for her to leave the room.

"No way are you going to take all those pills!" she declares in true Gallic fashion that brooks no arguement.

She goes to the bathroom and flushes the toilet. Later that day the nurse comes back with more pills. These follow the previous ones down the loo. By the next morning, the diarrhoea has slowed and the fever is abating. The nurse proudly tells us that she is responsible for diagnosing my sickness and it is clear that the prescribed medicines have worked. Three days later I feel sufficiently well to be discharged. We are now in the Easter break, so I have a few days to recover completely before returning to the classroom. We never did learn what my ailment was.

Returning to the University after the Easter break, I get an official message from the Housing Committee stating that we have finally been allocated a house with three bedrooms on Road-10 of the housing estate. The letter instructs that I should collect the keys, go to visit the house and put in a list of any work that needs doing to the Works Department. One week later, after odds and ends of repairs have been carried out, we move into our new home.

Our front garden is six metres deep and the width of the house plus a couple of metres on the side where I can park our car. We cross the garden and go up three steps to a small front veranda enclosed by metal bars and through the front door. I assume that the house is raised to protect us from flooding or perhaps to make entry difficult for snakes. The entrance door leads into an L-shaped room with the sitting area immediately in front of the door and a dining area off to the right. There is an open hatch that leads from the dining area into the kitchen, meaning that food can be passed directly from the kitchen via the hatch to the dining table. The kitchen itself is reached by passing down a small corridor and turning right. It contains a gas stove and a few built-in cupboards made of cement with wooden doors and covered by a cement work surface covered with 'made in China' tiles. A small corridor outside of the kitchen entrance goes both to the right and to the left. To the right is the back door and just outside is the electricity connection, meter and fuse board plus a big 45 kg gas cylinder with a pipe leading through the wall, into the kitchen and connected to the back of the cooker. To the left, the short corridor joins a longer corridor which opens into two of the three bedrooms. Both are sufficiently big to contain double beds with a toilet and bathroom opposite. Importantly, the bathroom has a bath; this will be our permanent reservoir of fresh water since, even in a region as wet as Calabar, where up to ten metres of rain can fall in a calendar year, there is a chronic shortage of fresh water. We can go days without a drop appearing from the taps. When the taps do deign to splutter water, we are obliged to tie a sock over the end to catch the larger pieces of muck that accompany the water.

Finally, at the end of the corridor is the master bedroom with *en-suite* bathroom, also with a bath. The bedroom nearest to the kitchen is to be a guest bedroom while the second becomes my office and our storeroom. We note that while each room has a ceiling fan, there are no air conditioners. The latter are only provided to professor-level academics (presumably because they suffer more from the heat!).

Outside the back door, the garden continues with a path that runs up the side of the house and includes a simple washing line and it then opens up to almost twice the width of the house and runs for another ten metres until it reaches a hedge composed of Coco yam or Taro. The garden is overrun by weedy grasses that are already up to knee height but I notice that the last resident of our house has planted six or so pineapple plants, and one is in flower.

Hanging down from the washing line to the tips of a couple of the pineapple leaves is the most amazing spider's web. The silk of the web is bright yellow, not white as we are used to seeing in Europe. And plonked right in the middle is an equally amazing spider. Apart from its large size, almost as big as my hand, it looks and is coloured just like an enormous wasp with long legs. I am told that it is probably a golden orb spider and not to let it bite!

Looking across the end of our garden, I can see John's beaten up Beetle parked outside a house in the next road; so we are neighbours and our back gardens back on to each other.

Furniture is basic but functional; all provided by the university. All the windows are screened and I have already gotten the Works Department to repair any screens that were broken. I notice that a couple of the sitting room window frames, made from wood, are only held together by several layers of oil paint. The termites have long since chewed away all the wood inside. I make a mental note to ask the Works Department to come and fix new frames.

We make a list of items to buy, including another water filter. No one would want to drink the water as it appears out of the tap, no matter how thirsty. In fact, we realise that even with a couple of filters, it is going to be hard to keep up with the quantity of drinking water we need because within a few days the ceramic candles of the filter – which actually do the filtering – become clogged and difficult to clean; also they are horrendously expensive to buy. As far as we can confirm, bottled water has not yet arrived in Nigeria, at least in our area of the Deep South. Eventually, we get a routine in place: this starts with improving the 'sock filter' on the tap, filtering the water from the bath through muslin, boiling it in a pressure cooker (that lifts the water temperature to close to 110 C, enough to kill most if not all bacteria), allowing it to cool, pouring it into the water filters, and running off the filtered water into screw top bottles – gin is our favourite as being square they are easier to stack in the fridge. I can hear our French relations chanting yet again, '*Ils sont fous*'.

We make a final trip from the guesthouse with the car loaded with our remaining effects. Removal is complete and we are home at long last. We have suffered the guesthouse privations for almost nine months and we laugh that is the same time as it takes to make a baby. But no little ones are on the road for us just yet, despite us both feeling quite broody; blame that on the cute little Anna Kemp!

Véro continues to work as the Secretary at Hillside School but soon after we move into our new home, she calls out to me as I walk in from the university: "I have a new job!" Apparently she is now a teacher of a class of eight-year olds. Having never taught previously, her first morning has been fun and rather funny.

Rosemary had asked her to start off by showing the children some long division; nothing difficult about that, of course. The only problem is that the French do not use the same method of long division as the Brits so the kids became totally confused when she uses her French method to arrive at the correct result. Step in Rosemary to provide Véro with a quick lesson in the British method. Becoming a teacher means that her salary has gone up by 50 per cent - such riches!

This is perhaps the moment to explain just how fixated all expats in Nigeria are to make their bimonthly cash transfers to home bank accounts. The Nigerian state allows us to remit overseas half of our salaries, after tax. The process is, in theory, relatively simple. It involves filling in a request in triplicate for foreign currency at the bank – pounds sterling in our case – and accompanying the request with three copies of an up-to-date tax card plus three copies of a current tax clearance certificate. There is always an unexpected shortage of the foreign currency request forms at the bank, unless some dash is provided, of course, and the tax inspectorate that provides the clearance certificates is always busy, except when dash is forthcoming. Then, when the completed dossier in triplicate is taken to the bank, the clerks are often unavailable to check them in without something to interest them. Luckily my friend Femi at the bank always looks out for me and now calls me 'uncle doctor' which is a bit off-putting because he is certainly older than me. Two weeks after requests are deposited at the bank, our sterling cheques should be awaiting collection. My salary has reached

Naira 465 per month and Véro's is now Naira 150 per month. After tax, which is modest, we have a total income of just shy of Naira 600 of which half can be transferred every two months. Naira 600 when exchanged for sterling comes out at about £550 and so, every two months, by living relatively modestly, we are able to remit that amount to our UK bank account.

Moving into our home and Véro being appointed a teacher coincides with a widening of our circle of friends but we still see more of Marian and Andy than anyone else. Marian is now pregnant – a Calabar-baby due to be born around the start of the new year.

Among the many parents Véro meets at the school are several southern Irish couples working for Harbour Works, the company building and expanding the Calabar Port. There is also a Romanian couple who have a cute little daughter of around eight. He runs a timber factory in Calabar for the Romanian government and has to deal with some very iffy-looking Romanian characters that work with him.

Many of the couples at Harbour Works soon become friends and via them we also meet other families working for yet more companies. One day while speaking to one of the Irishmen, I mention that we have waited several months for admission to the Palm Oil Club since we would like to play squash and badminton as well as have somewhere to go in the countryside. A few days later I receive a message saying that our membership is confirmed. Calabar is amazing like that; someone always knows someone else. In this case the Irishman, plays golf with Frank, the Scotsman, who runs the Palm Oil estate and manages the club. Such an incestuous society can be very positive in good moments but also negative if a cross word is spoken to the wrong person. We, especially I, learn the good lesson during my

Calabar days that it is better to avoid people one finds annoying rather than react to them. This simple lesson has stood me in good stead many times during my subsequent career!

Nigeria lesson number nine: Expatriate societies are often incestuous so it is better to avoid the more annoying people than react to them.

The Harbour Works families drive their children from their village compound to Hillside each day in a small bus, a round trip twice a day of more than an hour in both directions. The non-working wives take it in turns to accompany and supervise the busload of kids. However, one has the brilliant idea of asking Véronique if she would voluntarily supervise the children during the trips to and from the school. This is great news for me because it means that I no longer have to drive Véro to and from school each day. Since the wives do not know that this is a bonus for us, they offer to allow us to enter their guard-protected village and use the swimming pool as compensation. Thank you very much.

In Western terms, the value of life is impossibly cheap in Calabar. One morning as Véro accompanies the children to school in the bus she sees a body lying on the right-hand side of the highway. The poor person must have been struck during the night by a vehicle and just left there. She mentions this to the driver who replies that the man, as indeed it is a man, was probably a 'fool' (Calabar term for a mentally challenged person).

"Well, yes" says Véro "but will no one take responsibility and report the dead person to the police?"

"No chance" retorts the driver. "If you report this to the police, they will assume you are responsible and may arrest you, so no one will take the initiative."

The poor soul stays by the roadside for at least a week until a garbage collection van arrives to pick up the pieces left over by the vultures and feral dogs. So sad. A few days later, Véro mentions this horrible situation to some of the workers from a dredger that work out of the Port of Calabar, ensuring that the approach channels stay open for cargo ships. They respond that they have a 'friend' who washes past the dredger with the tides; another dead body for which no-one takes responsibility. Speaking later to our doctor friend Doug about the dead bodies and the number of obviously mentally sick individuals that walk naked around Calabar, he explains that many are in the later and untreated stages of syphilis. Obviously there is significant work for the authorities to get to grips with.

The Irish couple from the Harbour Works company are great friends with the manager of Calcemco. Since Harbour Works owns a speedboat, they are often to be found out on the river at weekends. One Friday evening when Véro drops the resident children back at the Harbour Works village after school, we are invited to join up with them the following day for a trip on the Calabar River, and the opportunity to try our hands at water skiing. All we need to bring is a cool box with a picnic and a considerable amount of courage. Neither of us has ever tried water skiing although Véro is an excellent (snow) skier and a good swimmer too. I cannot claim any skiing skills; in fact, on the ski slopes, I am considered a danger to life and limb – my own and anyone around me. Also I am not a very good swimmer either, so I am a little concerned about this new adventure.

Early on the Saturday morning, we are picked up from our house and driven to the new Calabar port, passing through two security checks and into the very heart of the port where the public is prohibited. Our boat is awaiting us, as are Calcemco friends. Within a few minutes of loading, the motor is started and off we speed along the enormous river, direction the sea. Drinks are passed around: coffee, soft drinks or beer while out comes a freshly baked cake.

We cruise at speed down the middle of the river and I point out a fish eagle that is perched high in a dead tree on the right-hand bank. A pair of pied kingfishers make a brief passage across the boat announcing their presence with a sharp cackle. We see several dugout canoes hugging the bank with the occupants fishing with hand-lines or nets. As we pass down the river and the wake of our boat reaches the shore, the poor fishermen start to bob up and down like corks until we have progressed sufficiently far downriver for the water to regain its relative calm.

After almost thirty minutes of travel, the motor is cut and the captain asks "so who is first to try?"

The Calcemco manager, by far the best sportsman among us, claims the distinction, slips on a lifejacket over his bare torso and pulls off his trainers. Without further ado, he jumps overboard and floats downriver at the same speed as the boat, quickly grabbing on to the side. We hand him first one and then the other ski which he slips expertly onto his bare feet. The tow rope is then lowered, and he moves away from the back of the boat as the engines roar and the water bubbles with the build-up of engine revs. We go at speed down the river and our friend, as cool as a cucumber, bobs up on to the surface and does a small wave with one hand, holding tight on the rope with the other. He is good, in our eyes anyway, as he begins to weave left and right behind the boat. He stays up for fully ten minutes until the skipper makes a hand signal to indicate that he is going to slow down and the cameo is over. He lets go of the rope and slowly sinks down into the water awaiting the boat to come to retrieve him.

Next up is Véro! And she does rather well, managing to stay up on her feet for around two or three minutes at a time, being pulled in a straight line by the boat. After she returns to the boat, receiving well done from us all, I am told that I should get into the water and see what I can do. I confess that once the skis are on and the boat is building up sufficient speed, standing up is relatively easy. What is more difficult is to remain standing. And I only last thirty seconds before tumbling down and the boat needs to do an about turn to come to my rescue. The second attempt is a bit better and by the time my allotted stint is complete, I have managed only to fall over six times. I am told not to give up my day job!

We are now in the summer term, and the university is moving rapidly towards second semester exams. Most of us have finished our teaching for the semester and many of the lecturers – at least those that have kept to their timetables – are starting to help their classes with revision. Teaching duties aside, I am also in charge of setting up the exam papers for all the ecology courses and so need to allocate portions of each paper to the lecturers who have taught on my different ecology courses. In this work I receive help from a brand new arrival in the department, Dr Alan Seddon. While Alan's name has been on the staff list since I first arrived in Calabar, he has only just made an appearance in Calabar after finally completing his doctorate. Alan is a kind and gentle person and immediately liked by everyone. Pleasingly, he is an animal ecologist and so complements my preference for the botanical side of ecology, and an expert in ...

errr ... midges; you know those little flies that form dense clouds of insects over grassy areas on balmy summer evenings?

For the first few months of his time in Calabar, Alan suffers an enormous amount of gentle ribbing from us all. This is because, during his interview in London, he had mentioned that he is an experienced diver and, since Calabar is on the coast (well sort-off), the selection panel employs him in the Biology Department, not only as an animal ecologist, but also as a dive instructor for marine biology students. Furthermore, since the department has absolutely no diving equipment, he is charged with buying, shipping and clearing the equipment through customs. Our experience shows that the first two parts are a little easier than the third.

Like all other expats at the university, Alan had never visited Calabar (probably never even heard of it until he was offered the job) and so knows little about the geography and obviously nothing about the water clarity either. The sad fact is that Calabar sits in the middle of extensive mangrove swamps and has a whopping big river that feeds into the swamps and a rainfall that some years approaches ten metres. All that combined produces a highly rich ecosystem for the life in the mangroves and shallow seas around but, sadly, such a dense water turbidity that it is impossible to see further than your nose when underwater. Poor Alan, after first struggling to get the equipment cleared through Lagos, is obliged to go no further than the local swimming pool to give diving lessons to a few brave students and it is only here that they can see far enough under water to observe the local 'wildlife'. This initiative dies a natural death a few weeks later. Indeed, the ribbing lasts longer than his diving lessons.

Term is soon finishing and that means we will be entering the long summer vacations. For the university, the summer break last almost four months; slightly less at the primary school for Véro. However, this year, we have to buy our own tickets since my university contract only pays a ticket at start and end of each two-year contract; so we will need to wait for next year, on condition that we renew, to get a paid round trip.

We have made friends with the Lobbs, Steve and Jane, a Kiwi couple of about our own age. Steve works for a building company while Jane is a font of knowledge about all things air-tickets. Like the Aussies, the Kiwis love to go 'walk-about' and visit the old continent and so many of them learn early in life how to find the cheapest and most flexible travel tickets.

Telling her that we need to buy round tickets from Calabar to Lyon then London, she says "leave it with me, I'll see what I can come up with."

We keep our fingers crossed because we do not have a lot of spare funds. She manages to find us an interesting flight for a five-week break; anything longer puts the price up sharply. She tells us that we must travel from Calabar to Lagos on Nigerian Airways as they are the only company that covers the internal leg, and then recommends that we travel from Lagos to Rome and on to Lyon with Alitalia, and then Lyon to London with Air France. Alitalia covers the return leg from London to Rome and Rome to Lagos. We purchase our tickets with considerable gratitude to Jane and are booked to fly out in mid-July, returning in early September. We will spend the first three weeks in the Lyon area with Véro's parents and then two weeks in Kent with mine.

Travel time arrives and Alan drives us to Calabar Airport in his new Volkswagen Igala, a step up from the Beetle, thanks to a car loan provided by the university. The flight from Calabar to Lagos passes without a hitch except the stomach-wrenching plunges when we hit air-pockets and the stomach repeating experience of the infamous sardine-filled rolls of Nigerian Airways. Our flight to Rome takes off in the evening, and on time, and we arrive the following morning in the Eternal City. Since we have around 24 hours before our onward flight to Lyon, Alitalia kindly puts us up in a very passable hotel in the centre of the city. Jane's ticketing skills have thus brought us an unexpected and free twenty-four hour stay in Rome.

On to Lyon the next day and after a short flight of less than two hours we arrive at Satolas Airport and straight through to the greetings of Belou and Mic, Véro's parents, with an excited but shy Nico, her ten-year old brother, hiding behind his Dad. Ooph, it's good to be on vacation.

That evening, after a typically enjoyable and tasty French supper, we sit around the garden chatting (as only the French can chat). How great it is not to have the sun disappear at 6 pm every night nor have mosquitos permanently whining in our ears. We start to tell stories about all our adventures during the past year spent in Calabar but, strangely to us, her parents seem uninterested, even bored, by the stories. A few days later we meet up with Véro's uncle André who had spent twenty or so years working in the Cameroons and then in Chad.

When we tell him that we were surprised at just how uninterested the parents seem to be concerning our time in Nigeria, he laughs and says "welcome to the club. My parents, your grandparents Véro, showed no interest either. You just have to accept that what you and I live is beyond their smaller worlds."

From that day on, we rarely spoke about our overseas lives unless asked.

The three weeks draw to a close and we move on to the UK, travelling from Heathrow to Kent where my parents live in a small house in the countryside. My dad works at the paper mill in the neighbouring small town of Aylesford, and he is on night shift when we arrive, and so asleep in bed. My mum is a secretary on a small fruit farm, a short walk from their home. After dropping our suitcase, we take a walk up to the farm to say hello to my mum.

My parents moved to their current home when I was not quite five years old. The first four years of my life were spent living in a tied cottage in the tiny village of Otham. The tied cottage came with my dad's job working as a labourer in a quarry. However, when the quarry owner heard on the grapevine that my dad was looking around for another job, he kicked us all out of the cottage. I understand from my parents, that we then spent a bad six months living apart with my two sets of grandparents until our current house was allocated by the council. Soon after we moved in, my mum started to do seasonal fruit-picking on the farm; strawberries in the summer, apples and hops as autumn began. Then she had the opportunity to work during the winter months in the apple wrapping and packing shed with twenty or thirty other ladies and a couple of men who were responsible for the heavy lifting and forklift and tractor driving duties. A few years later she was asked to do secretarial duties (she had trained as a secretary several years before) in the farm office.

As a very young child I spent all my school holidays with my mum playing in the orchards with the other children during the nice weather and inside the pack-house during the winter months. As I got older, I became less interested in playing around with the other children and more in helping the ladies with their work. One summer holiday when the ladies were overstretched and a load of cardboard boxes had to be made up from flat-packs, the pack-house owner, who was only ten or so years older than me, asked if I could make up the boxes while he stapled them. Of course, I did happily and at the end of the week was surprised when he presented me with my very own pay packet containing four shillings; a fortune when my pocket money was only sixpence a week! I was not quite eleven years old and as happy as a sand-boy.

Each school holiday thereafter, I was given more and more work to do with increasing responsibility, and I loved it. At the age of twelve, the farm manager, Mr Brown, told me it was time that I learnt to drive a tractor. The farm had one small tractor for use in the strawberry fields, and it was this one I was to learn on. I was taken into the middle of a pasture, shown how the engine started and stopped and how the gears worked – and left to practice. Unfortunately, after thirty minutes I found the one damp, boggy patch in the field and the rear wheels sunk down into the mud! Nonetheless, that was a great experience and as I got older, I did more and more of the same work as the permanent farmhands. I believe that those early, idyllic years on the farm laid the basis for my love for nature that has always underpinned my career.

Véro and I arrive at the farm office to see my mum after almost a year away from the UK.

Hearing my voice, her boss calls out from his neighbouring office "have you come for a job then? I need your help in the pack-house."

The next morning, I am working eight-hour days stacking full apple boxes and taking them to the cold store with a fork-lift truck. With my weekdays full, time goes quickly and the two weeks in the UK are soon up. Time to start travelling back to Nigeria.

~ 6 ~

OUT OF THE DITCH BUT NOT OUT OF THE WOODS

We arrive back at Fiumicino Airport in the late afternoon and, since we have only a couple of hours to wait for the Lagos flight, decide that we will go straight through formalities and then make ourselves comfortable at the gate. We find the waiting room already quite busy and are amazed at the quantity of hand luggage that many of the Nigerian passengers are carrying. While we have only our two small cabin suitcases, I see a number of ladies with airport trollies piled high with their ubiquitous red and blue traders' bags. These must be almost a metre long, fifty centimetres wide and eighty centimetres high. They seem to be made of some plastic-based material and are closed at the top by a long zipper running between the two red cloth handles. I shudder to think how much each weighs. I point out to Véro a particularly corpulent lady who seems to believe that she is allowed to bring half a dozen such bags on board with her.

In response, she points across the room and says "better still, look over there."

We both roar with laughter as we see a scrawny and rather elderly gentleman with a pompom hat squashed to his head by the small refrigerator that he has balanced on top. We follow his progress with amazement as he walks, hands-free across the waiting room, occasionally bobbing his head to maintain balance, and sits down in a spare seat still with the fridge balanced atop. A kindly compatriot comes across to help lift the fridge off and place it on the floor beside him.

Just as we approach the appointed boarding time, a dozen or so Italian soldiers, each casually carrying machine guns, march towards the boarding gate and form a queue back down the hall. All passengers will have to walk past them in order to show their boarding passes. With our small amount of carry-on baggage, we are relatively quick to join the queue but fall in behind a few quicker passengers, some carrying those ominous and large trading bags.

A slim, pretty, and very chic Alitalia lady (how do Italians always manage to look so good?) calmly and gracefully walks down our queue saying "you go, you stay, you stay, you stay, you go" efficiently selecting out for boarding those with reasonable amounts of baggage while detaining the traders.

One trader begins to argue with her which prompts a soldier to move forward and, without needing to hear a word, the trader falls silent.

We board and find ourselves sitting close to the front of economy class. Only a few of the passengers, following behind us into the plane, are carrying their traders' bags and no gentleman appears with a fridge on his head. What happened to all that surplus? I have no idea but we do manage to take off with only half-an-hour delay.

The flight goes without a hitch and we are well looked after by another very chic hostess. She seems to be giving us special attention, stopping to chat every time she passes but ignoring many of the Nigerian passengers, who all seem to have flashing red overhead lights. She is interested to know what a young couple like us is doing on the Lagos flight because she hates this route and cannot imagine anyone wanting to live there. She has never even heard of Calabar. It appears that passengers on the Lagos flight are often very demanding, so she finds it simpler to ignore them. One gentleman has just asked her for six cans of beer and four little bottles of whisky!

I ask what happens to all the bags that people try to bring on board and she laughs and says "and did you see the fridge?"

She explains, as we thought, that these people are traders and they always have bundles of cash with them. The airline charges a fixed amount per bag for the excess luggage to be taken off them and stored in the hold. All the traders know the ropes and simply hand over the cash without too much protest while the soldiers keep order. But the company decided to carry the fridge for free because the elderly gentleman seemed totally lost when told that he could not take it on board.

The following morning, we touch down in Lagos, and go through formalities, again with little hassle although on passing our two passports to the policeman at border control, he says "where is your passport?"

"In your hand, sir" I reply.

He looks at my dark blue passport and says "this is not a passport; this is an empty document. Put something into it and then it will become a passport."

I laugh and say "an honest man like you should not be joking with me about dash."

He laughs too, stamps the passports and hands them over saying "have a nice day sir."

After picking up our suitcases, we travel the well-known road in a yellow taxi to the domestic airport and check the cases back in, receiving our boarding passes in return. We have four hours to wait so settle down with a couple of novels.

An hour or so into our wait, so still three hours to go, there is an airport announcement: "all passengers must leave the terminal. The airport will close in thirty minutes for a military exercise by the Nigerian Air Force. We repeat all passengers must leave the terminal immediately."

We watch many of the other passengers begin to gather their travel materials and start to walk towards the exit. Véro asks me whether we should leave too.

"Sit tight," I say, "you know how things can change."

But fifteen minutes later the same announcement comes across the airport's public address system but this time telling us that the airport will close in fifteen minutes. Still, we sit tight. Another announcement five minutes later, now the airport will close in ten minutes for the military exercise. We remain stubbornly in place. Then five minutes later another announcement telling us that the airport shuts in five minutes and that this is the last message.

Just as we are gathering up our bags to leave, a Nigerian Airways hostess comes across and says "quick, go out through that door," she indicates the door behind her, "and onto the tarmac. The plane for Calabar is leaving in less than five minutes."

We rush outside clutching our boarding passes and travel cases and climb on board. Our seats are close to the front but a couple are already in our allotted places. A hostess tells us to sit anywhere as we are soon taking off and must get airborne in a minute or so. From our seats on the aeroplane, we faintly hear the airport communications system from the terminal building saying that the Calabar plane will leave in three minutes, stopping at Ibadan and Nsukka. There is a mad rush of passengers from all around the domestic terminal building and soon they are pushing and shoving as they climb up the aeroplane steps. Rapidly all seats on the plane are filled and there are at least a dozen passengers standing in the aisle, trying to find a handhold on the overhead compartments. Others are trying to share seats; a real pandemonium of noise.

The pilot, a young Brit by his accent, emerges from his cockpit and roars at the melee. "Everyone without a seat, off now. This is not a bus service, off, off!"

Many of the seated passengers join in his demand, embarrassingly, me included – where are my manners? The surplus passengers sadly leave the plane, a hostess closes the door and off we go. Once in the air, the pilot informs us that we have made it with thirty seconds to spare.

Absolutely no one going to Calabar cares that our flight time is now doubled due to the two unanticipated stopovers, and we are compensated with TWO sardine-filled rolls each and, I swear, less turbulence.

Alan, in his Igala, picks us up from the airport and drives us home to Road-10. We are back in Calabar, and our second year is about to get underway. Still three weeks or so until the term starts and so I have time to do some organising work in the botanical gardens and nature reserve. In the former, I want to get the shade house built so that we can use it both to increase our research facilities and provide a wider variety of plants for practical classes. Personal experience has shown me that the lecturers tend to scramble around for sufficient numbers and varieties of demonstration plants; which is really not good enough for a university.

On arriving at the gardens, the day after we returned to Calabar, I find a new staff member. He ranks equal to the Chief on the associate staff pay scale but has a far broader botanical knowledge and speaks excellent English.

I take him away from the gardens with the explanation to the other staff that we need to discuss his work. Instead, we drive to the Green Onion Annex and have a quiet beer so that we can get to know each other a little better. He has a university degree and is interested in being involved in staff research. I explain that there are only a few lecturers carrying out any research in the gardens and the most active is myself. He tells me that he would be very interested to work with me and learn; so I have found a well-qualified research assistant. Great.

We then go to my office and I show my plans for the Shade House. He gives a few good suggestions and modifications. From the measurements, we make a list of all the materials we need for the construction and go off to a couple of merchants in the market to get estimates. We find two merchants who have all the wood, nails and shade material (really rolls of green mosquito screen) we need and so ask for quotes. Both provide very similar prices and both tell me that if I buy from them there is 20% dash for me; as openly as that. I select the second trader, who can deliver immediately, and tell him that he can write me the estimate but at the end of the estimate signify that there is a 20% discount for buying bulk.

Frank laughs and says that the trader will never understand what I am saying, and so he explains in Efik. He tells the trader that he does not need to pay dash and so should remove the offered 20% from the prices. The trader writes out the purchase proforma with a big smile on his face and completes the order by saying just one word 'M'bakarah!'

The following day I collect the Chief from the gardens – I do not want to undermine his position despite finding our new worker a far more competent technician and interesting person

– and take him to the nature reserve beyond the student residences; still empty of students. We walk for at least three hours, following several of the larger trails occasionally coming across poachers' snares, which we remove as we go along, and several small patches of vegetables being grown where the forest has been cleared in the last year or so. I can see that Chief is embarrassed that I have found the snares and the vegetable plots so easily. For the moment I make no comment. At the end of our extended tour, we return to the staff hut which is a copy of the large shed in the botanic gardens and take out two plastic chairs. I collect two cokes from my car and we sit down to drink.

After a while I ask the Chief what he considers are the main functions of the Reserve. He reels off the correct responses: protect the animals and plants, allow species to breed, provide specimens for practical classes and lectures, provide research sites, and so on.

I tell him, very frankly, that I am disappointed to have found the traps and the cultivated areas. Did he know that they were there? Initially, he tells me no but when I suggest that he is therefore not doing his job correctly because he cannot have been making frequent rounds of the reserve, he changes his plea. He then admits all knowledge and says that there are people from surrounding villages who come in to trap and cultivate. He has tried in the past to forbid them but they keep coming back.

During our walk around the reserve, we note that a number of palm oil trees are being tapped for their sap in order to produce the same fermented liquid that I had drunk with the students. The process seems to be simple. The tapper waits until the palm begins to flower. It does this by producing a large bunch of flowers from the very top of the trunk, its apex, and, as the flower bunch grows and becomes heavier, the flower stem bends down. The tapper climbs the trunk, slits into the flower stem and ties a plastic bottle to it. The palm 'bleeds' sap and this is caught in the bottle. The tappers empty the bottles regularly into jerry cans and it is the contents of these containers that we see being sold to the students.

As we chat about the poaching and cutting and clearing of the forest for vegetable patches, Chief says that he presumes that wine tapping should not occur either.

This makes me pause for thought and I eventually reply "no, I think that is OK because the oil palms must be from an old plantation or have naturally regenerated from the seeds of a plantation. Of course, it would be better to have less oil palm and more natural forest species. But you have given me an idea how we can perhaps reduce vegetable planting and stop a lot of the poaching. Can you set up a meeting with the palm tappers and any poachers and vegetable growers you can find? Perhaps say in a week's time?"

A week later I go back to the reserve and find close to a dozen men standing outside the reserve's hut, several with wine tapper paraphernalia spread around their feet. Chief introduces me to the men and tells me that most are wine tappers but this one is a poacher and also grows vegetables and this man has one of the larger garden plots we had found. I realise just how poor the men are and I know I cannot simply ban them from the reserve because of the impact this would have on their families. Instead we need to find a way of harnessing their needs to help us in protecting the wildlife of the reserve. One thing I noticed on my first visit to the reserve, a year ago, is that someone in the past had cleared the forest for about a kilometre either side of the access path to the hut and then abandoned the ground. The land is now overgrown with Awolowo Weed and does not resemble at all the rest of the forest reserve as it has only shrubs and almost no trees left standing.

With Chief translating, I offer those that have been making vegetable gardens hidden within the forest – this involves the destructive cutting down and burning of trees – to come instead and garden either side of the access path. We offer to allocate anyone currently gardening in the reserve a generous plot of land and they will be given permits to cultivate there for ten years at a time. The only conditions for accessing this land are that first they must spread the word to others who garden in the reserve, and second promise that they will stop cutting trees and planting crops outside of the areas I am offering.

They chat together, and then with Chief, and eventually I am told that they agree providing that they can harvest the crops they have already planted within the forest. Fair enough, I agree. After this they promise to abandon their slash-and-burn practice and report any further instances they see. To seal the deal, I tell them that if they produce excess crops (it will be mostly yam and cassava) I will help them to sell at the university for a better price than can be obtained in the local markets. However, the poacher remains a little reticent and says that he needs the money from the small deer, bush rats and porcupines that he occasionally catches. But he admits that he catches very infrequently and keeps losing traps. I offer him two plots of land instead of one, and the deal is settled. We allow the two men to leave but retain the palm tappers and tell them that we will allow them to continue to collect palm wine in the reserve but in return we wish them to be our eyes and ears for any future poaching and gardening. I also offer to buy, for a small sum, any poachers' traps that they find and bring in to me.

Our meeting seems to have been a success and I, in hindsight, now realise that we have just undertaken perhaps the first community management agreement in Cross River State history!

We are now almost at the start of the new academic year and several new faces join the biology staff while a few of the older ones who have been at UniCal for at least two years have received promotions. Another Indian lecturer with the room next to Maurice, has jumped from being a senior lecturer to a professor and is now third in rank in the department after the head of department and Prof. Tambiah. He is a very quiet and polite gentleman, an animal physiologist who does research on the regrowth of lizards' tails, coming up with some interesting specimens with double tails and y-shaped ones. Whoever may have previously laughed at my research on wild lettuces or even Alan's on midges can have a bigger laugh about his research interests!

Unofficially, the word is going around the department that the Head is facing problems with the entry procedures of some of the students. He is no longer Dean of Science; that post has passed to Professor Tambiah while the new Indian professor is stepping up to become head of department. These changes are a surprise to us all.

A few days before the term is due to begin, all the lecturers get a call to an urgent union meeting; this is the first time that I even knew there was a union at the university. However, most of the department turns up along with staff from other departments and we are told that the National Union of Lecturers is declaring a strike for better pay and conditions. The strike is to start immediately and we are forbidden to teach any classes. The union representative, a humble and usually quiet lecturer, warns us all about the dire consequences that await anyone who dares break the strike, which makes many of us burst out laughing; much to his displeasure. The negative side of the strike is that our poor students will likely experience a blank year while the positive side for the lecturers is that the government has agreed in advance to pay us in full providing that lecturers turn up to the office each day.

I walk back from the strike meeting with Alan and we discuss using our unexpected free time to do some joint research work on *Chromolaena odorata* (the Awolowo weed) and its big predator, the grasshopper, *Zonocerus variegatus*. The research we hope to do will need considerable research assistance for data gathering. Another fortuitous knock-on of the strike, therefore, is that my botanical garden team will have less work in support of departmental teaching and so, once trained, can help us in what we both consider important and interesting research. The crux of the work we plan is to determine how *Zonocerus* and *Chromolaena* interact and whether this interaction can be used in controlling *Chromolaena*. At this stage, we do not know the degree of predation of the grasshopper on the plants' flowers, whether there are specific times of the grasshopper's life-cycle when predation is the most important, nor whether the presence of *Chromolaena* is not giving a significant boost to the grasshopper's population by providing a plentiful supply of food at critical points in its life-cycle. All interesting things for us to study and, eventually, to share with the wider academic community.

Meanwhile, my personal research work on the several species of *Compositae* that have two different types of seeds in the same flower head (termed dimorphic achenes) is ongoing and starting to produce some interesting results while I am also beginning to study characteristics of buried weed seeds (called the seed bank) and the timing of natural germination in groups of agricultural weeds. These linked pieces of work, I believe, will possibly demonstrate periods in the life-cycles of these weed species that are the most susceptible to organic weed control and require the least physical effort from small-scale farmers.

As with all of my colleagues at the university, I am only too aware that if I wish to apply for promotion at the end of the current academic year (at which point I will be up both for contract renewal and consideration for promotion), I must publish a few scientific articles.

In the jargon we say 'Publish or Perish', a term which is self-explanatory and a little unfair. Why do I consider this unfair? Because one of the characteristics of ecological research is that it almost always takes a fair amount of time to generate meaningful results; say a couple of years. Add to that, the time – one to two years – that most, good quality scientific journals take to publish research papers and it can be seen that starting a research project from scratch, as I am doing in Nigeria, and seeing results eventually published can easily take up to five years. So, rather than a vain attempt to get papers out of my Calabar research, I turn instead to the considerable pent-up data that I collected and analysed for my PhD thesis. The lecturers' strike gives me time to do some additional analyses and also write up the papers. In this way, I am now well advanced in the development of two papers from my thesis. The first looks at the germination characteristics of the wild lettuce while the other shows the impact of germination date in the field on the fecundity (seed production) of plants. The first draft of each has been sent to my old supervisor and co-author at QMC for his comments. I have chosen the journal of the Nordic Ecological Society (called Oikos) for eventual submission. With luck and a speedy and safe Nigerian postal service, I can get the proposed papers to Oikos during the upcoming semester and their eventual acceptance letters back in time to add to my submission for promotion at the end of this academic year.

On my drive back from work I notice that the new bakery is almost complete. When we had first arrived in Calabar and were obliged to eat the sugared bread with a delicate covering of mould, we had dreamt that one day a French Master Baker would 'ride into old Calabar Town and set up a bakery'. Well, guess what? The baker has ridden into town (in a four-wheel drive, of course), care of a local Chief who is an important businessman in Calabar. The Chief is just starting to build his new bakery business in Lagos and Calabar but is destined to expand to many Nigerian towns in future years and make all those involved a fortune.

The new baker and his wife are from Marseille, in southern France, and have arrived with two small boys. While the baker proves to be an excellent bread maker and pastry chef (*pâtissier*), he fails as a natural linguist! Despite being in Calabar to set up, install and run a large bakery with a considerable team of local workers to carry out the installation and to train them in baking, he only speaks a smattering of English and usually expresses himself in a loud and frightening voice. When this is combined with the fact that he is a big and rather swarthy-looking gentleman, most of the Nigerian workers are scared stiff of him. To make matters worse, only a handful of people in the whole of Calabar speak French and, of course, none of his workers do. This has and will lead to many hilarious as well as a few dramatic moments during his early time in Calabar.

We meet the bakers by accident in a local shop as he and his wife try to find the right English words to communicate with the shop assistant for the articles they wish to buy. Step up Véro and Malcolm as translators ... and a new friendship begins.

Just as we had been helped to learn the ropes more than a year ago, we have the pleasure to help them as they install into their first-floor apartment, not far from our old guesthouse. One of the difficulties on arrival in Calabar is obtaining good quality meat. The chicken we obtain from the university chicken farm run by the lecturer in my department. Funnily, the first time I visited the farm to meet my new colleague and to buy chicken, I also asked about buying chicken livers and gizzards, a delicious addition to a cold salad, and was told that they are thrown away, not sold. For several months thereafter, my colleague would send me plastic bags of liver and gizzards for free that we stored in the freezer and ate at leisure. Sadly, we told too many friends from outside the university about the chicken farm ... and the livers, so that the farm soon came to realise that 'there's gold in them thar offal' and the bags of liver eventually become more expensive per kilo than the chickens!

To source other meat, we had met 'John-the-Butcher' while we were staying in the guesthouse and he provides us with beef and pork. The beef is priced per kilogramme, no matter which cut is ordered. We found that most of his meat is tough enough to have walked the whole way from Kano in the north to Calabar in the south, which indeed it has. We tend therefore to buy only whole fillets – Naira 5 per kilo – and avoid all other cuts. With pork, he will only take orders for a whole leg of pork. Here, I am not talking about the leg joint you might order from the high street butcher back in Teddington, I am talking about a piece of meat that weighs at least ten kilogrammes and drips with blood having been chopped off with a machete at the abattoir from the still warm carcass; yucky, I know.

One Saturday, soon after we moved into our house in Road-10, we returned from morning shopping to find Rose looking at a great haunch of meat sitting on the kitchen counter, slowly accumulating a following of blowflies. The only way I can describe the leg is as though a Troll has ripped the leg and most of the side off of a wild boar. The skin is dark and covered with bristles and the bubbly fat is at least six inches thick. John-the-Butcher has left a note that reads pork: 14 kg – Naira 70.

I calculate that once I have taken off most of the skin, all the fat and the bones, we will be lucky to be left with four or, at the most, five kilograms of meat. While I do not mind butchering such a large hunk of meat, I do mind handing over so much money for a piece of pork that is nothing but skin, fat and bones. So, I slam the hunk into the car boot and go off to look for John, only having a vague notion of where his house is located. I just know that it is close to the abattoir. Of course, John is only his *nomme-de-guerre, so* when I ask for him at the abattoir, I get only blank stares. Finally, a worker puts the M'bakarah and the butcher together and realises who I am talking about. Eventually I arrive at his house and hand back the lump of meat. He nods, smiles a little bit in embarrassment and says he will bring me a better piece the following day, which he does. All good.

So, going back to the bakers, I introduce them to John-the-Butcher and all seems to go well for the first few weeks. But one evening, as I arrive at the baker's apartment for a drink, his driver greets me at my car door saying "Boss, come quick, big trouble-O." Once outside the car I can hear bellowing in a strange and confused mix of French and English. I run up the stairs and enter their apartment without knocking and see John sunk into a chair and the baker standing menacingly over him, still bellowing.

I speak rapidly in French, "what is happening, what has John done?"

John looks up and says in panic "save me boss!"

I then start to receive the explanation in French and what he tells me is that he asked for two fillets that had been delivered at Naira 5 per Kg, correct, and also meat for the dog (*de la viande pour le chien* he tells me) which John is trying to bill at a ridiculous fourteen Naira per kilogramme. With the telling of the amount so the Gallic temper flairs again and John cowers further down into the chair. Now, apart from the first pork delivery, John has always been very honest with us, so it is hard to imagine what is now going on.

So I say to the baker in French "dis-moi exactement ce que tu as dit en anglais" (tell me the exact English phrase you used).

To which he replies "*j'ai dit* ... bring me two beef fillets and dog meat." *Et voila*, we have the answer to the high price of the second meat item. Instead of my poor dough-kneader asking for cheap cuts of beef to feed his dog, he had inadvertently asked for the meat of a dog, considered a delicacy in southern Nigeria and very expensive. For one reason or another, dog meat goes by the nickname of '504' named after the famous Peugeot model that ply the intercity taxi routes of Nigeria. Having finally understood his error, my Gallic buddy roars with laughter then apologises to John, pays him, and gives us both cold Champions.

Early during his stay in Calabar, my buddy experiences severe problems controlling his temper; I think mostly because he cannot understand his workers and they certainly cannot understand him! On another fortuitous (for the worker) occasion, I stop at the Bakery to say hello and check how the installation work is advancing and as soon as I walk inside, his wife shouts "quick, go to the back."

I run through the shop section and into the enormous backroom where the bread-making equipment is being installed. I first see a pandemonium of scattered cardboard boxes, polystyrene wrappings and around a dozen workers calling out in Efik.

From the far side of the room I can hear someone whimpering under the bellow of the baker. I see that he is trying to push a worker into the newly installed bread oven and has almost succeeded! One or two of the workers, all far smaller than he, are trying frantically to pull him back.

I push them away and grab a very hairy arm, telling the baker to cool down. Hearing French, he relaxes and begins to stand back. I pull him away from the oven and help the worker out. "Mon ami, what the hell are you doing?"

In his Marseille-accented French he tells me "I caught him stealing and so I wanted to frighten everyone by putting him in the oven. All the other workers think the oven is switched on and that I want to cook him – but it's not plugged in yet!" and he roars with laughter. What a character but I would never want to cross him.

Soon after, the bakery opens with his wife in charge of the customer-facing work while the baker works on cake and bread production at the back. We go to the opening day and are amazed at the array of cakes and breads on sale. Also amazing is the queue of Nigerians waiting their turn and the prices are far higher than I had expected – will local custom continue at this rate, given the expensive cakes? I do not need to have any concerns for the baker or his Nigerian backer; Calabar residents have a sweet tooth and the bakery provides expertly to their needs.

Once the bakery is up and running, they move from their flat to a house on our estate, about one hundred metres distant from us.

Marian left with Anna a couple of months ago to await the birth of her baby in the UK. She has been staying with her parents and now that her second daughter, Helen, has arrived at the start of January, we anticipate her arrival back in Calabar sometime in March or April.

In the meantime, both Alan and I are only too aware that our own perception of the quality of our teaching is hindered by our shared lack of experience in the vegetation of the more northerly parts of Nigeria. As an undergraduate at QMC, I had taken courses in plant geography offered by the Geography Department that were co-lectured by Peter Wanstall from biology. The courses focused on the striation of vegetation zones that run East to West across West Africa. In their simplest form, these striations in Nigeria, start from Sahel Savanna in the North and run via bands of Sudan and then Guinea Savanna into Rainforest in the South. Mangrove forests provide the vegetation boundary between the rainforest and the sea. Each band has different vegetation types, plant species and their associated animal, bird and insect populations. These bands match pretty precisely with the quantity of precipitation that falls on each with by far the most intense rainfall in the south. Calabar boasts one of the highest annual rainfalls in West Africa, hence we have rainforest and mangrove vegetation but the quantity of rainfall steadily declines with distance north until in the far north of Nigeria, annual rainfall is only sufficient to allow vegetation of the semi-desert Sahelian savanna to grow. Going still further northwards, into Niger, the Sahara Desert proper begins as the Sahelian savanna thins out. Of course, man has drastically modified the vegetation bands over the millennia and, I suspect, has dramatically affected the rainfall too.

Alan and I agree that we need to improve our knowledge of the other vegetation types in order to ensure that we bring the best teaching to our individual courses; reading books is simply insufficient and even then the university library is not over-endowed with relevant texts.

I put this issue to the Dean of Science and he is in agreement that I should develop a position paper for him to share with other senior staff. He suggests that most likely, on the basis of that paper, we should start planning for a trip north to visit a couple of universities and see what solutions we can bring.

Within a couple of weeks, we are ready to set off to the University of Kano via the universities of Jos and Ahmadu Bello, Zaria. The university provides us with an air-conditioned Peugeot 504 saloon, a real luxury, and a university driver. Our itinerary is planned ahead for a seven-day trip which includes a lot of driving. On the first day we head towards the University of Jos, a distance of some five hundred and fifty kilometres and a full day's driving. Alan sits in the front and Véro and I occupy the back seats. We make frequent stops so that we can take drinks, eat lunch and stretch our legs. We also worry for our driver, whose name is Akpan, since the distance is long and the roads out of Calabar heading north are not brilliant. Our worry intensifies when he tells us that he has never driven outside of his home State of Cross River. Ninety minutes or so out of Calabar and we are going well on a narrow but tarmacked road that contains the inevitable potholes that cause severe jarring of our backs whenever the driver is going too fast and does not have sufficient time to slow down. We take it in turns to tell him to slow down and anticipate the potholes but in true driver stubbornness (me included if I am honest!) he listens for five minutes and then goes back to his normal driving style.

At one point in the far north of the state where the landscape is hilly and abuts the Oban Hills (where I am convinced that there must be a population of gorillas), we see a sign indicating a deviation, but crazily no barrier, that takes us off the main road and along a dirt track through the forest. We follow the track, running parallel to the road and see why the deviation has been put in place; the road has been completely eroded and all there exists is a deep gully into which any vehicle that ignores the deviation would fall. The deviation soon leads us back onto the tarmacked road on the other side of the gully.

As we continue northwards into areas that experience less rainfall than us in Calabar, we see that the vegetation really does begin to thin out, the trees become less dense and shorter while the quality of the road improves. We start seeing signs for Jos and the road seems to be on a permanently upwards trajectory as we start the climb towards the Jos Plateau.

Jos is considered by many to be the most beautiful and liveable part of Nigeria since the climate is milder due to the altitude. Every Sunday, a Calabar-based trader called Bassey comes south from Jos with a truckload of 'European' vegetables. He has a building in the centre of Calabar market where, on Sunday afternoons, he sells his produce – at highly inflated prices – to a mostly expatriate clientele. We go along most Sundays to purchase tomatoes, lettuce, bell peppers, aubergines, peas, potatoes, onions and so on with nothing priced at less than four or five Naira a kilo. But if you want such vegetables in Calabar, you simply have to pay the price. The saving grace is that the seller is affable and knows all his customers by their first names. Once an established customer, he will put aside some nicer vegetables rather than oblige you to plunge hands through big baskets of squashed tomatoes to find one or two that are of an acceptable quality.

With an ooph and thank God, we finally arrive in Jos. The daylight is just ending so we are pleased that we set off early from Calabar and thus manage to avoid finishing our travel into Jos at night. Tonight we are staying in a government guesthouse built during colonial times for the British Governor of Jos. Everything is comfortable, the evening meal is good and based on European vegetables but the beer on offer is only Crown, a Lagos brand, and in our opinion far inferior to the Champion of Calabar!

For dessert we have strawberries and cream, "just like Wimbledon" enthuses Alan. He gets gently ribbed for that remark since, just like us, he has never been to Wimbledon either for the tennis or the strawberries.

The following morning after breakfast we do a tour of the gardens surrounding the guesthouse. They are magnificent and tended by an old man who tells us that he had worked for the British when they governed Nigeria and he regrets their leaving.

"Corruption and tribal politics is all that replaced the Queen" he bemoans. "I feel so sad about the politics of my country and I cannot see this civilian government lasting too long either."

Prosaic words and a prediction that we hope does not come true too quickly.

We spend much of the day at the University with national and expatriate staff, explaining our hopes for cooperation between our two universities; and potentially with the other universities we will soon visit. We are making two alternative suggestions. Either that we do an annual lecturer exchange with the Calabar team teaching about the mangroves and rainforests to University of Jos students while the Jos staff teach about their extraordinary climate and its impact on Jos vegetation and fauna to our Calabar students. Or we could exchange groups of students who would follow relevant courses. This second alternative is harder to imagine as it would involve sending a coachload of final year students to Jos for extended periods, say two weeks, and receiving a similar number in Calabar. Our Jos counterparts ask to be allowed to consider our suggestions and take them up with their head of department.

The next morning, we are to head northwest towards our second destination of Ahmadu Bello University in Zaria, just under 250 Km away and a driving time of approximately five hours. Since the distance is not great and we have no appointments fixed for later today, we find ourselves in no great rush to leave. All of us appreciate the beauty of the guesthouse gardens and the perfect climate (at least in comparison to Calabar) that the Jos Plateau offers.

Véro asks me "why didn't you get a job here instead of Calabar?" Why indeed?

Driving off the Jos Plateau and onto the well-made road towards Zaria reveals just how rocky the plateau is. There are sheer rock faces bordering the sloping road that takes us rather gently from an altitude of around 1,200 metres in Jos down to about 400 metres on the road to Zaria.

Rather than larger houses built of concrete breezeblock and imported brick, as in Calabar, many here are constructed instead of local stone mined on the plateau. But Jos generally does not appear, at least to our new eyes, to be any richer than Calabar with the vast majority of the population living in similar, mud-built huts with roofs either of corrugated steel or thatched with palm fronds or local grasses. However, the huts are round in this part of Nigeria - not square or rectangular as predominate in Calabar - and the people seem taller, slimmer, and more brightly dressed. We have not yet arrived but we will soon be entering the Hausa-dominated areas and their influence appears to stretch up the Jos Plateau.

As the drive to Zaria is predominantly straight north with only a slight lean to the west, we see clearly the influence of latitude on the vegetation banding that we have come to study. This is particularly visible in the rural areas where the vegetation is now very different from that in our home state. Here, the trees are smaller, further spaced and most of them are prickly. The most common types are from the enormous Acacia group. These belong to the *Leguminaceae* family which we know in Europe as the pea, bean and clover family because almost all our species are herbs with only a couple able to boast any wood in their stems, most notably the gorse. However, in Nigeria and particularly in the more arid regions, various species of Acacia and its closely related genera dominate as tree species.

Having had a late and rather leisurely breakfast, we stop to buy some fruit and a couple of baguettes – yes really; the French are spreading their influence even this far north – for lunch. We choose to stop at a grove of Acacia trees that provides a perfect umbrella of shade while allowing the breeze unhindered access. While our thermometer shows that the temperature under the trees is close to 32C, none of us is sweating or feeling uncomfortable from the heat. All the proof that we need that it is the extraordinarily high humidity in Calabar that makes us always feel damp and uncomfortable rather than the temperature, which is no higher than here in the shade of the Acacia.

Can the Garden of Eden really be sitting on a blanket, chewing on a banana under a canopy of Acacia, and being bathed by a cool breeze? Probably not, but at that moment as we watch the yellow and green weaver birds in their colony high up in the trees weaving simple grass into elaborate homes, we could almost be in paradise. That is, if it was not for the long grey snake that the driver espies slithering up through the branches as it heads towards a newly completed nest, presumably to collect its own lunch.

We leave in a leisurely hurry; none of the M'bakarah tribe wanting to show fear to the driver or to each other but all of us feeling it. I cannot recognise with any certainty the ferocious and deadly Black Mamba but I do know that it is long and grey, lives mostly in trees and is pretty quick off the mark. By the way, is anyone wondering why black mambas are grey? It is actually because they are named after the colour inside their mouths. Generally, you see the colour that gives them their name at about the same time as they bite. Not the ideal way to identify them, as the local carpenter knocks up a coffin and you are being carried off to your last resting place.

We arrive at the Ahmadu Bello University guesthouse in the late afternoon and once we have dropped off our bags and left Véro to relax, and the driver to go off and see friends from his extended family, Alan and I take a leisurely stroll around the campus. This is Nigeria's largest and most academically renowned university, but Ibadan might disagree with the second. Although we are not expected until the following day, we are surprised to find the campus totally empty. We eventually see someone working in an office, so knock at his door and enter. After some friendly introductions and explanations about what two Calabar lecturers are doing in Zaria, our newfound colleague explains that since the lecturers are on strike – of course just like us in Calabar – they do not often come into the university. And that is exactly what we find when we arrive for the meeting the following day; no one bothers to turn up. Put a cross through any hope of cooperation with Ahmadu Bello then.

The positive side of this letdown is that it gives us a free day before going on to Kano to explore and sightsee. After all, we have come almost eight hundred kilometres straight north and the cultures of the Efik and the Hausa are as different as between say the English and the Egyptians. We take a taxi to the main Zaria market and leisurely walk around for an hour or so. Our driver has asked for permission to visit his family again, which is fine by me. He has driven a long way and we want him to be refreshed for the next part of our journey.

Once inside the market, the three of us discuss what strikes us as the greatest difference between the Calabar and Zaria markets. For Alan the main difference is in the fragrance: Calabar mostly stinks, which I can confirm, it really does, while Zaria smells mostly of the different spices that are on sale everywhere. For Véro it is the colours, so bright with varied yellows and reds on display while Calabar seems dull and grey; an impression not helped by the piles of yam that seem everywhere in the Calabar market. In Zaria, we did not spot a single yam. But for me the biggest difference is underfoot. Walking through Calabar market on just about any day of the year means wading through noxious mud, formed not just by earth and water either, while in Zaria one could be walking along the beach on fine sand – if not for the piles of camel droppings that are to be avoided at all costs!

Our final leg north takes us from Zaria to Kano, a distance of a little over 150 Km or about three hours driving, allowing for a few stops. We set off at around 10 am and so arrive in the early afternoon. The drive has been easy and simple. As we enter Kano and proceed along a boulevard towards the centre of this ancient city, we see a traffic light that turns red in the distance while we are still about fifty metres away. This is the first traffic light that the three of us have seen since our arrival in Nigeria; perhaps the novelty is what saves us because I notice that our driver is approaching the lights at normal speed rather than starting to apply the brakes.

I say to him loudly "Akpan slow down, the traffic lights are red!" He comes to a jarring halt still twenty metres short of the lights. I suddenly think perhaps he has never seen traffic lights before if he has never previously left Cross River State.

Alan sitting in the front passenger seat, instructs him, "drive up to the white line and wait for the lights to turn green, then you can go."

Once we are safely through the lights, I ask "do you know what that red light means?"

"Yes sir" answers Akpan in full confidence "red means 'get ready to stop' and green means 'get ready to go'. I remember that from my driving lessons."

"And so what does orange mean?" I query.

"Oh, I do not remember that one sir." The three of us become a little warier from then on!

We follow the road signs and soon find ourselves approaching the entrance to Bayero University and its attractive entrance that moulds architecturally into the semi-desert surrounds. The university became independent from Ahmadu Bello in 1977 and so, by the time of our visit, had existed for only three years or so. In such a short time it has built a growing reputation and has designed and installed some very lovely buildings, including the staff housing.

The signposts indicate the Biology Department and, as we draw up, four young people emerge from the entrance. This is our welcoming committee – and what a contrast to Zaria. Two of the reception group are Nigerians and the other two prove to be British. They have already agreed among themselves that we will not be lodged in the university guesthouse as we had anticipated but rather Alan is invited to stay with one of the Brits and us with the other. We are told that in the evening, since everyone lives within one hundred metres of each other, our Nigerian hosts will come round and we will have a barbecue and drinks together. This will allow us to chat more informally as they are very keen to visit Calabar for a vacation trip dedicated to bird watching. I have, by accident, fallen on a dedicated group of twitchers.

After greeting the head of department, we are guided across the campus to the staff accommodation. After the Calabar concrete apartment blocks where Alan lives, what gorgeous housing the university has designed and built for its staff in Kano. The two Brits are next door neighbours and both have small two-storey houses built of stone, from Jos I presume. Each even has a fireplace and chimney where they light small wood fires during the winter months. Their gardens are well kept with lovely manicured green lawns surrounded by well-trimmed bushes with beds of beautiful flowers. Now this is something different to our surroundings in Calabar and shows what adequate watering can do in the near desert.

The evening arrives and the other lecturers walk across the grass to join us. All is relaxed and I cannot describe how wonderful it is to be able to sit outside in the garden with spotlights lighting our places and not be attacked by hungry mosquitos, drenched by sudden downpours or soaked to the skin simply by the intense humidity.

In conversation, Véro reveals that when I was interviewed in London, it was mentioned that Kano had been interested in offering me a job but that Calabar had got the offer in first. Our hosts laugh and tell us that they are well aware that Calabar had pinched me from under their noses!

The next morning Alan and I walk into the university and hold meetings with different levels of the department hierarchy. The first is with the head of department and other departmental professors and is rather formal but friendly nonetheless. We explain the broad lines of our proposal for an exchange between Calabar, Kano and potentially Jos. We develop the reasons behind our ideas for the exchange especially the lack of opportunity to adequately teach the vegetation and ecology of the whole of Nigeria while living and working in only one ecological zone out of the several that exist in the country. A professor tells us frankly that they have exactly the same type of problem in Kano as we experience in Calabar. The meeting ends with a broad consensus that our proposal is doable and necessary.

The second meeting is with the four more junior lecturers that had received us yesterday as we arrived at the department, including our hosts. This meeting starts off by assuming that an exchange can occur and so orients around how to physically organise the exchange. An exchange of lecturers is far simpler and more practicable than busloads of students heading in either direction. Our hosts state that they will now get official approval from their head of department for the exchange of lecturers. Then the group of lecturers from Kano will make a trip to Calabar to check out our system and university as well as to meet with our own departmental hierarchy. They tell us that this will allow two things to occur. First, to draw up a memorandum of understanding for signature by the two universities, three if Jos comes in with us, and second, to wangle a birdwatching trip to the forests and mangroves of the south!

After a pleasant lunch at the university, I go back to collect Véro from our hosts' house, leaving Alan to relax for the afternoon. Not so relaxing for me because Madam wishes to go shopping in the famous Kurmi Market that she was hearing about at last night's barbecue. We have directions from the university, so get Akpan to drive us there. He seems strangely offhand, but we simply put it down to nerves about driving in a more modern city than Calabar.

However, when we arrive at a suitable parking area, fifty metres or so from the market entrance, I ask "do you want to walk around the market with us Akpan?"

He replies in a very soft voice "I will stay with the car, boss."

"Will you be OK here for an hour or so?" I ask with some concern because I notice him fidgeting and not looking at all happy.

He lifts a sharpened machete from the side of his seat and says "I will be OK with this doctor."

"Akpan what's the problem? I've seen you have been nervous since we left the house. Do you need some money to buy gifts or is there another problem?"

He looks at me with a gathering of tears in his eyes and says "Boss, these are bad people here. You know what they did to us in Calabar during the war? I am frightened."

So more than ten years after the Biafran War ended there still exists this distrust and fear; at least for the southern people against the northern tribes.

I tell him not to worry, that we will be quick, and that he can relax. Kano is a lovely town and the war finished a long time ago. I promise that he will be fine while we are gone.

In Calabar, we frequently get visits in the evenings from itinerant Hausa traders that have already made their fortunes by selling all manner of local crafts to my expatriate colleagues and their wives. We are less good customers as we realise – and this is strictly our opinion – that while African crafts may look great in our African homes, they transfer and sit less readily in European homes. Especially as we are both fans of antique furniture and baubles. Nonetheless, we have bought northern fabrics from our traders and a few trinkets under the guise of jewellery. But our itinerant traders in Calabar, while being amusing fellows to chat to, are often a bit crooked, to say the least. The beautiful blue cut gemstone that I was sold as a sapphire turned out to be a zircon as was the lovely 'diamond'. But since I paid almost nothing for them, I knew what I was buying despite the trader's frequent comment of "Hhaba Hhaba". To this day, I have never understood the meaning of this Hausa expression but I always assume something around 'on me life, guv'ner'!

But what the Hausa traders hawk around Calabar has nothing in common with the arts and crafts on display in Kurmi Market. I am eternally grateful that we are travelling in a salon car and not an estate or, God forbid, a large 4-wheel drive. Our boot is already full of our suitcases – and Véro never travels light – so there is only room for several Hausa woven blankets and some tie-dye material. I have gotten off lightly on this occasion!

We arrive back to where the car was parked, but it is no longer there. Oh my goodness, has Akpan been abducted? Of course not. We spot the car across the road, parked under a large Flamboyant tree covered with numerous and bright orange flowers. He tells us that a gentleman had knocked on his window and advised him to move the car into the shade across the road. Akpan confesses that the gentleman, a Hausa, was most polite to him!

Another pleasant evening passes with our hosts but we all turn in early because of tomorrow's trip south. The next morning, we feel sad to be leaving our new friends as well as the much pleasanter climate and town of Kano. No matter, they promise to travel south to see us in the not-too-distant future and finalise the agreement around an exchange of lecturers.

The first part of our journey home sees us stopping for the night just south of Jos. In distance this is more than halfway to Calabar but we calculate about equal in travel time. The first leg goes smoothly except that as we leave Kano, we enter an enormous hailstorm.

"Ice blocks" Alan informs Akpan since the hailstones are so large. Akpan laughs and tell us that this is the first time he has ever seen ice blocks falling from the sky. We tease him that during this trip he has seen traffic lights, ice blocks from the sky, and a kind Hausa.

Our final day arrives and we are all looking forward to getting home to Calabar. I always enjoy travelling and seeing new places but after a week on the road and sleeping in a number of different places, it will be nice to get back to our routine. The journey goes well with Alan and I playing naturalist's I-spy, trying to be the first to see the tree and shrub species that signal the changes from one vegetation zone to the next and the last examples from the previous zone that have managed to spread too far southwards.

At around midday, we stop in a small town, eat a simple meal, and allow Akpan to stroll around and relax for a while. We then set off, knowing that this is the final leg of the trip. We enter the north of Cross River State and the vegetation is now truly back to dense forest. The journey seems to be going smoothly until Alan notices that we have just passed the sign indicating the deviation that goes on to the dirt track, into the forest and cuts around the deep gully where the road has collapsed.

He says gently "Akpan, you just missed the deviation."

The next thing we know is that Akpan jerks the steering wheel hard to the right and we tip sideways and at speed into a deep drainage ditch. The engine cuts immediately. Luckily Alan has insisted throughout the trip that seatbelts be worn by all. Why Akpan reacted in such a silly way instead of simply stopping and reversing the thirty metres or so back to the deviation, we have no idea. Was he beginning to doze off? Did he panic? I do not know.

Akpan and Véro are on the left side of the car, which is now deep in the ditch, while Alan in the passenger seat and me at the back are on the right. My door is undamaged, so I can open it and clamber upwards and onto the bank at the side of the ditch. I lean back in and grab Véro's offered arm and pull her up through the gap. She is very light and so comes out easily.

Alan's door is jammed shut by the force of the crash and held in place by the ditch which is narrower at that point. He winds down the window, gives me his right arm to hold while he uses his left hand to unclip the seatbelt. He is not so light but with me pulling and him climbing, he soon emerges out of the window beside me. We both realise that we need to get Akpan out quickly. This is a petrol vehicle and there is at least half a tank of fuel. We have no idea what damage has been caused to the engine by the crash and we are both fearful of an explosion of spilt petrol.

Akpan, of course, is further away from us than was Alan so I cannot simply reach in and pull him out as I had done for my buddy.

Alan seems more shaken than me and keeps repeating "we could have been killed" so I go back in through the window while Alan and Véro hold on to my two legs.

"Akpan, come on, give me your arm and we will pull you out." But he will not move and stays glued to his seat still enclosed by the seatbelt and whimpering. Poor guy is terrified. So rather than continuing to speak softly, I shout "You have to move now, petrol is leaking." That works and he pops up through the window with little help from me.

So what a too-doo! We are miles from anywhere, it is 3 pm, the car is stuck in the ditch and there is no way that we can possibly extract it; and even if we do, we doubt it will start. Umm.

And then, as always seems to happen wherever you may be in Africa, a bush moves here and another across there and suddenly groups of villagers of all ages emerge into view. Within fifteen minutes of escaping from the car, there are at least thirty people standing around and taking in the accident. Alan estimates that there are easily enough men plus us three men to push the car out of the ditch and get it the right way up. He tells Akpan his plan, this is translated to Efik, and within ten minutes our battered, mud and grass-covered car is back on the road. Not surprisingly, it refuses to start. I suppose we are out of the ditch but not yet out of the woods.

Then in quick succession, a four-wheel drive turns up, driven by two friends from Calabar. They stop to help at the accident but when they see who we are, offer us a lift home. Then a mammy wagon truck pulls in and offers to tow the car back to Calabar. By 3.30 pm we are all on our way home.

~ 7 ~

CROCODILES IN THE GARDEN

A Saturday weekend pleasure for us and our friends the Kemps, now that Marian is back in Calabar with baby Helen, is to go for most of the day to the Palm Oil Club and meet up with other friends there; especially the families from the Harbour Works company. Andy and I play games of squash for much of the morning, interspersed with cold beer, while Véro and Marian play badminton with the other ladies. Anna is busily colouring in a book and little Helen is sleeping contentedly in the shade.

One Saturday, Frank Fyffe, the Palm Oil Manager, comes around with a sheet of paper and asks "are you and Véro here next Saturday?"

"Yes, sure."

"Great", says Frank, "then you are both playing in our Pro-Am Golf Tournament."

"Neither of us have ever played before!"

"That's OK, it's the idea behind pro-am, after all."

The following Saturday sees us both lined up for the start of the tournament. By chance, we have been paired with the two resident Catholic priests, Father Michael for me and Father

Colum for Véro. We play our very first rounds of golf on the nine-hole course that weaves in and out of palm trees. Many holes need a drive down the fairway calculated to miss the trees that have been deliberately left between the tee and the hole. If the unlucky drive hits the tree, you can say goodbye to your ball since it disappears off into the shoulder-high shrubs – the so-called rough but 'scrub' would be a better name – and no amount of looking will turn it up. Add to that the hordes of local children who have discovered that golf balls are valuable currency. They make a useful amount of extra pocket money by standing on the side of the course, watching where the balls land and then waiting for the M'bakarah to give up searching before pocketing them (or taking their feet off them). In the evening they appear at the bar and sell back the lost balls to their original owners.

The Calabar golf course does not have 'greens' it has 'browns' and these have been produced by putting a sand and oil mix that congeals to a mush, dries out hard in the scorching sun and then re-mushes with the next rainstorm. The perfect wedge shot that is popped up onto the brown generally stops dead and slowly sinks into the quicksand-like surface rather than rolling on to the hole as one might anticipate. This means a good golfer who has never played the course has little chance against the local ringers, like the two Fathers.

Father Michael and I play quite well together. I can hit the ball off the tee in a pretty straight line and do not miss the ball entirely too often. At school and at university I played a lot of grass hockey and also while at school I was known as 'slogger Marks' and made captain of the gentleman's eleven at cricket; so I have a reasonable eye for the ball. The Father is a great player on the Browns, so we get around in only a little over par; which is only 29 for the nine holes. At the end of the afternoon, the results are announced along with the prizes. The overall winner is the manager of the cement factory and his partner. The partner is a young, bearded and bespectacled guy that has just arrived in country to work on the building of an enormous paper factory outside of Calabar. He claims to have never played golf before but, a few months later, he is down to par. Is he a natural or just economic with the truth? Their first prize is two weeks at a tourist resort in the Cameroons; offered by the local Calabar travel agency. Second prize, a week at the same resort, is won by Frank and his partner. Father Michael and I come third. No mean feat. A special prize goes to a German lady by the name of Erma. Erma is a frequent player, along with her British husband, and she made her round along with her partner in the company of Father Colum and Véro. The reason for the special prize? Well on one hole, her partner's ball bounced at the edge of the fairway and settled behind a palm tree so she went with the intention of chipping it back onto the fairway to give her partner a straight shot to the brown. But just as she brought the club behind her head, a cobra reared up in front of her and, rather than strike the ball, she lopped off the cobra's head with her seven-iron. Father Colum would not hear that this was a life-saving stroke and insisted that it was a missed ball and so has to be counted as a shot on her scorecard. Everyone agrees that this is truly bad sportsmanship from the good Father and so awards her the special prize.

While Father Michael is a gentle, quiet man; perhaps just as one might expect of a priest, Colum is a real character with a very large capital C. After Michael and my third place finish, Colum comes over and asks if I would like to play a round of golf the following Wednesday.

"Yes, of course", I reply, "but you do know that today is the first time I have ever played?"

"I know, see you on Wednesday at 2 pm."

The following Wednesday I duly turn up, borrow a bag with a few clubs from behind the bar and spot Colum arriving in his old car. As we walk over to the course, he says in a very matter-of-fact voice

"Naira 2 a hole and Naira 5 for a birdie (one under par)."

"Eh, Colum, don't forget that I have never played!"

"That doesn't matter." No, right, it doesn't matter, to him, because on the first hole he scores a birdie (Naira 5 to the priest). The second hole he wins (N7), and the third (N9). On the fourth, by a fluke stroke from the tee, I land in the middle of the fairway close to the brown. My next shot is a seven-iron chip (I have no sand wedge in the bag) and the ball lands only a foot from the hole. This has to be a birdie for me on this par-4 hole and so my debt will be reduced by Naira 5.

However, the Father does not bother to take his next shot saying simply "I give that one to you but since you have not sunk the putt, it only counts as a win, not a birdie." Come on Father!

We play on until the end of the nine holes and I have to hand over Naira twenty; still feeling sore about the poor sportsmanship on the fourth hole when I was denied the birdie.

Later in the bar, I am chatting to Frank, the estate manager, who is a lovely character but always plays the gruff Scot. He tells me that everyone appreciates what I have just done to give Colum some pocket money. I mention the denied birdie and he tells me in all seriousness that it is a small price to pay. The father is a very good and proud man who lives on nothing except what his parishioners from small rural villages contribute to the service offertory. This small amount is augmented by gifts of food from his many expatriate friends, mostly the Calabar Irish Catholic community, and what he wins at golf. Although I have only a small salary, I feel humbled at what I hear and a little embarrassed to have worried about the lost birdie.

Frank then tells me that he has been the British High Commission representative in Cross River State with the title of Community Liaison Officer for several years now. However, since so many British have started to work at the University, he and the British High Commissioner in Lagos think it might be a good idea to place the CLO within the university community. Frank has recommended that I take over the role. I am surprised, honoured, and delighted in equal measures. Two weeks later I receive an official UK High Commission letter appointing me to the role of CLO for Cross River State. There is a second 'To whom it may concern' letter enclosed, which I am told to keep with my passport, that states 'It would be appreciated if Dr Marks could be given every assistance in his capacity as Community Liaison Officer'. Because of the importance of the role I may be required to play as CLO in the university, I take the letter to the Registrar.

He is always very polite to me and, on this occasion, he grips my hand, bows his head and declares "Your Excellency."

This meeting will prove very important when I need to apologise for a later misdemeanour.

On another early evening at the club, Véro and I see the good Father arrive and so place a Champion on the bar ready for him. He starts to chat openly to us for perhaps the first real-time and tells us that he has lived in his Calabar village for over twenty years, built his house from scratch and even stayed there throughout the Biafran War. After his second Champion is almost finished, he opens up even further, telling us of the horrors of the war both that he heard about but particularly what he had witnessed first-hand. The government forces – mostly from the northern tribes – came to all the small villages of the forest-dwelling inhabitants and meted out atrocities on the entire population, most of whom had nothing to do with the war itself but were suspected of collaborating in one form or another. They killed, raped and burnt indiscriminately. Things got so bad that the forest inhabitants began to form a self-protection militia but armed with only traditional weapons and antique shotguns. The father was persuaded to show them how to make Molotov cocktails.

When we expressed puzzlement as to how a priest would know how to make such devices, he merely grinned and said "I'm Irish." Better not to dig deeper, especially as many of the southern Irish in Calabar had an inherent dislike of anything British; rather disconcerting to a young person like me.

We take to inviting Colum to eat with us at our home every month or so, while he takes to inviting himself about once a fortnight. Luckily we know he comes to town every Wednesday, after the golf, to buy provisions; with his winnings, I presume. Thus, in advance, Véro would ask the three other couples who frequently invite Colum if he was eating at their place on the Wednesday and, if not, we make sure to have more food ready, a lot more, just in case Colum turns up – which he often does, on the stroke of 7pm.

Another frequent visitor for meals is our neighbour, John, he of the beaten-up green Beetle. He reminds me of his favourite animal – the snake – since his appetite is just like a python; he will eat an enormous meal one day and then not eat again for a week, simply digesting off his last significant meal. We love having John around and seeing him relax during an enjoyable meal cooked by my resident French chef and washed down by a Champion or two.

One evening, he tells us, in passing, that he did his research in the USA and got bitten by a rattlesnake. Of course, we ask what happened and he tells us that he drove quickly back to his laboratory and then passed out on the floor. The next thing he knew was when he woke up in hospital with a drip in his arm. It seems that he was extremely lucky, not just to have recovered from such a dangerous bite but because he was correctly diagnosed in the first place. When he was first discovered passed out on the floor of the lab, the person who found him thought that he had taken a drug overdose. Luckily his lab colleagues knew that John did not take drugs and said that it was more likely he was suffering from prophylactic shock from an animal bite since, even then, he was well known always to be out chasing snakes and other reptiles.

Coincidentally, a few weeks later, one Saturday afternoon when we are relaxing at home, John comes to the door looking deathly white. "Heh John, what's happened to you?" I ask.

He sits down on the sofa and simply says "can you watch over me for an hour or so? I have just been bitten by a snake that I caught last night and I have no idea if it is poisonous or not. If I pass out, get me to the clinic and tell them it's a snake bite." We pass a strange hour trying to make small talk while I watch the colour slowly coming back to his face. Obviously the snake is non-venomous!

John's girlfriend is from Calabar and a market trader. She is a slim, pretty, young woman full of character and as tough as nails. We always feel that John, who is a little naïve, is out of his depth in this partnership – but then that is none of our business. While listening to Neil Diamond and 'Sweet Caroline' on the tape recorder one Saturday evening, we see him drive past with his lady in the passenger seat.

The next morning, we have a leisurely breakfast in bed, go off to the Harbour Works village for a swim and then come back to start cooking the food for a 2 pm lunch. Suddenly all hell seems to break loose on the other side of our coco yam hedge. First, we hear a roar from John, then a door slams and soon after, a woman's high-pitched scream rings out over and over again. Given the repetitiveness of the screaming, the lady is still alive, but has something happened to John? Not another snake, please.

I run down our back garden and jump over the coco yams. I can see her face at a window staring through the bars, just like a prisoner, as she continues to scream. I say hi to John's rather bemused-looking Indian neighbour as I run past him and burst into the house. John is standing inside with a pleased smile on his unshaven face.

"John, what the HELL is going on", I shout at him.

He just stands there laughing and laughing while the lady's screaming continues, becoming more acute as the moments pass. The sound is coming from the toilet and when she hears my voice, she calls out "help me, help me."

"John, calm down! This is not funny; you are disturbing the whole neighbourhood on a Sunday afternoon. What the hell is going on?"

Slowly his laughing subsides, as do the screams from the lady; these are now reducing from shrieks and squeals to wails and whimpers.

He then tells me, "she stole money out of my wallet; that's why you heard me shout. Because I shouted, and she knew I had caught her, she locked herself in the toilet and now refuses to come out. I warned her that I wanted my money and she just laughed, so I slipped a snake under the door; it's only a grass snake, not poisonous, but she doesn't know that." And he begins to roar with laughter again.

I go to the door and call to her "it's OK, the snake is not poisonous, open the door for me."

After a few moments hesitation, I hear the key being turned in the lock but still she does not emerge. So I gently push the door and see the little grey snake peering out from under the toilet pipe and the lady standing on the toilet seat.

"Jump," I say holding up my hand towards her, "the snake is under the pipe and is more frightened than you. Come on." And she grabs my hand, jumps off the toilet and slams the door shut leaving the snake trapped in the loo.

She rushes at John to dish out some instant Nigerian justice. Luckily I manage to get between the two of them.

"Give him back his money" I say, and she grudgingly takes a folded Naira 10 note from her jean's pocket and hands it over to John. "Say you are sorry, John. I want to get back for my lunch and not listen to you two squealing all day."

We have been watching our one and only pineapple steadily grow in size near the washing line at the back of the garden. Soon, I believe we can pick it and taste the sweetness of our patience. But I think perhaps another week or so. Since we both like pineapples, especially madam, we frequently buy them from itinerant traders who hawk different vegetables and fruit, depending on the season, from door to door. A few days after the John incident, there is a faint knock at the door and on opening I see a little tot of perhaps eight years old with a large pineapple balanced on top of his head (how do Africans do that so easily?).

I ask *"okuk ifan?"* which means how much? And he asks for fifty kobo, which is cheap, so I hand the money over and he goes off with a pleased smile on his little face.

We carve the pineapple and sit down for a snack. Suddenly, Véro says "you don't think …?" and I am thinking the same at that precise moment. And the reader, who has been concentrating, will have guessed already!

After the shock, horror and disappointment of the theft and resale of our single pineapple, I rather let the line of plants get overgrown by grass; and they eventually die. Occasionally, an old man does the tour of all our gardens and, using a sharp machete, cuts the grass and weeds down to an inch or so. However, we have not seen him for a couple of months and the grass has reached knee height. Véro has reminded me on a couple of occasions that the grass is getting too high near to her washing line and I really must learn how to lawn mow with a machete. Luckily, a violent rainstorm on one occasion and the need to go and buy Champion on the other has saved me from acquiring the necessary skill set.

On a memorable day – that is one without a tropical downpour – Véro is hanging clothes on the line. I hear her shout "John, get out here now!"

Now, my wife is not known for being loud and aggressive, so hearing her shout means that something has certainly not pleased her; I wonder what is happening and so walk out to see. She tells me to go back and bring the machete – the situation gets more ominous by the minute! I hurry back with the machete and she indicates a large, metre-long log lying in the long grass where the pineapple plants used to be.

"Do you want me to chop it up for the BBQ?"

"No, nitwit, tap it on the head!" 'Ze plot sickens' as they might say in 'Ello-'Ello. I then realise that this humble piece of wood is, in fact, a less-than-humble Nile crocodile – I am deadly serious – and when I give it a light tap on the head, it shows me a double array of teeth that would do some even more serious damage to an unprotected calf muscle or a stray hand.

I join the chorus calling for John and he eventually appears, rubbing two tired eyes, saying "sorry, but I was out all night in the forest. What's the problem?" We show him the crocodile and he beams with gratitude.

"Oh great, thanks, I thought that I had lost her."

He goes on to explain that he had been given the casing of an old, broken fridge-freezer by the Works Department and buried it in his garden to make a pond. This had housed a couple of crocodiles, caught some weeks previously, without incident until the torrential rain of the last couple of days had caused the pond to fill up to the brim and overflow. The crocs had made their escape.

"How many got away John?"

He looks at me with a very sheepish regard "only two and I caught the other one in my neighbour's garden."

"Time to take them for release John." He agrees and we believe that is the end of the story.

Marian and Andy announce that it is time to christen little Helen. They ask Alan to be the Godfather and Véro and Rosalind to be Godmothers. Marian has fixed the date of the ceremony at a local Protestant church in Calabar. We all take the occasion to dress up smartly, even Andy, and, along with Simon, go off to the church. It is packed full with our little group only numbering seven adults but there are perhaps one hundred local worshippers in the Sunday congregation. The ceremony is a little odd because the vicar speaks throughout the service in Efik but the hymns are in English as is, luckily the christening ceremony itself. After the first hymn, the collection plates do the round and we all add one or five Naira notes. The vicar offers a prayer in Efik followed by another hymn. The expatriate contingent is surprised to see the collection plates start to do a second tour as we sing. The Calabar part of the congregation then stands up clapping, and dance around the church, belting out the hymn and so avoiding the collection plates. They do not avoid us. Andy rumbles about having run out of small notes, so I pass him my last one.

Helen is welcomed into the church by the vicar who places the perfect liquid cross of Holy Water on her brow. She does not cry but simply gazes up at her rather nervous Godmother. Alan stands well back, just in case anyone has the foolish notion of handing him the baby to hold.

We retake our places in the pews and organ music strikes up for the final hymn. And what do we see coming around again? You guessed: the collection plates are making another circuit. We are almost all out of small notes. Simon passes me five Naira, Alan rattles in a couple of coins while Andy smiles, as only Andy can do, and hands the collection plate straight back, as in pass-the-parcel, to the rather startled church assistant.

One item lacking in Calabar is a hairdresser for European hair. The Calabar hairdressers have absolutely no trouble caring for Nigerian hair because they simply take an electric shaver and shave everything off. However, the Yul Brynner style does not appeal to many expatriates, especially the younger ones. Some of our friends notice that I manage to keep my hair short and tidy and so ask where my hairdresser lives. The answer is that Véro has actually always cut my hair and is rather good at it, although baldness in my later years does eventually drive her to redundancy.

Straight off, our closest friends ask her to cut their hair too; which she does happily, usually on a Sunday morning, and always refusing any of the proffered payment. But progressively, the message spreads and more and more people turn up unexpectedly. The crunch comes early one Sunday morning when I struggle out of bed to make us breakfast and find four strangers from the paper mill sitting patiently in my lounge, each drinking a Champion; thanks to a generous Rose who supposed that, since they were M'bakarah, they must be our friends.

A quick chat with Véro and we agree that she cannot spend her Sunday mornings cutting the hair of strangers while they drink their way through a case of beer. So when the hair of the first unknown gentleman is cut and he asks "what do I owe you?" Vero replies Naira 5 and so the M'bakarah Barber Shop is born and Rose is warned that we are the only ones to hand out beers!

I am working in my office preparing a couple of lectures for later in the semester when Frank and Chief from the botanical gardens come to find me.

"Doctor, can you come with us to the nature reserve please? It is urgent."

Curious, I drop everything, grab my car keys and take Frank with me while Chief zooms off in front on his motorbike; throwing up a cloud of dust on the laterite track. On the drive down, I ask Frank what all the panic is about. He tells me that they have just found the body of a dead person in the reserve and that better I should see.

The ten-minute drive sees us arrive at the reserve storehouse and, no, to me it cannot be possible, there is a body hanging from the front roof joist.

"Chief, have you sent someone to call the police?" I ask.

He replies in the negative that they wanted to inform me first and find out from me what they should do next.

"OK then, go straight away to the police station." Off he roars kicking up more dust along the nature reserve trail as he drives away at high speed.

Frank asks if we should cut the body down but since the person is obviously dead and this could be a crime scene, I tell him to leave well alone and not approach the body in case there is any evidence nearby. However, something strikes me as curious (probably not the best word to use at such a moment) about the body. So approaching from the side so as not to disturb the several footprints under the body, I glance at the victim's face. While the eyes are staring, I see that the face is relaxed in death and this is not what one would expect from someone who has committed suicide by hanging. We will see.

After a wait of about thirty minutes, Chief roars back with a pillion passenger – my old friend, the Detective Sergeant. He looks at the body, disregarding crime scene protocol by scuffing all the footprints in the sand under the body, and declares the victim dead; murdered. A few moments later, a police van arrives with a driver and a rotund officer. The body is cut down, put into the back of the van, and driven off. Sadly, a few days later, another body turns up lying next to our small sacred stream where animists from the villages around come frequently to make offerings of eggs and small denomination coins. And a further body is found on the campus, not far from the student halls of residence.

Does Calabar have a serial killer? It turns out that the straight answer is 'no' because, in reality, Calabar is suspected by the population to have a gang of serial killers – acting together with a common aim.

Obviously having three murders within and around the nature reserve is worrying for staff safety, to say the least. So I call a botanical garden staff meeting and tell the nine ladies and men that until the situation settles down, they should avoid going to the nature reserve and stay working within the botanical gardens. Iyamba starts to talk, first in his very poor English and then shifts quickly to Efik, asking Frank to translate. He is from the old town of Calabar and he tells us that at night everyone in his neighbourhood is locking and barricading their doors. People are only going outside in the evening in groups as several more dead bodies have been found in the vicinity of his house.

I ask "what on earth is happening to bring about so many murders?"

Iyamba tells us that a rumour is going around the old town that Edidem Esien Ekpe Oku V, the Obong of Calabar, has died and animist tradition holds that he must be accompanied to paradise with forty souls. This, Iyamba is convinced, is the reason for so many murders.

He sneers as he looks straight into my eyes and finishes with the statement "be careful doctor. One M'bakarah would count as five people from Calabar!" The entire team roars with laughter and this is the correct moment for the meeting to finish. I never did get to like Iyamba!

Deaths continue to be reported in the local newspapers and by the Calabar radio station until an official announcement is made that the Obong sadly passed away on 14th January 1981. Following the announcement, no further cases of these mysterious and numerous deaths are reported. Coincidence or was Iyamba correct about the animist tradition?

Speaking of Radio Calabar, we often listen to the English language parts in order to learn the local news. But the highlight of our listening is when the broadcaster changes to a deeper tone of voice and announces "and here is the international news." This is followed by a copy of the BBC's bonging of Big Ben except, no matter at what time the international news is read, there are always the same number of bongs. And the international news invariably starts with the mention 'the Bamboo Bar of the international hotel is now open!'

Soon after the announcement concerning the Obong, the baker's wife asks if Véro would home-tutor her two boys as she cannot cope with trying to teach them and helping to run the bakery at the same time. She has brought all the home-tutoring books for their ages from France and so the job is made that much easier. By coincidence, a few days later, we get a visit from George, a young Lebanese who owns and runs the only Lebanese restaurant in Calabar with his two brothers. George is the youngest and has just returned from Lebanon where he married a beautiful young Lebanese lady. The only problem is that she does not speak a word of French and the family uses French as the language of the household in Calabar. Can Véro please tutor her in French?

A decision therefore requires to be made. Say no to the bakers and George and continue working at Hillside or say yes and resign. Véro decides to go for the home tutoring and so a few months later she resigns from her teaching job at Hillside.

Fast forward a year and Véro is still tutoring the baker's two children. They are lovely young boys of eleven and nine but do suffer from the fact that their parents work hard and very long hours. Plus, madam baker is now very pregnant and so quality time for the boys is further reduced. From time to time I take them out for nature walks and fishing trips. I have gotten to know the nature reserve very well by now and found a slow-moving stream that is full of brightly coloured fish that I believe are a type of *tilapia* and, luckily for the boys, are very easy to catch.

When not at our house for lessons, they stay at their home, looked after by their maid while the parents work. Sadly, the maid does not care to play with them and so they are mostly left outside to their own devices wandering in the fields and wasteland around their home. On the opposite side of the road from their house is a deep drainage culvert, more like a big overgrown ditch, with a little access bridge built across the top leading from the road to the field beyond. The boys often ask me if we can fish in the ditch, and I expect there are a few small fish in there, but I tell them that it is not a good idea as the water has a thick coat of duckweed floating on the surface. But what worries me the most is that there may be snakes in the dense vegetation around the ditch while the stagnant water attracts clouds of mosquitoes and black flies.

One morning the children arrive early for their lessons and the eldest tells me that I should come with them to see the giant frog that lives in the ditch. I am intrigued and so Véro gives them permission to take me quickly to see this giant frog. As we walk the short distance to their house, the eldest tells me that although he has never seen the frog outside of the water, he knows it is huge because its eyes are this far apart – and he spreads his hands almost 20 cm apart. That would be some frog. But I have a deep suspicion that it may be some other creature instead! We arrive and the 'giant frog' is in its usual position, in the middle of the ditch covered in duckweed, with just the eyes showing above the surface. My suspicions are confirmed and so I walk the children back for their lessons at our house.

John gets my immediate attention, and he meekly admits that he had actually lost three crocodiles from his makeshift pond, not two as he had told us a year earlier.

From inside his house he collects a big net, a wire slip noose on the end of a bamboo pole and a machete; "just in case" he tells me as he gets into the battered green Beetle and drives off.

He returns about an hour later with the 'giant frog' trussed up in the front boot but still able to move sufficiently rigorously to make the car bobble on its old suspension. Over the course of the year, this third crocodile has almost doubled in size and would have been very dangerous to any young child that might have wandered too close to the water's edge.

~ 8 ~

THREE'S COMPANY

The bakers' gorgeous baby girl arrives. Since they could not go back to France for the birth, they were advised by many people to have the delivery in the Catholic Missionary Hospital which is about a two-hour drive from Calabar. We visit as soon as we receive the news of the arrival from the baker and find a radiant mum sitting up in bed nursing her new baby. She has a screened-off room on her own but as we walk down the corridor to visit her, we pass general wards packed with new mums, babies and assorted family members. The place is alive with humanity and everyone seems happy, chatting and colourful. Half of the ladies are nursing their newborns while continuing their loud conversations and no one is stopped by modesty; this is Africa and everyone is vibrant, noisy and relaxed.

Many of the nurses are nuns, wearing grey habits, as are the doctors in their white coats, and all have their Holy Crosses prominently displayed. There seems to be an approximate equal mix of white, Irish by their accents, and Nigerian nuns. As we chat and cuddle the baby, the senior gynaecologist comes in to say hello. She tells Véro in her sweet Irish brogue that she delivered this baby and also followed the pregnancy of the wife of the cement factory manager.

Véro confides in the Sister that we have been trying for a baby for almost a year without success, to which the Sister asks "would you let me exam you? I am sure there may be a simple reason why you are not getting pregnant?"

Véro looks at me and I shrug my shoulders, leaving the decision up to her because I know such examinations are uncomfortable. Off they go to a nearby room. After a brief internal examination, the doctor tells Véro that she has a slightly misplaced or inverted uterus and there are two schools of thought on what to do. Either leave well alone, which is the advice usually given by young practitioners or insert a stitch to straighten the uterus. She recommends the latter approach and says that most older doctors would agree with her suggestion. As the academic year finishes in a month or so and we are returning to Europe for the summer, we promise the Sister that we will see a senior gynaecologist in France for a second opinion.

We soon leave new mum and baby, walk back down the corridor and, by mistake, exit by a different door. This actually leads to a broad and shady veranda on which the hospital staff have arranged the new babies, in their cribs, in a series of parallel lines. The babies lie sleeping and each has a piece of paper with his or her name handwritten on it. These have been laid on the babies' chests. As we watch this beautiful sleeping mass of new humanity, a light breeze blows off several name tags and they turn and twist in the wind as they fly off the veranda. We see a nurse coming over to check on the babies and we tell her what has just happened. She laughs and says that this is a frequent occurrence. We laugh with her but do wonder if these gusts of wind will be responsible for any future adolescent identity crises!

With the realisation that the summer vacations will soon be upon us, we have many things to finish. I cannot believe that we have now been in Calabar for almost two academic years and that my contract actually finishes at the end of June. The Dean, together with the Head of Department have already asked me to renew for another two years and told me to ensure that I complete my promotion forms in the next week or so. By good fortune, I recently received letters back from the Nordic Ecological Society telling me that my two papers have been accepted and will be published in their journal Oikos, the first later in 1981 and the second in early 1982. Thus on my promotion form, I am able to say that I have published three papers already and have these two others in publication. I also recently published some short articles on the dimorphic achenes that I am studying and on the genetics of budgerigar colour inheritance (don't ask!). With my additional work for the department in the Botanical Gardens as well, I am quietly confident about my prospects.

I soon receive some good news. My contract renewal has been approved and I am promoted to Lecturer I from the coming September. This is accompanied by a second piece of good news: the Government of Nigeria has agreed to the university lecturers' demands and has approved a doubling of salaries from the start of the coming academic year. The promotion together with the salary increase means that from September I will be receiving a very nice pay rise.

I book our round-trip flights with the university picking up the bill. This means that we can travel on a full-price ticket and not cut our vacation short as was necessary last year. This time we are off for a full three months. Although the university usually requires that we travel the long haul with Nigerian Airways, since our first destination is Lyon, they agree to let us travel from Lagos to Zurich to Lyon with Swissair and then on to London.

In advance, Véro's mum gets her an appointment with a Lyon-based gynaecologist. Within a few days of us arriving in the gastronomic capital of France, that is the beautiful Roman city of Lugdunum or Lyon, she is being examined by an eminent and rather elderly gynaecologist at a private clinic. He agrees with the diagnosis of our Irish Sister.

Luckily, there is a slot free the following week in his clinic near to Tassin-La-Demi-Lune for the minor operation and this is to be followed by a three-day stay in the clinic. By a pleasant coincidence, the timing coincides with Wimbledon. Not only can I stay all day with Véro as she recovers, but I can also watch John McEnroe's infamous 'You cannot be serious' antics while playing Tom Gullikson as well as another game as he progresses towards the final. For the record, he wins Wimbledon in four sets against my favourite, Bjorn Borg. We are fortunate to have Véro's godmother and aunt, Jacotte, living not far from the clinic. I stay with her at night and can walk to and from the clinic each day to visit.

Obviously, Véro is a little sore after the operation and so we go back to her parents in Crémieu for recuperation. All goes well. At the end of the following week, another aunt, *la tante* Poupette, then kindly gives us the keys to her Lyon apartment while she packs off to the family country residence in Panossas; about an hour's drive away. She promises to pick us up in a week and take us back to Véro's parents' home in Crémieu.

We have a further plan for this long vacation: we want to find and buy a holiday home that we can use during future long vacations. We are only too aware that we cannot impose on our two sets of parents during three-month vacations but neither do we have sufficient funds to rent or stay in hotels for such a long period of time. We look carefully at our finances, composed of what we have managed to save and remit during our time in Calabar and the excess we have accumulated from the rental of the Islington flat. In France, the process of buying is more expensive than in the UK so on top of the purchase price one must add about a further 10 per cent mostly in government taxes as well as pay the conveying solicitor (*le notaire*). Our sums show that we can afford very little and, indeed, must try to get a small bank loan to have enough even to purchase a dilapidated property in a lost village (as all Brits seem to do). Véro's first idea is that we should look in an area of France called Les Cevennes which is a hilly region to the south of the Massif Central where apparently there are ruins aplenty and the prices are low. However, a few days before we are due to leave for the drive south from Lyon to the Cevennes, I am looking in the 'for sale' section of a local newspaper and see '*Maison à vendre, mauvaise état. Brégnier-Cordon. 76.000 francs*' (house for sale in bad condition in the commune of Brégnier-Cordon. 76,000 francs or about £7,000 at that time).

"Where's Brégnier-Cordon?" I ask.

"Absolutely no idea, why do you ask?"

"There's a house for sale there and it's on the market at 76,000 francs. Interested to have a look?"

Véro rings and makes an appointment and off we go to the most southerly village in *le Bugey* to visit the property. As soon as Véro sees the house she is over the moon about it, especially as there is not too much land to look after (remember we are away in Nigeria for nine months of the year). The house is square in shape, about fifty metres square on the ground, and built of local limestone that bears a close resemblance to Kentish ragstone from my area of Kent. There is just a small amount of land at the side of the house and a further few hundred metres squares that goes with the house, a short walk away down a little lane that leads into woodland.

The house to my mind is very odd, to say the least. It dates from around the early 1800s – perhaps earlier – and has not been lived in since the 1950s and, as the advertisement clearly warns, is in very bad condition. It actually covers three floors but the estate agent taking us on the visit can only show us the ground floor because there are no stairs to get to the second or third floors. In fact, there is not even a trapdoor to pass through even if we had a ladder!

"How on earth do you get to the other floors?" I ask.

"The upper floors were lofts where the farmers would have stored hay or dried tobacco or maize. In the past there was an outside wooden staircase but that rotted years ago and was taken down for safety reasons. But the door is still there so we would need a ladder to pass through it from the outside, at the back of the property."

"And you have no ladder?" I query. Of course, he does not. But, the next-door neighbour, a charming, elderly gentleman who must be in his 80s, does and within five minutes, we are clambering up a homemade wooden ladder, through the rickety old door and into the first-floor loft, again of some fifty metres square.

The agent does not follow us up the ladder but calls up to us from the safety of the ground warning us to be careful of the floorboards which are probably in a bad condition. While I am tutting and remarking about the rotten floorboards and the bloated nature of some of the thick stone walls at the back of the house where water must have been percolating for years, Véro is tugging my sleeve and saying look at the window, "c'est une fenêtre à meneaux" which is a style of window with stone surrounds that apparently dates from the middle ages and should rather belong in a chateau not a peasant's cottage. From this floor, we can look up, through an opening, to the second-floor loft and see that sadly (or luckily?) the roof has so many missing tiles that the sunlight penetrates sufficiently to show me the most magnificent oak beams holding up the deeply sloping roof. Roofs of this type are common in the Bugey region and were built with such steep slopes to stop excess snow from accumulating on the roof during winter snowstorms.

We return carefully across the rough floorboards and down the ladder. Back inside the house I ask the agent about water and am shown a tap that stands alone fixed to the inside wall. The waste pipes? There are none so no toilet, sink or anything else.

"Is there main's drainage?"

"Eh, no but there is umm ... electricity."

The agent points out to us a couple of cloth-covered cables that surely date from the 1930s running across the wall, held in place by bent nails hammered into the crumbling plaster. The wires connect to a couple of ceramic fuses containing fuse-wire so thick that it would need a lightning strike to break it and so, of course, the fuses are absolutely useless as circuit breakers. There is one ceramic wall plug flopping about at the end of more cloth-covered cable and two ceramic lamp holders nailed to the ceiling but no bulbs.

There are four small rooms downstairs which the agent proudly announces as "the two bedrooms, the sitting room and the kitchen." One of these rooms has no windows, so it is in complete darkness when the door is shut.

In summary, the property is 'Ripe for conversion and needs plenty of love and care' as a UK estate agent would certainly have told us but our agent simply says that we are the first viewing for a year and the owner would certainly listen to an offer.

We thank him for his time, saying that we will reach a decision quickly and get back to him.

As we drive away, I ask Véro what she thinks and am surprised to learn that she is enchanted by the property while my unexpressed opinion is that the house is a dump, would be impossible to restore and, in all truthfulness, a danger to life and limb. How wrong could I be?

She looks at me with her beautiful green eyes that I have never been able to refuse and says "it will be perfect for us, my love. I can imagine spending our holidays here. We can soon start the repair work, and you will be able to do most of it anyway." Oh My Gosh.

How can I get out of this one? I quickly think and reply "I think we should not pay the asking price but make a much lower offer."

"I agree, and the agent says that the owners will take 65,000 francs."

Deal done. After a trip to the local *notaire* in Saint-Genix-sur-Guiers followed by a visit to our local bank in Crémieu to ask for a small loan, we sign the *compromis* (in France there is a two-stage buying process). We also give power of attorney to Véro's parents to sign the final purchase contract for us in a few months' time, because we will already have returned to Nigeria. The house eventually goes through in November 1981 and we are the proud owners of an ... errr ... ruin.

Our plans for this vacation are to stay a little more than two months in France and the remainder in the UK. We soon realise that we cannot continually borrow Véro's mum's car and so look around for a cheap run-around. Step up her uncle André, the uncle who lived a couple of decades in Chad and the Cameroons. He finds us an ancient Renault-Six for about £150 from his local garage and we become a little more independent.

Everyone knows that vacation time passes twice as rapidly as work time and so we are soon saying goodbye to Véro's family at Satolas Airport and taking the plane to the UK to be with my parents in Kent. This year I have promised Véro that I will not accept work on the farm and instead, I will show her around the beautiful Kent countryside, visit my sister and her family as well as meet up with old friends in London. I also want to check in with some of my old school friends who live in and around Sutton Valence. Another thing we need to do, as a priority, is to visit a dentist as we both have a lot of work to be done on our teeth. Stupidly, I had tried to match Iyamba, he of the Botanical Gardens, by cracking a palm oil nut with my back teeth and had managed to crack a molar instead.

We go to see my parent's NHS dentist in the neighbouring village of Loose and he gladly books us in for the following day, blocking a whole late afternoon as private patients (yes, you can ALWAYS get an appointment if you go private).

As we settle side-by-side into two dental chairs the dentist asks "madam, before I take x-rays, is there any chance you might be pregnant?"

"No" says Véro, answering rather quickly.

"Wait," I reply, "you said that your period was a couple of days late, so there is a small chance."

"No, don't worry, it's often a bit late" she insists. But the dentist replies that he is not going to take the risk, so no x-rays for madam. Well, to cut a long story short, a couple of days later, we buy a home test kit, and, of course, it is positive. We are both so happy. And just how successful was the advice from our Irish gynaecologist in Nigeria?

We sit my mum and dad down to give them the baby news by declaring "we want to tell you some news and it starts with 'Three's Company' – we're going to have a baby!" They are delighted, especially my mum who loves little ones while my dad sees the Marks name being perpetuated; until I remind him that we might just have a girl.

In fact, we are already convinced that we will have a daughter. Let me tell you why but first remember the fact that it is the male who determines the baby's gender. My mum is one of ten children, and all are girls, so the 'fault' lies squarely with my dear late grandad Ted! The odds of a run of girls like that is 2 to the power of ten (or one chance in 1,024). And not only did we have that run of girls in my mum's family, it continues with the male descendants of my mum's sisters. Two of my male cousins have managed to produce a further three girls and so that brings the odds up to a staggering one in 8,192. If our baby happens to be a girl, those odds will rise to one in 16,384. Patience will tell.

We also tell my parents that we have started the process of buying an old house in France. My dad splutters on a mouthful of milky tea and most of it sprays on to the old Pekinese sleeping contentedly in his lap.

"My son, are you sure you know what you are doing?" he asks with real parental concern. "You already have a mortgage on your flat in London and now you are telling us that you are taking another one on this old house in France. What happens if you cannot pay?"

The reader has to realise that my dad is a proud, working-class guy and very old school where having a loan is tantamount to a one-way ticket to the workhouse. Indeed, there are the ruins of a Victorian workhouse in the eponymous road that runs at the bottom of his village; a permanent reminder to the incautious, he believes! My dad is 55 and, aside from a little hire-purchase on a sofa or TV, he has never had debt in his life; a noble achievement. But what this also means is that for all his adult life he has lived in rental accommodation. Since I was four, so not far off twenty-five years, their home has been a little two-bedroom council house in the village of Coxheath.

In response to his question about what happens if I cannot pay the mortgages, I reply simply that I would sell one of the properties.

He looks astonished and asks seriously "can it be really that simple?" I nod and he turns to my mum and says "show him the letter Kath."

The letter turns out to be a missive from the Kent County Council that informs all tenants that the government of Margaret Thatcher has decided that council tenants are to be given the right to purchase their homes at market value less a percentage for the length of time that they have been resident. In my parents' case, they can have a 50% reduction.

"Go for it dad" I advise him. And they do. After thirty years of marriage, they finally buy their first home and discover that the mortgage has a tax rebate attached and the amount they pay each month is cheaper than the amount they previously paid as rent to the council.

From that day on, Thatcher can do no wrong and the Conservative Party can count permanently on their two votes. My dad is now the most house-proud man on the road and during the next several years there are workmen permanently making more and more changes to the house.

All vacations come to an end and so we make our way back to Calabar. The trip goes smoothly with absolutely nothing of interest to report. Sorry to have to record that there are no fridge-carrying gentlemen, God forbid. After all, this is Switzerland we are travelling from. Similarly, we are not asked for dash in Lagos and the military does not try to close down the airport. The only similarity with our previous trip is that Alan Seddon in the VW Igala meets us at the airport in Calabar and of course, we were offered sardine-filled rolls on board the Calabar leg.

Alan had a foreshortened vacation since he had to purchase his own ticket – as we had done last year – and so had already been back in Calabar a few weeks before our arrival. He mentions that there are more new arrivals from the UK at the university, including a young bearded man, Barry, who is joining our ecology team on the animal side. There is also an older and more senior lecturer called Peter Bacon who will join us after Christmas from the Trinidad Campus of the University of the West Indies. All newcomers have already been given housing in the same recently built block of flats that Alan occupies on the university campus. I joke that newcomers are getting it soft now, no more passing through the guesthouse as we had done! Marian and Andy have also come back from their vacation looking tanned and relaxed.

All our old friends are happy and surprised to know that we are expecting our first child but are, of course, a little worried about Véro being pregnant in such a hot and humid place as Calabar.

We spend the first few days back in Calabar getting settled back into our lives. Véro restarts her tutoring and I catch up at the university with progress on my research as well as checking in at the Botanical Gardens. The shade house is now fully functional, and it looks perfect while Frank has been looking after my weed research in my absence. All looks good.

On the drive back towards the University, I spot a dead python at the edge of the newly tarmacked road. It must just have been killed by a car and is at least two metres long. I know John will love to dissect it and see what it has been feeding on; rats I presume. So I stop and lift it into a large plastic bag that lives in my car boot. The snake is heavier than I imagine. Since it is around midday (and I do not want a large snake putrefying in the boot) I drive home for lunch. As I walk through our front door carrying the large and bulging plastic bag, Rose, our maid, who is as curious as a cat, runs forward and tries to take the bag off me.

Knowing that many people have a mortal fear of snakes, I tell her "It's OK, I will carry the bag" but she pulls and tells me that it is her job to carry the shopping.

I tell her again that I will carry the bag and that it is not shopping. She insists and insists so I gently and teasingly start to open the bag and she puts her eyes to bag level to get a better look at what is inside. When she sees the snake, she squeals and at the same time (I swear) literally flies back across the room, lands against the far wall and starts shaking and gibbering. I gently tell her to look and I start to lift the dead snake out of the bag. Her panic subsides but her annoying curiosity remains.

The only current 'ick' in our lives is that Véro has severe morning sickness with a capital S. Each morning I rise before her, make breakfast on a tray and bring it to her in bed. (I can hear gentlemen in the audience braying at such male subservience but I do ask them to remember those beautiful green eyes and the sexy French accent).

As always, her food is wolfed down twice as quickly as I can ever eat. (My theory on why she eats so rapidly puts the blame squarely on her mother who always forgets she has four children to feed and seems to prepare just enough for two. The quickest eater in the household gets the chance to grab a second helping). But I digress, fifteen minutes, if we are lucky, after the breakfast has disappeared, there is a rush to the loo and a total regurgitation. Back to the kitchen and a second breakfast is served on the platter, fingers crossed. It usually stays down.

One evening when I arrive home from the university, I find two friends, Rex and Sheila, having sundowners with Véro. Rex and Sheila are a middle-aged couple who have lived in Calabar for several years longer than us. They are both keen golfers and spend considerable time at the Palm Oil Club too. Sheila has heard about the pregnancy and so has come to make us a beautiful offer. In a nutshell, they have given us the key to their house and there is a bedroom always prepared for whenever we have long electricity cuts on the housing estate, which is about three times a week. Rex is an experienced engineer and mechanic and his company has installed a large generator at his home that cuts in as soon as NEPA decides to switch off. Often they have no idea whether the house is running on NEPA or on the generator, except for the hum that the generator produces when running. This is one of many examples of the way friendship functions in the Calabar expatriate community. Frankly, without such displays of friendship, I doubt that we would have stayed as long as we eventually do. Their kind gesture makes Véro's pregnancy a little more bearable in the stifling heat and humidity of Calabar.

The students start to return; it has been fifteen months since years two to four were last on the campus. They find a lot of changes: there has been some considerable staff turnover, especially among the various expatriates, and substantial building work has been started, ongoing or completed, especially in staff housing on the campus but also they are finding some new teaching facilities. The teaching staff themselves are happy with the pay increase while some, like me, have received significant promotions and so have in effect received two considerable pay rises.

Given my new lecturer-1 status, the courses I am now covering are the more advanced ecology courses targeted to students who have chosen this specialisation from their second year onwards. And, since yesterday, I have a postgraduate student – my first! His name is Tony and he hails from Port Harcourt. He is starting a two-year Masters in the brand new course of Agricultural Ecology that I was able to design and develop during the previous year. Tony will hopefully be able to progress from the Masters eventually to do a full PhD; time will tell.

In addition, I have a dozen or so students from the final, fourth year who have enrolled with me to do either a library or a research project. For the library project, the students are obliged to arrive with an idea of what they wish to investigate. The role of the supervising lecturer is to ensure that the topic proposed by the student is adequately focussed to allow a detailed report to be written within the semester and, of course, to guide the student during the bibliographic research and report writing. Choosing a subject that is sufficiently focus is not as easy as it may sound.

I remember back to my final year as an undergraduate at QMC where I chose to do both a library and a research project. The first was supervised by Mike Swift (the Mycologist who eventually went off to Papua New Guinea). I had gone to him with the idea of doing a library project on 'Apple Diseases'. Since I had spent all of my childhood running about the apple farm where my mum works, I thought this might be both an interesting project and perhaps a useful one too. However, when I went to Mike to ask him to supervise it, he said "yes in principle but first write out for me a list of all apple diseases and bring the list back to me tomorrow."

I realised why Mike had set me the task when my list reached four A4 pages and I still had not finished. The following day I went back and suggested that the project be reduced to look at only two diseases caused by fungi: apple scab (caused by *Venturia inaequalis*) and apple rot (caused by the *phytophthora* group of fungi). He laughed and told me "just go for apple scab or you will end up writing ten volumes of (apple) rot!"

One student arrives at my office with the idea of writing a report on 'Food Crops Originating from Africa'. Remembering the useful lesson that Mike had taught me, I agree in principle but sent him away to write me a list of the crops involved. He returns the next day agreeing that he had been a bit over-optimistic and now suggests that he add the word 'Some' at the start of the title. We are good to go, although I was surprised at how short his list actually was. We both discover how many of the stable food crops in Nigeria originate from other continents, especially from South America.

Students who wish to do a practical project do not have to come up with a well-defined idea but it is always pleasing when they arrive, at least, with some sort of an idea. This is the case of Callistus, a student who comes from Kaduna in the NW of Nigeria. He is only three years younger than me and I know he will go far. He is quiet but friendly, extremely polite and he always makes Alan Seddon roar with laughter (perhaps the reason that he ignores Alan and comes to me to be his project supervisor!). Callistus has the habit of always replying 'this is very true' no matter what we say to him; even if it's only 'I'll see you in five minutes after I go to the loo'.

Alan cannot (and never did) get to grips with Callistus' verbal tic. He tells him completely idiotic things like 'the sky is a beautiful shade of green today' and dear Callistus will of course reply 'this is very true.' After these frequent encounters, Alan has to lean up against a wall until he finishes laughing while Callistus always keeps a straight, serious face.

Callistus comes to me with the idea of working on the dimorphic achenes that he has seen me frequently collecting. Indeed, the way I first got to know Callistus outside of the lecture theatre was during such a seed collection moment. I could not help but notice that whenever I collect seeds, bending down to pick them from the plants that grow in the disturbed soil around the sides of the campus roads, students – at least those who do not do my classes and so do not know me very well – would cross to the other side of road. At first I had not noticed them doing this and then, when I did notice, I put it down to good manners, a Nigerian characteristic. But with time, it was so obvious that they were avoiding me.

One day, Callistus comes up to say hello and to check out what I am doing. He asks me "doctor, do you notice that the students always cross the road when you are collecting seeds? Do you know why?"

I reply by singing: "The natives grieve when the white men leave their huts, because they're obviously definitely nuts! Mad dogs and Englishmen go out in the midday sun."

To which he replies "This is very true." Thank you Callistus!

But this quirk aside, he is a great student and because of his excellent work, I am able to integrate his results to my own and write for the two of us a nice little article about the ecological significance of dimorphic achenes. This is accepted by the Journal of Tropical Agriculture and is eventually published in 1984. Callistus leaves the university in that year with an upper second class degree and goes on to build a very successful academic career in Nigeria as a university professor. I am proud that the very first publication that is to be found on his *curriculum vitae* is our joint paper.

Another fourth year student that I am very fond of is called Emmanuel, also an ecology major. He is doing another project with me looking at growth patterns in a selected group of plants. We have started with a selection of two weeds of interest to me: *Imperata cylindrica* or spear grass (a really invasive pest of grasslands and agricultural fields) and my old favourite *Tridax procumbens*, one of the plants that produces dimorphic achenes. He succeeds in his project and this helps him, like Callistus, to receive a great BSc and go on to a successful career.

Meanwhile Tony gets on with his Masters. This involves both receiving lectures from me in various aspects of agricultural ecology that I have been developing, and doing research on the seedbanks of a number of weeds that we have identified. I confess that having a postgraduate student feels like a real luxury! As a lecturer and researcher, one can come up with a half a dozen or more ideas a day but time only allows a fraction of these ideas to be developed any further. Having Tony eager to get going on the research side – always so much more fun and rewarding than boring old lecture classes – especially now Frank has spent almost a year helping me in the area of seedbanks, we can together follow so many more leads. Which we do.

One course I enjoyed preparing and now teaching is a new course in biogeography to my second year ecology students. Of course, I draw partly on the experience that Alan and I had been able to glean during our drive through the different vegetation zones of Nigeria while travelling to Kano and back. Part of my course is to give some background on the characteristics of the different groups of animals from fish through amphibian, reptiles, birds and lastly mammals found in each zone. Today I arrive for my hour long lecture to be met by a crowd of enthusiastic – more enthusiastic than usual – students.

"Doctor, come quick, we have captured a strange reptile to show you."

Not knowing quite what to expect, I follow them into the laboratory, frankly presuming to see a chameleon or a rainbow lizard. What I did not expect was to see a very cute, sleepy and curled-up pangolin.

"You see doctor; this is assuredly a reptile because it has scales," exhorts the proud captor of the poor pangolin.

"Err, no, sorry but this is a mammal," I reply.

"But you taught us that reptiles have scales and the pangolin has scales. So it must be a reptile" my enthusiastic student continues. At that moment, the pangolin decides that siesta time is over and slowly begins to uncurl and take a stroll across the lab bench. Just in time for me to grab it carefully and turn it over quickly.

"What do you think those little lumps on the underside are and what about the hair?" and, as it tries to nip me, "what about those different shaped teeth? Are they not mammalian features?"

The now less enthusiastic student receives a playful clunk on the head from one of our less ladylike ladies who tells him "foolish boy, everyone told you that it was not a reptile but you refused to listen."

This was one of the many hilarious incidents that my kind and respectful students provided me during my years at the university. Indeed, the same student, when writing his exam at the end of the semester, decided to inform me in a response to one question that 'my doctor believes that there is likely a population of guerrillas living in the Oban Hills.' At that time, I had actually thought that gorillas might be present in the hills although today he might finally be right with his spelling of the word!

Another hilarious incident with a large class of some 150 second-year students was when talking about age structure within animal populations. As I am explaining about the need in animal populations for balanced ratios of infants, adolescents, adults and elderly, I notice some confused faces so, instead of continuing, I decide to use, as an example, the age structure of my present class of students. The intention being to draw a graph with their data and then show how to collect the mean, median and mode as well as calculate some other simple statistics.

I start with the question "who here is 17 years old?" The answer is 0 which was not surprising. "so who is 18" again 0. Slowly we progress up the age scale, and I am finding that even at 20 and 21 there are very few of my students who belong to this category. We quickly reach 28 and this heralds the raising of seven hands. I also raise my own (because I am also 28).

The class erupts in fits of laughter and one student shouts "oh yeah, and pull the other one doc" (that certainly sounds like a Seddonism not a Nigerianism!).

"But no, I promise you, I am 28."

Again roars of laughter and calls of "that is not possible sir!"

"Of course it is, I left school at 19, got my BSc at 22 and my PhD at 26. Then you all know I came straight to Calabar. I am 28."

The shocked silence restored the order and we manage to collect the remaining data and do some simple statistics with them. With around ten minutes or so left with the class, I ask for their stories and, what many students have to tell me, leaves me feeling very humble. The doyen of the class is 42 years old and his story can serve as an example of what many of the other students share with the class. He did not enter primary school until around 12 or 13 years old. He told me that he remembers shaving the morning of his debut at primary school. He had some years when he went to school and others when his father needed him to work and help with the family income. He finally managed to start going to secondary school when he was around 20. Once he obtained his school-leaving certificate he was obliged to start again working in the fields or at any manual job he could find. All the time he tried to save small amounts of money to eventually pay his way through university. When he was in his late-30s, the village chief told him that several of the 'richer' families recognised his intelligence and had decided to help him go to the university in Calabar by providing the funds necessary to enrol and stay in the student residence. Of course he is grateful for this help, but knows that payback will come once he graduates. He, like many of my other students, will be obliged to share what they hope will be a superior salary with the families that had originally sponsored them. That one incident left me with an eternal respect for so many of the people hailing from so-called developing countries and an equal dislike of the 'moaning minnies' that are just too frequent in our own society.

The Botanical Garden staff continue collecting field data on the interaction between the *Chromolaena* bush and the *Zonocerus* grasshopper and so either or both of Alan and I are frequently checking in on the staff and collecting their latest data. One day we decide to go together in my car to check on data gathering in the field. We chat about the sort of things that young guys chat about as we proceed past the remains of Trevor's infamous ditch. Suddenly, and by a marvellous feat of magic, Alan disappears from my view.

Of course, I screech to a halt fearing an alien abduction but instead find that my floor has given way and my best buddy is continuing his journey with me as though on a luge. Out of the pure kindness of my heart, I stop and allow him to go to the back seat as we progress very slowly to Samy's workshop for repairs.

A few days later, Samy has welded in a floor of tank metal (storage tank not Israeli military grade, I hasten to add!).

Talking of dear Samy, one beauty spot popular with Calabar residents of all nationalities is Kwa Falls. While the waterfall is nowhere near as large, high or impressive as the Cascade de Glandieu in our new commune in France, it is an uncrowded, relaxing and cool site to visit. We have been thinking of making a visit for a few weeks now and so finally set off one morning when the weather forecast is favourable. The drive takes about two hours to get to the Falls followed by a short walk through a forest. The outward trip goes well, the falls are as lovely as we had been told, and the fish in the river do not bite!

As we set off back towards Calabar on the little country roads, I realise that the brakes of my car have stopped working. I can pump the foot pedal as much as I like but there is no resistance. Worrying to say the least. Luckily most of the road to Calabar is not too hilly and I find that I can slow down relatively well by using the handbrake and switching to lower gears. However, the handbrake is only feasible when the car is not going too fast – so I keep my foot off the accelerator as much as possible. We only experience one frightening moment. We drive down a sharp incline to a very narrow bridge over the river that produces Kwa Falls and as we approach the entry to the bridge, I see a car approaching the other side of the bridge. Of course, I cannot stop so I flash my lights to warn the oncoming driver but he decides that he wants to play chicken – so he flashes his lights back at me and accelerates. I make the bridge a few seconds before him but that does not stop him from continuing the game. He drives on to the bridge and again flashes his lights. Frantic now, I put my arm out the window and gesticulate while Véro does the same from her side. After an agonising wait, he decides that he is a bigger chicken than me and reverses off, just in time for me to drive off the bridge, narrowly avoiding him. As I pass, I shout out the window "Sorry, no brakes!". He gives me a thumbs-up sign and we continue on to Calabar without further incident. Samy kindly fixes my brakes.

While it is fun being back in Calabar, and we are now into our third year, I have a serious concern staring at me that I need to resolve as soon as possible. Véronique is due to have our baby around mid-May and we both want to ensure that the child is born in France and, of course, I want to be present for the delivery. The anticipated date of birth means that legally Véro must travel before she reaches the seven-month stage (i.e. by early March at the latest) while I will have to arrive in France, to be on the safe side, by the start of May. The Catholic Mission hospital where the baker's baby was born is good but we have too many concerns about climate, sanitation and general health to want to risk having the birth in Nigeria. Also, quite logically, Véro wants to be near her family following the birth.

The issues facing us are therefore threefold. The first and most pressing is how can I leave the university at the start of May since second-semester exams are in June?

I call a meeting of the ecology lecturers at the Green Onion Annexe and get some cold Champions placed on the table and a few bowls of goat meat pepper soup ordered. Present with me are Alan, John and Barry, the new ecology lecturer. All are well aware of our upcoming joy due the following May but none have given any thought to the consequences for me; why should they?

When I explain the dilemma, Alan says "of course you have to be there for Véro." John nods in agreement.

The new lecturer, who is perhaps the deepest thinker among our group, asks "what are your options, Malcolm?"

"Well, accepting that I must and will be present, I have only a few real options. First, I can resign and leave by May." All say that this a bad first option both for me, the department and our students, as well as for the ecology team as a whole. "Second, I can leave in May and come back after the birth, say in June."

Alan says "arriving back in June would be a crazy idea both for Véro's sake and also for sheer timing purposes since the University will close for the summer vacation as soon as you get back."

"And third", I add, "I can do double teaching in the first semester and none in the second. That way I will have no exam duties in June when I will be away. But that means that the three of you will have less teaching in the first semester but more in the second. What do you think?"

The new lecturer scratches his chin under his bushy red beard and replies "but we are three covering for you in the second semester, so the amount of extra work for each of us will be pretty insignificant." The others agree, so it looks like we have a deal.

But then the second issue is how do I tell the university? I go to the Dean of Science, and speak to him very frankly. I inform him of the chat I had with the rest of the ecology team and he agrees with our conclusion. However, he advises me that since I propose to do a double amount of teaching in the first semester and that I will not be taking off the second semester entirely, the best thing to do is to keep quiet and say nothing to anyone. That is then the route I will follow but I do feel nervous about simply keeping quiet rather than going to see the Registrar and asking for formal permission to be away.

The third issue, once back in France, is where do we stay following the birth? Clearly the terrible state of our recent purchase in the hamlet of Cordon means that we cannot camp in the house with a newborn baby. My initial suggestion of buying a caravan and putting it on our small piece of land sounds as stupid to my ears as I speak it as it does to Véro as she listens. She more logically suggests that we should find a place to rent for six months or so before coming back to Nigeria. To this end, she sits down to write identical letters to all the local councils (called *Mairie* in French) close to Cordon asking if there are any furnished properties to rent for six months or so. The only *Mairie* that replies is from the village of Lhuis, about fifteen kilometres from Cordon. We exchange with the owners by post and we have our rental starting from next April.

One Sunday morning Marian comes to see us in Road-10 and she is in a real state. Andy is being held at the police station and obviously she is very worried for him. We sit her down to get the whole story clear. Apparently, Andy was driving back late on Saturday evening and he had an accident. In Calabar, no matter what time of year, night falls at 6 pm and, if there is no large moon, everything on the road is in total darkness. On this particular evening, around 10 pm, it was pitch black. Andy was driving down the highway and suddenly struck or was struck by an object in the road. The highway has two lanes in each direction, separated from oncoming traffic by a concrete barrier. This has small openings every half-kilometre or so. After the accident, what he realised had happened is that a motorbike had tried to cross the highway through one of the gaps, and with its lights switched off. For unknown reasons, the motorbike driver had chosen the exact moment Andy arrived along an otherwise empty highway to execute this foolish stunt. The result is very sad. The pillion passenger, a young woman, was killed and the driver is seriously injured and in hospital. Andy is being held without charge awaiting a court appearance set for the next morning.

I go to the police station; taking with me the letter from the British High Commission that appoints me H.M. Community Liaison Officer for Cross River State. On the basis of the letter, Andy is released until a court appearance the next day, timed for 10 am.

We arrive at the court in good time and sit on one of a row of benches that line the courthouse. The magistrate arrives and a steady stream of cases pass in front of him; all in Efik of course. Finally, at around 11.30 am, Andy's name is called and so he moves to sit in a seat in front of the Magistrate's bench. The police then say that they have had insufficient time to prepare a case and ask for an adjournment. A new hearing is set for two weeks hence.

This scenario is repeated on umpteen future occasions, always a long wait in the courthouse for the two of us, always the police have not produced a case, and always a next adjournment. To my knowledge, the case is never settled and Andy leaves Nigeria with his family a couple of years later.

Although the case is never settled, the families of the deceased woman and the injured motorbike driver make frequent contact at first requesting, then demanding reparation. CalElectric is switched on every night as a safeguard against reprisals.

One of the sad facts of expatriate life is that there is a regular turnover of friends. The normal expatriate contract duration is around four or five years and that means an average turnover of 20 to 25 per cent of expatriate friends every year. The positive side to this is that a similar level of less nice people are also likely to leave while among each new influx there are bound to be some exceptionally nice people arriving! And that is just the case. We meet up with the Cornish, Roger and his wife, and they are destined to be among our best friends in Calabar and that friendship goes on well after our Nigeria days come to an end.

Roger works as a trainer in a bank recently set up and headquartered in Calabar called Meridian Bank. It sits just along the road from the Standard Bank that we use. Roger is from Kent, like me, and he has a little girl with another baby on the way. He works for an international training organisation called ORT, based in Geneva. ORT (*Organisation pour Rehabilitation par Travail*) is an interesting outfit that was set up in 1880 in Russia to help train unemployed Jewish people in crafts and agriculture and has subsequently opened branches in many countries of the world helping people from all nationalities and religious backgrounds.

Roger works in the bank with two colleagues from ORT, one of whom is the local boss and also named Roger, Roger Marre. He is older than us and hails from France. Both Rogers are equally nice but in very different ways. In the early days of their arrival, we spend a lot of time with the Cornish showing them the Calabar ropes and helping them to get membership of the Palm Oil Club. In return, Roger-the-younger introduces us to the new Managing Director of the Meridian Bank, a rather rotund, pleasant and real English gentleman. This latter lives on the edge of our housing estate, in a magnificent villa with a beautiful swimming pool, surrounded by well-kept gardens. He loves to host curry parties in his home, and lays on really marvellous spreads. We are always grateful to receive an invitation and amazed at how he manages to get all the ingredients necessary.

During one of his first curry parties, we are all sitting around drinking coffee after the incredible meal and chatting about our experiences in Lagos. Véro and I tell our two stories about clearing our luggage and running across the tarmac pushing the luggage trollies, plus the one about the military exercise and people trying to stand in the corridor of the aeroplane. These are received with a lot of laughter and 'well done' and 'trust you two' from the assorted gathering. Then we hear a few other similarly unbelievable stories from the other people present. Our host then tells us all that our stories are rather pedestrian in comparison to his; and this is what he narrates:

He was appointed Managing Director of the Meridian Bank after interviews in London and had actually never been to Nigeria when he accepted his job. On his first trip out to start work, he was met at Lagos International Airport by the company 'fixer' (all large organisations, and in most countries, have a fixer to speed things along at the airport for their important staff). The fixer came with a driver in a plush company car. After all, this was the new Managing Director arriving. The new MD tells us that he watched as his suitcases and bags were loaded into the car boot and he then took his place in the backseat while the fixer sat in the front with the driver. The air conditioner was switched on, there was some bottled water to drink and a pile of mail for him to go through as the car made its way to his five-star hotel in the nicest part of Lagos.

As the car sped along the airport road, direction Lagos, the driver noticed that there was a checkpoint up ahead, manned by people in uniform, either the police or the military – he could not tell from that distance. Such checkpoints are frequent around the airport so the driver slowed the car down as he approached and an officer stepped into the road with his arm up, signalling the car to stop. The driver opened his window to tell the officer that he had an important passenger in the vehicle and that is when he found himself staring into the barrel of a pistol. The three people in the car were ordered out and more 'officers' surrounded the car and began to remove everything from it. All the new MD's bags, his briefcase, wallet, watch and papers were removed. Since he was wearing an expensive London suit and leather shoes, he was told to take them off. He was stripped down to his socks and boxers and then the car was sent on its way. A mile further along the road, the car was forced to stop yet again and, this time, the officers were manning an official checkpoint. When they heard the story of the robbery, they told the car to wait while they went back to check the unofficial blockade. Too late the crooks had already left. Our poor MD proceeded to his five-star hotel in a state of undress! When the raucous laughter subsided, we all had to agree that his story was by far and away the most enjoyable of the day. The poor, red-faced, podgy and knobbly-kneed MD was royally welcomed to Nigeria.

The time arrives for Véro to have her first pregnancy check at the Catholic Mission Hospital. We heard that the pregnancy clinic is complete pandemonium and so best to arrive with plenty of time and armed with considerable patience. We set out early from Calabar for the two-hour trip and the journey goes smoothly until we reach the outskirts of the small town where the mission is based. Still two kilometres or so to go.

Over the past few days we have had typical Calabar downpours which have to be seen to be believed. In our part of Nigeria, the rain is frequently so heavy that drivers are obliged to stop on the road itself because they turn into rivers, and wait for the storm to pass. Often it is impossible to drive with any safety or see sufficiently clearly where the road ends and the kerb starts; and remember those deep culverts that run alongside most roads.

We have just arrived in a town that boasts no tarmac and the road we must take is a one-car-wide track that undulates every thirty or forty metres. The hilly parts of the undulations are water-free but then they descend into massive puddles of unknown depth that are fifteen, twenty and even thirty metres across. Arriving at the first hillock, I stop and look down into the water that awaits us. I know of no other way to get to the clinic, it is either through the puddles or walk and wade there, and it has started to pour with rain again.

"Love, I have no option but to try to get through. Are you OK with that?" Véro nods in agreement and tells me that I will be alright. At the same time, a kindly and very soaked pedestrian knocks on my window and indicates for me to continue. Obviously the water is not as deep as I think.

Nonetheless, the VW Passat of the 1970s is not built for such terrain, being very low to the ground, at least in comparison to the Peugeot 404s and 504s that predominate the Nigerian car fleets. Knowing that the biggest danger to getting water into the engine is via the exhaust, I tell Véro to hold on and not to be concerned over me revving the engine. My logic – probably wrong – being that if I keep the revs high, the extra exhaust fumes will stop water going up the exhaust pipe and into the back of the engine. I have decided to use only first gear, to keep the revs up and, especially, not to stop until I get out the other side of the puddle. I notice from my right that the pedestrian is still in the same place and still gesticulating for me to go forward. With heart in mouth I descend the slope and the muddy brown water comes just up to the top of the wheel arches and remains at that level until we start to emerge out from the other side of the puddle. That was not too bad. At the next puddle, I repeat the manoeuvre with the same result, we are through that one too. I notice another soaked pedestrian standing on the puddle's edge waving me on; strange.

The third puddle we arrive at has me very worried because I cannot see the other side of the water since the road, just in front, takes a right and goes behind a partially flooded building. Pointless saying anything but I do notice more wet pedestrians that are gathered at intervals along the roadside beckoning me forward. High revs and down we go into the water. This time the wheel arches are covered and water is beginning to lap on to the front of the bonnet – and still we are going down. I rev the engine even more and finally the descent flattens and we are slowly moving forward through dirty brown water that is slopping over the surface of the car bonnet. I know that if we stop now, we are 'dead in the water' and so I keep revving, play my foot on the clutch to stop the engine stalling and keep moving forward. Finally, after at least five minutes of tension, the road slowly starts to rise and the water levels sinks below the bonnet and then the wheel arches. We are out.

The rest of the journey to the mission goes without any further dramatics and we pull into the hospital's pretty compound. There is no mistaking the pregnancy clinic as we pass several very pregnant ladies walking towards a building with a raised veranda and spot several more enormously pregnant ladies sitting in white plastic chairs on the veranda with their legs spread wide apart – no need for modesty here.

Véro tells me that she feels a fraud as her bump is barely visible. We climb the three steps on to the veranda and the ladies indicate that we should go through the door. We can already hear the usual pandemonium coming from inside but as soon as we walk through the door, we are greeted with complete silence apart from the two slowly rotating fans that zoom-clunk-zoom-clunk overhead. The ladies are almost in shock. Not simply to see a pregnant M'bakarah lady but to see a man in the clinic too. I realise that I am the only man in a room of at least sixty pregnant ladies.

I say to Véronique that we will indeed need to be patient with so many ladies in front of us but I had not counted on the friendliness of the Nigerians to strangers; especially from the women. Two brightly dressed and very pregnant ladies come over to us as we wait by the door and each takes Véro by a hand and together they lead her across the room to the front. When the nurse comes out for the next patient, they tell her to take M'bakarah. Véro is examined by our Irish gynaecologist and she tells us that all is going well with the pregnancy. The morning sickness is deemed unfortunate but nothing to do but continue the TLC that I provide every morning on a tray. The doctor walks with Véro across the room towards me, exchanging pleasantries in Efik with the pregnant ladies she passes. Shaking my hand, she tells me that I have been a busy boy. Congratulations!

Seemingly not at all pushed for time, she sees my mud-splattered vehicle parked near the entrance and asks us which road we had taken to the mission. When Véro mentions the road with the puddles, she laughs and inquires how many times we had to pay for a push-out of the puddles. It seems that the wet pedestrians are actually waiting for cars like mine to get stuck and need a push out; for a fee of course. Luckily she tells us of a different route to take that avoids that stretch of road, and we are soon off on our return trip.

On the way back we have an invitation for a late lunch with a couple that we have got to know well at the Paper Mill site. We have known them for a year or so and find them lovely people. The husband is a bearded bear of a Scotsman with the accent to match and one of the sweetest guys around. He absolutely adores his petite wife, who rules the roost in their household.

While chatting about the progress of the pregnancy, Véro mentions about the morning sickness and our friend immediately gets up beckoning me to follow. Attached to the outside of his house is a garage and he disappears inside and calls for me to follow.

"Here, let's put this in the back of your car", he indicates an air-conditioner, "it is surplus and an older model but it works fine."

This is one of the nicest presents that we could possibly receive as the high humidity, even at night, makes sleeping so difficult and sweaty.

Just to give an idea of how bad the humidity is, we noticed very soon after moving into Road-10 that any clothes and shoes left unworn for more than a week, started to gain a film of grey mildew. Leather is the mould's favourite surface but they are also partial to cotton and rayon. Simon had told me several months previously that the only way to stop mould on clothes is to install an incandescent light bulb in each cupboard. The heat, the drying effect and perhaps the light itself certainly does work well although I doubt that modern LED would be enough to stop the march of the mould.

On my first morning back at work after the maternity visit, I put my head around the door of the Works Department and ask if someone could kindly go to my house and install the air-conditioner. These machines are put into a hole in the wall and have the cold air blowing part facing into the room and the heat exchanging hot part facing outwards. Modern A/Cs, so-called, 'splits' are almost silent because they have the cold-blowing unit tucked away in the room while the noisy, hot unit is usually placed metres away outside. Not the A/C of this time. In order to get the cold air, you suffer the permanent clunk-clunk-clunk of the machine and the only ways to stop the noise is either to switch it off or alternatively allow NEPA to provide a power cut, as NEPA strives to do several times a day. But without too great an exaggeration, our A/C is a life changer. We gladly listen to the clunk-clunk-clunk in order to have sweet cool air, with a reduced moisture content. Now we sleep much better covered with a blanket rather than lying in nothing but sweat-soaked sheets. The A/C also helps to reduce the level, if not the frequency, of the morning sickness. Thank you our dear friends from the paper mill, what a marvellous present.

Time is passing rapidly and Véro has grown a bump that allows her to pass muster at the 6-month visit to the maternity clinic. All the better, the local government in the Mission's town has graded and raised the road, so there are no longer puddles to be negotiated, but this has led to a significant rise in distraught and unemployed car-pushers. They now try to make ends meet by placing their wives or daughters at tables selling bananas and manioc along the roadside to the clinic.

Our kindly gynaecologist declares all is well but insists that Véro must not delay any longer to leave for France. So her ticket is purchased with the oh-so-efficient Swiss Air and off she goes to the next stage in our family adventure. As usual, the first leg is with Nigerian Airways and that remains as interesting as always. Neither the sardine rolls nor the extreme and violent turbulence travelling across Nigeria change. Véro does suggest, however, that it might be preferable not to travel on Nigerian Airways when around seven months pregnant!

~ 9 ~

ENVIRON DE RIX (ADOLPHE APPIAN)

After arriving in France, Véro initially stays with her parents waiting for our rental to be vacated. She learns that the little house we are to rent belongs to a middle-aged farming couple living in the tiny hamlet of Rix, about fifteen kilometres from our new purchase in Cordon. We are only a stone's throw from the beautiful River Rhône and in a village full of old stone houses in the lovely region of the Bugey. Our area is also beginning to appear on the map for the quality of its white and *péttilant* (sparkling) wines.

After a couple of weeks resting at her parent's home and catching up with friends and family, Véro travels with her mum to be shown around the future rental by the owner, a lovely lady named Marie-Rose. The little village house has two bedrooms and an open-plan kitchen with a comfortable sitting room. It is relatively private as it opens onto a wide terrace area with only a *grange* (barn) belonging to the neighbouring family, the Joly's, in front of it. The house even has an open-fronted barn attached to the side where there is a 'summer kitchen' that we can use for BBQs and receive our friends during the balmy summer evenings to come. Perfect.

Marie-Rose and her husband André, although he appears at first to be rather shy, are absolutely charming people and are to become lifelong friends.

The house dates from the sixteenth century and still has its beautiful *'plafond à la française'* which is a ceiling composed of small, closely-spaced beams with the floorboards running over the top. This type of ceiling is typical of this area of France and usually found in wealthier households. When ceilings were installed, centuries ago, poorer people would simply use the wood to hand – often using lengths of poplar or pine chipped roughly to shape with a hand axe as the beams. However, the beams in this house are square and all of the same shape and dimensions; clearly a carpenter would have spent a significant time cutting them with a hand saw so that they all matched. Véro learns that several centuries ago, the house was a *douane* (customs or toll house) where people crossing the Rhône from France would be obliged to pay tolls for goods and safe passage. Most of the department of Ain where Rix is located was, from the fifteenth century, a part of the Duchy of Savoy. It remained as such until 1601 when it was ceded to the Duchy of Burgundy and so became a part of what is modern France. Interestingly for us, our own house at Cordon had historically served exactly the same function and leads us to name our house 'la *Maison de la Douane'*.

The recent history of our new rental is interesting. For two decades it has been rented out as a holiday home for a peppercorn rent to a gentleman living in Lyon; a bookbinder by trade. However, the rumour mill tells us that he recently lost an elderly aunt who left him money in her will with the caveat that he only has access to the cash if he uses it to buy a house. This he does, purchasing a beautiful watermill in the next village and into which he has recently moved.

The house we are renting has been little touched for the last twenty years but Marie-Rose promises that it is to be repainted and other odd jobs done too. She even asks Véro which colours of paint she would like for the various rooms. A couple of weeks later with the house complete, Véro is ready to move in as soon as I arrive in France.

Meanwhile, back in Calabar, I have a couple of months or so of enforced bachelor life but it is impossible to be lonely with so many friends around the town. I have been enjoying the company of Peter Bacon who joined the university from the Trinidad campus of UWI. At the moment he is a bit depressed with guesthouse accommodation so I invite him to come to stay with me for a few days. He tells me that he is having trouble both settling into Calabar and into the University – after Trinidad most people would! He misses his wife and grown-up children who are back in the UK and he is seriously thinking of quitting Calabar. As our few days together go smoothly, he asks if he can move in, offering to share the house costs. I have less than a dozen weeks or so before I am off to France, and it would be nice to have the company and also someone to look after the house while I am away. Peter moves into the spare bedroom.

Back at the university, I get a visit from three scientists who have been told about my presence at the university and my work in ecology by Kurt, a German friend who lives in Calabar with his wife Gerda. Kurt runs an aerial photography and survey company; a field that will later beckon my career. Two of the visiting scientists work as consultants for a company based in Frankfurt-am-Maine and they are in my office along with their boss, Klaus Voelger. His company recently won a contract from the Nigerian Government to develop an Optimal Land-Use Analysis for Cross

River State. Klaus tells me that he has a very impressive team of top German scientists but he lacks a presence on the ground to do some local research. He also believes that it would be seen in a favourable light by the state government if the university was somehow involved; hence his visit today. At that moment, Peter comes into my office and Klaus invites him to take part in the discussions too.

After considerable talking and exchange of needs and ideas, Klaus offers Peter and I consulting contracts in which we will collect and analyse water samples from the tidal parts of the river courses of the state. Our brief is to identify at which geographic locations rice might be grown and this will be partly controlled by the levels of water salinity in the river courses. An interesting and not impossible task, we judge. Eventually, Klaus also wants me to go to Frankfurt to edit the English of the sector reports before they are submitted in their final forms to the Nigerian Government. Although the different volumes of the report will be written in English, Klaus is a little concerned that the quality of written English may vary between the different authors because, of course, his team are not native English speakers.

I am particularly excited to do this work because all lecturers try hard to get on to the consulting ladder as a means of subsidising their relatively low salaries. Also, I see the fieldwork as a challenge and one that if done correctly will hopefully benefit the agricultural sector in Cross River State. Of course helping with rice cultivation also ties back into my university research interests in agricultural weeds.

Peter and I plan to get going on the work as soon as possible and so, via my friends in the Harbour Works village, I manage to get hold of tide tables for Calabar. Peter and I then purchase large-scale maps from the Cartography Office in Calabar Town.

Sitting down with the maps, we highlight areas along the rivers where we can get relatively easy access by vehicle, either my Passat or the department's Land Rover. Then by reference to the tide tables, we determine reasonable times during the coming days when we can travel to these sites at both high and low tides. In this way, we plan to collect a total of about one hundred water samples from different locations and analyse their salt contents back in my office cum laboratory.

As might be expected, the collection of water samples does not always go as smoothly as it should. On five or six occasions, we find the maps incorrect and are required to walk long distances or hire pirogues to get into the larger rivers to collect the water samples. On another occasion, after we have collected the two water samples in separate bottles and a third as a backup sample, we are challenged by a group of angry villagers who ask for *dash* in order to allow us to take 'their' water. By luck, I am carrying the backup sample in my hand while Peter has stowed the other two samples in his shoulder bag. On this occasion, we have gone with the Land Rover and so have our Efik-speaking driver, Akpan, with us. He translates the angry demand for money and so I ask him to apologise on our behalf and I make a big scene of tipping the water from the bottle back into the river. We all keep quiet about the two samples in Peter's bag.

We finish the salt analyses work for Klaus over a six-week period, Peter shows me the correct way to write up a consultant's report and we pass the finished version to Kurt for onward transmission to Klaus in Frankfurt. In all we are owed for fifteen days of work each.

While chatting over a glass of beer about the salt analyses work with one of our Kiwi friends, he asks if the same type of analysis could determine whether well-water on his building sites is sufficiently saline-free to be used for cement production.

Currently, they are bringing water onto the sites in tankers because of concerns that the salt load in the wells might be too high to make good-quality cement. I am told that the literature recommends not to use water above a maximum salt content and also that higher levels of salt in the water can damage the iron rods and make the cement itself crack over time and allow water infiltration. For the next several weeks I receive regular shipments of well-water from across the south of the state. These I analyse for their salt content and get the results back to the company. They insist that I be paid as a consultant because the saving they make by using local well-water, rather than bringing in tankers, far outweighs my small fee.

During breakfast on April 2nd Peter and I, as is our habit, switch on the World Service of the BBC and are both shocked by the news that Britain has declared war on Argentina after the military junta, who govern the South American country, invade the Falklands, a British Overseas Territory. Since the Falklands are grassy rocks with many more sheep than inhabitants, the reasons for the Argentinian invasion is unclear; especially since the islands are some 500 km from the Argentine coast. The BBC reports throughout the day on little else and we follow the news in our offices as the story unfolds. Although the military junta is unpopular with the general Argentinian population, the Generals seem to be playing to the country's emotional attachment to the islands that they call *Los Malvinas* in an effort to improve their own popularity. They are gambling that the Falklands are too far away and of too little value for the British to respond militarily. Peter and I believe that the Generals are seriously miscalculating the British bulldog attitude in general, and one British bulldog in particular: Margaret Thatcher, the Iron Lady. At this time, Mrs Thatcher is herself going through a popularity crisis as the repercussions of her previous battles to break the unions, especially the Arthur Scargill-led miners', begin to unfold in the shape of rising unemployment and strife within her own party.

I must own up to being a fan of Margaret Thatcher, who followed the weakly Ted Heath as Conservative leader. Singlehandedly she has overcome the Conservative tradition of money, landed-gentry, Eton, Harrow, and the Guards and, by a stubborn force of character, has shaken up the snob elements of her party. We both agree that if she can bring the Conservative traditionalists to heel, she should have little problem in chewing up and spitting out the Argentinian Generals. And that is precisely what she does. She forms a naval task force composed of the most powerful elements of the Royal Navy. Freight ships and liners are commandeered to act as transport and hospital ships and they are packed with thousands of our best troops. Special forces are dispatched behind enemy lines in the Falklands to cause problems and turmoil. Ten weeks later, the Union Jack is seen once again flying over Port Stanley while thousands of sheep go back to grazing on British, not Argentinian, grass. Meanwhile, the Argentinian people sweep the Generals away after their humiliating defeat, Rule Britannia returns yet another Thatcher government to power.

Time passes and I am getting anxious to get to France to see Véro and, knowing her, she will be getting fed-up waiting for the birth. Luckily, Spring in our region of France is a beautiful Goldilocks season; not too hot nor too cold. In fact, perfect for a very pregnant lady to sit in a deckchair and read and relax.

Nonetheless, and despite Véro being looked after by her parents, I am worrying more and more about her as the pregnancy advances. Of course, we regularly exchange letters but this is not a satisfactory way to check in on each other because of the very significant time lag between posting letters and receiving the replies.

One of the big issues with Calabar is that it is almost totally cut off from the rest of the world. There are no international phones, so it is impossible to call and check on people outside the country. In fact, there are only two means of communication in Calabar. The first is by letter, and the post invariably takes around three weeks to get to or from Europe; that is if the postmistress at the university post office does not strip off the stamps from recently posted letters and try to sell them to the next customer at a cut price. The letters so bereft of stamps are then binned. Sadly, I am not fabricating this, hand-on-heart. Indeed, the post can sometimes take so long that my paternal grandmother died, was buried, mourned and then started to be forgotten by relatives in the UK before I received the letter from my parents announcing that she was deceased.

The second means of communication is to get an invite for the evening on to the dredging ship that anchors at the Port each night and then to ask to use their ship's radio to call a European telephone number. Only two drawbacks here. First, in order to have a conversation, one must speak and then say 'over' at the same time releasing the radio clip. This allows the person at the other end to say their piece and then announce 'over', and so on until the conversation concludes. A simple sequence, I agree, but not for elderly parents or relations and certainly not for the French who, as a nation, neither like to cede the conversation nor know the meaning of brevity. The second and very serious drawback is the cost. On one previous occasion, we called for a short conversation with Véro's parents, wasting half our allotted time explaining what 'over' meant (well they are French) and then were faced with a bill for around £40. On the plus side, the crew always kindly provide fish and chips with real malt vinegar to their invitees!

My departure day finally arrives at the start of May and I travel on a Swiss Air flight from Lagos to Lyon via Geneva. I arrive fully 24 hours after I left Calabar to be met at Satolas Airport in Lyon by my father-in-law, Belou, and my lovely wife, looking as slim as always, except she appears to have swallowed a football.

The next day, we have a lunch invite at our uncle André's house so we can also collect our beaten-up Renault-6 that has spent the winter tucked away in his barn cum husband's hideaway. He even has a sign on the barn door reading 'Ze Dog House' that I had gifted him on a previous visit. We also get to see André's wife, Paulette; the only other member of the French family who seems at all interested in our Nigerian life. They are now in their mid-fifties, and André has recently taken early retirement. Because of all his years in colonial Africa, his retirement has been given a considerable bonus top-up by the French Government and so he can retire early and receive a very comfortable pension. The sadness in their lives is that they never had children of their own. André's father, Véro's paternal grandfather, was known as the 'Paternal' which is basically the equivalent of the patriarch in English. A little man with a force of character that he used to override the wishes of most, if not all, of his seven children. Although he died before I met Véro, I have heard so many stories about him and he seems to have been a bully (except strangely an equivalent to that word does not exist in the French language) and all his children appear to have feared him. Thus, at an early time in their marriage, when it was clear that André and Paulette were having trouble conceiving, André had discussed the possibility of adoption with his father. The Paternal told him certainly not, that he already had enough nieces and nephews to look after, so he should not bring a stranger's child into the family. Thus this lovely couple are destined to grow old without children of their own.

I am incredibly fond of André and get fonder of him as I know him longer and my French improves so that we can chat more intensely. It is becoming interesting and a real pleasure to be able to have proper conversations with him without having to reach every couple of words for the English-French dictionary or call for Véro to translate a difficult phrase. Today, we chat about some of the incidents that I share with you in previous pages and, at the same time, we reconnect the car battery that he has had on trickle-charge throughout the winter. Two turns of the ignition key and the engine magically fires into life as a year's worth of soot is expelled from the exhaust. We do a couple of turns of Saint-Jean-d'Avelanne, the village where he is deputy Mayor, just in case there is an issue with the car, and then drive off to the local garage to fill up with petrol and pump the tyres.

Over the course of the next two weeks we make several trips to Rix getting everything prepared for our new arrival. The cot we are to use belongs to Véro's family and is at least one hundred years old. Its last occupant was her younger brother Nico, now twelve.

We also make several visits to Cordon deciding where on earth we should start with the repairs to our house. Obviously the roof is a priority, especially when one-day, sitting in the ground floor (to be) lounge area, I look up and realise that I can see the sky via holes in two levels of floorboards and up through gaps in the tiles!

We call in two companies based nearby for estimates and both quote us figures that are higher than the price we paid for the entire house; they are clearly no-go as we simply do not have the necessary funds to proceed.

Then, one lunchtime, Poupette comes to visit us in *Cremieu*. She is the aunt who had lent us her apartment in Lyon during our vacation last year and is the sister of Véronique's dad and her uncle André. To put it mildly, Poupette is eccentric. A real character, barely five feet tall and a very talented interior designer. Indeed, she is one of the guiding lights for the popular and national magazine called '*Maisons Paysannes de France*'. After the meal she asks to visit our new house and so we drive over to Cordon. Immediately she gets out her camera, tape measure and a block of paper. We leave her measuring, drawing, making notes and clambering up and down the ladder that *le pépé Parcoret* has kindly lent to us again. Poupette spends about an hour going backwards and forwards occupying herself with checking where pipes can pass and inside walls must be knocked down and others rebuilt, measuring where the stairs can eventually be best placed so we can access the first and then second floors without needing to clamber up a ladder outside the house. Since the house has no mains drainage, we need to put in a septic tank – which basically decides where the toilet, and therefore bathroom, will go.

A couple of days later, Poupette arrives with a dossier full of architects' plans and drawings as well as, critically, the phone number of the Franco Brothers who come highly recommended by some of Poupette's clients. The Franco brothers are composed of Gilles (the silent) and Henri (the chatterbox). They are of Italian origin, coming to France as children, and excellent workers and totally honest builders cum roofers. We meet up with them in Cordon and I show them around the holes in the roof, explaining that we just cannot afford the estimates that we have received from other private companies. They ask if they can see the estimates and declare *"ils ne se fatiguent pas"* (basically that the companies 'have not made much effort' since they simply propose to take the complete roof off and replace it with a new one. The Francos tell us that the main structure of the roof is very solid and in fact beautiful with all its original main beams, mostly oak and ash. They believe that these date back at least two hundred years and possibly longer. The roof is covered with local handmade tiles that resemble overlapping fish scales hence their name here of *'tuiles d'écailles'* with *écaille* being a fish scale. The other companies simply wanted to bin the old tiles and replace with modern, and expensive, cement tiles.

What the Francos propose is that they will remove the tiles, panel by panel, working across the roof, and replace whatever of the structural wood is not sound. As Henri explains and Gilles smiles and nods in agreement, I receive a rapid lesson in the structure of roofs.

The main elements of the roof that run across the sides are called *'poutres'* (beams) and these do most of the heavy support work. The beam at the very top of the roof is called the *'poutre maîtresse'* and it holds the shape of the roof. When this starts to rot, the roof can be seen sagging in the middle; a common sight in the French countryside. Running downwards from the *poutre maîtresse* and across the parallel *poutres* are the rafters or *'chevrons'*. Finally running at right angles to the *chevrons* are the *'liteaux'* or battens on to which the tiles hook with their short protrusion on the underside. For our type of tile, there are approximately eighty per square metre and so in the region of 12,000 on the whole roof, each weighing one kilogram. Clearly traditional roofs are heavy!

We re-join Véro, and Henri declares that he will send us a precise estimate but we should anticipate that redoing the roof will cost around 8,000 Francs (about £800). We cannot believe our ears. This is not far off ten times less than the other companies are quoting us. The only drawback is that Henri tells me that I will need to find about three thousand second-hand tiles to make up for the missing and damaged ones on the roof. But after the pleasant surprise of their estimate, what is finding three thousand, one hundred-year-old tiles?

Up steps Poupette again, putting us into contact with another of her clients who also needs tiles for a house he is personally renovating. He lives in the town of Morestel, only ten kilometres from us in Rix, and has a plan with his wife to renovate the old house they purchased a few years previously and build an ocean-going boat. They already have the hull but need to build the entire superstructure, and then sell the house and use the money raised to go around the world in the boat. Some people have such extreme projects that they put me to shame!

Together we scour adverts in local newspapers for people looking to sell tiles. We have agreed to work together on finding and collecting the tiles and to split them equally, at least until I have the three thousand I need then I will help him get the remainder he requires. My new friend owns an old Renault Estafette – basically a shed on wheels – that serves as a mobile wheelbarrow. Together over the next three months, we go to various homes and building sites to bargain for and pick up the needed tiles. Before the summer is out, I have my three thousand tiles at an average price of seventy centimes, about seven pence each.

Véro's due date is 18th May and so we stay with her parents as they live significantly closer to the clinic we have selected for the birth. I, naively (typical male?) imagine that on waking on the 18th, we would pack off to the clinic.

"Not at all", I am told by my mother-in-law, "you have to wait until the baby decides it's time to arrive."

However, we do go to see the gynaecologist at the clinic on 18th and she declares all is fine. She asks that we wait five days and then, if the baby has still not given notice of arrival, we should come back to see her. The 23rd arrives and still no sign of a baby so we keep our appointment and are told that all is still good but perhaps we should do some mild exercise to give baby a small nudge.

The next morning being fine and sunny, we decide to take a gentle stroll in the Crémieu countryside. We walk down the *chemin de Prajot*, across the D65 and along the *Auderu* parallel to a little stream that runs through a fenced-off meadow and towards the ruins of a watermill fed by the stream. We have driven past the watermill on many occasions and often ask ourselves why no-one has ever bothered to restore it? Just after the mill we turn left along a wooded footpath and loop back in a circle towards the D65 and then the *chemin de Prajot* where the in-laws live. I do not know whether it was simply the walk of about a kilometre that got things moving but I suspect that it was more likely us clambering over a fence that the farmer had kindly placed across the public footpath. No matter really. Twinges start at lunchtime and so off we drive to the clinic in Décines. Décines is a small, nondescript town on the outskirts of Lyon that will one day become famous thanks to *Olympique Lyonnais FC* building their new stadium there after deciding to desert the *Gerland* suburb of Lyon.

At 10.20 pm on 24th May, our beautiful daughter Mélanie announces her arrival with a very particular cry. Remembering the concerns that we had for those Nigerian babies who had lost their name tags in the wind; we both now realise that parental recognition goes much deeper than a name tag. I could find my little Mélanie in the dark by the sound of her cry alone; not to mention her cute little turned-up nose. For the record, Mélanie arrived five years to the day since I had first met Véro in 'La Poubelle'. Romantic, no?

After getting over the very pleasant shock of realising that I am a dad and now responsible for this lovely but so tiny bundle, Véro suggests that I start back to her parents' home, a drive of some forty minutes.

Off I drive, direction Crémieu, it is well after 11 pm by now. Being a disciplined driver (well, I am British, don't you know?), I respect the fifty kilometre limit as I drive from the clinic and out of the town. Someone less disciplined than me decides that I am not going fast enough and so he sits tight behind me and intermittently flashes his headlights. I know that if I brake brusquely, he will crash into the back of my car, so I am concentrating hard. At that moment I approach traffic lights and just five metres before I arrive, they turn orange. Nothing to do really. If I brake, he will crash into my boot, so I accelerate through the orange lights. Bad luck for me because there is a police (they are called *gendarmes* here) checkpoint just ahead. An officer steps into the road and waves me to the side. Blast (that is not the expletive I used!).

"Good evening sir, you just went through a red light." The gendarme addresses me in French.

"I am sorry to disagree but the light was actually orange when I passed. Also you will have seen that I had an idiot behind me who was far too close. Normally I would stop at orange but I was afraid he would crash into the back of me."

"Your papers please sir." I hand over my folded green UK licence, my dark blue British passport and the car's insurance and registration papers. "Ah, you are English. What are you doing here?"

"My wife gave birth to my daughter at 10.20 pm at the *Décines* clinic, now I am on my way back to my in-laws' house."

"What? You have just become *un papa, mais c'est formidable, félicitations*. And, by the way, my colleague is verbalising the '*conard*' who was driving too close and flashing his lights at you. We saw him coming a long way off. *Vous pouvez aller et encore félicitations, monsieur.*"

With that he steps into the road, hand in the air. All the traffic stops and he waves me out. This is my first encounter with the French police and I am impressed by their kindness and understanding. I arrive at Belou and Mic's house and am on cloud 9. A quick call to the UK to inform my parents that they have again become grandparents, that's twice in less than three weeks for them, and it's off to bed. I am shattered. The gentler sex do not often realise that being an expectant dad for nine months and then helping to give birth takes a heavy toll on us poor guys too. I sleep like an ... err .... Baby!

The next morning, I am up early and back to the clinic. As I walk through the door of the section where Véro has her room, I hear the distinctive cry of my little girl. No mistaking her. Mélanie is an angel of a child, she sleeps well and feeds well.

One of my chores this morning is to register the birth at the local *Mairie*. So armed with the necessary paperwork, armfuls of it – France and its wretched *dossiers* – I stroll up the road to the *Mairie* and announce the birth. Of course, being so close to the clinic, this must be a common occurrence – not unique as it is for me – and so when I announce that I am here to register the birth of my daughter, I am met with an '*eh ben*' which translates in this circumstance as akin to 'so what'. Welcome to the world of the French public civil servants. They are usually lovely people but please do not interfere with their peaceful days.

I am asked for the child's name: 'Mélanie Marks'. "*Et encore?*" (and what else?) demands the lady from behind the counter.

"Well, nothing else. That is the name that we have chosen", I reply.

"*Mais non monsieur. Ce nom est impossible !*"

Now why should the name we have chosen for our perfect little girl be impossible? I understand that there might be objections if I wanted to call my child Attila-the-Hun or Boris-the-Unruly but we believe that the name we have chosen is cute and will serve both in UK and in France.

"What is wrong with Mélanie" I query, and am told that one name is insufficient. In France there has to be a *deuxième prénom*, a middle name.

Gosh, we have never spoken about a middle name. The lady then takes pity on this *pauvre 'rosbif'* as the French have nicknamed the Brits in revenge for us calling them 'Froggies'. She kindly tells me that in France we often use the name of the maternal grandmother for girls. Unfortunately, my mother-in-law's name is Michèle which would give initials of MMM – that sounds like a zip company – or worse mmm and that sounds too appetizing (if you get my drift). Back a generation, we have Mélanie's great-grandmother, called by everyone *Minouche* (kitty or pussy cat) but really named Isabelle. That will do fine as I consider my new little lady 'is a belle' and her initials are now MIM. 'Mim' becomes a personal nickname that only her adoring dad ever uses for her. A few days later I pick up my two ladies from the clinic and we drive with a feeling of bliss back to Crémieu.

Two days later and Véro is feeling in good form. I pack the car, we say goodbye to Mic and Belou and set off for our rented house in Rix, about 35 kilometres from Crémieu. Mélanie sleeps peacefully in her travel basket. The sun shines down on us as we pass through the little villages that crop up sporadically along our route. Several kilometres away from the town of Morestel we can already spot its twin landmarks vying to be the tallest building for many miles around. The honour is now boasted by the *Eglise Saint Symphorien,* built in 1425, that added an extra spire to one corner of the clock tower in the nineteenth century thus overtopping the Medieval Tower. Morestel has gained the nickname of the '*Cité des Peintres*' (the city of artists) with its most famous son being the impressionist, François Auguste Ravier.

After stopping to buy bread in the main street, we turn left into the *Route d'Argent* (the silver or money road – I have no idea where the name comes from) and then left again at the horse riding stables into the road leading to Brangues. This small village is perched on the crest of a hill looking down on the broad River Rhône on one side and Morestel on the other. Its claim to fame is that two famous French authors set up home in the cute village, namely Paul Claudel, a poet and diplomat and Stendahl (his nom-de-plume) who wrote the classic tale '*Le Rouge et le Noir*' set in the time of the French Revolution. From Brangues we cross the broad river Rhône at Groslée on its majestic suspension bridge. The first half of the Rhône belongs to the department of Isère but after halfway we enter our home department of Ain. Coming off the bridge, we take a left and then four or five kilometres further along the D19, on the right, we see the tiny sign indicating Rix. Sometime in the past, some idiot has used the enamelled sign for target practice almost obliterating the 'i'. Up the steep little hill, left turn at the *lavoire* and we arrive at our home for the next three or four months.

Véro has already visited the house on two or three previous occasions and met the nearest neighbours in this hamlet of about fifty souls. The grand house next door to us is owned by the Jolys, an elderly but very welcoming couple. She has also met the equally elderly brother of M. Joly, called Leon who lives just down the lane. He is famous for his enormous patch of wild strawberries that grow against a wall in his back garden. And of course we know Marie-Rose and André who rent us the house and live next door to Leon.

Once unpacked and relatively well installed, we make a quick and typical French lunch of mixed salad, ham and cheese, washed down for me, by a light red wine from our Bugey region, all eaten at an outside table in the late May sunshine; heaven. Mélanie sleeps soundly in her crib after polishing off her lunch of a tiny bottle of milk.

The washing up finished, we have just settle down to read when there is a knock at the door. On opening it, I am greeted by a smiling gentleman of about my height but twice as broad with a thick brown beard and twinkling eyes. He must be about 35 or so.

"*Je viens te dire bonjour*" he says to me. "*Je m'appelle Bruno et j'habite la maison à l'autre côté des Joly. Tu veux jouer aux boules?*" (I've come to say hi, my name's Bruno and I live in the house on the other side of the Joly's. Do you want to play 'ball'?). *Boules,* sometimes called *pétanque,* is a typical pastime enjoyed in France; a type of bowling.

In general, the French can often be a bit reticent to break the ice, especially with a foreigner, and so I am very touched by Bruno's friendliness. Not surprisingly, he turns out to be a very nice guy, a cheesemaker by profession, and a good *boules* player too. The team of he and I beat his two friends and then we sit down on an outside bench to share glasses of pastis. After the second glass of this popular aniseed drink, with the ice cubes chinking as we swallow the yellowish liquid diluted in cold water, he tells me that I look like a rugby player.

"Well", I reply, "I did play rugby as an undergraduate at university but have not played for a good six years."

"Great!" he responds, "I am the captain of the Lhuis team, we need extra players and training starts on Tuesday evening. Will you come?"

Well, how can I refuse? And just like that, within an hour of arriving in this cute little hamlet, I have made new friends and I am to play for the local rugby team. I feel a little less enthusiastic about the training part though. The heat and stickiness of Calabar is not very conducive to training and so I must be very out of form; and the hills around Lhuis are pretty steep!

We quickly settle into a rhythm that turns around the need to keep the Little Miss fed, cleaned and slept. We consider we must be the perfect parents because Mélanie is absolutely no trouble. She feeds when she should, she would sleep all night if we did not wake her for feeding, and she goes back to sleep afterwards. All is easy. Except at 'cranky hour', around 6 pm when she will not sleep, feed or settle. She simply cries for no apparent reason; we believe she is just letting off steam. That is the signal for me to put her in the back of the car and drive around the block in Rix resulting in an instant snooze.

Prior to her birth, Véro had purchased a book considered the 'bible' for child raising in France called *J'élève mon enfant* by Laurence Pernoud. Within a few weeks of her birth, we are already pretty sure that Mélanie has somehow read the book because every time that the book mentions a milestone, she achieves it on the due date. You know the sort of thing: baby will smile from 4 weeks on (she smiles on the exact day), first tooth will appear around the fourth month (it does), baby will walk around one-year old (she does on her first birthday) – but more on some of those milestones later.

The in-laws are frequent visitors; Mélanie is only their second grandchild after all and their first granddaughter. Rix is little more than thirty minutes away from Crémieu (when I drive) and considerably less when Mic is behind the wheel. She usually manages to stay in second gear all the way no matter what speed her Renault-4 is doing.

Véro's dad, Belou (really Réné) worked until recently for Oldham, the UK battery company, as a sales representative but he has just retired on reaching the age of sixty. He is an excellent handyman and spends most of his free time working for his wife, Mic. This is because Mic bought a small house in the centre of Crémieu in early 1975, two doors down from the church and opposite the general store. The house dates from the fourteenth or fifteenth century. With Belou's help, she has converted the downstairs into a very chic boutique in which she now sells classy table lamps, mostly made from antique bases that Belou transforms in his workshop. The bases seem to be made from anything suitable, all that is needed is good skill and an incredible imagination. Candlesticks are the obvious items to be transformed but he has turned wooden shoe lasts, piles of flat pebbles, ancient blowlamps, and many other fascinating objects into unique and beautiful lamps. Mic spends most of her free hours, including while in her boutique awaiting customers, to sew the lampshades to go with the lamp bases. Her designs are really beautiful and, not surprisingly, she has a faithful clientele not only from Crémieu but from much further afield, including Lyon where she supplies high-end shops. Her boutique also has a stock of paintings, mostly of interesting sites in and around the medieval town of Crémieu, painted by Belou's older brother Ferdinand. Ferdie has won many local painting competitions and is an artist in every sense including being laid-back, antisocial, scruffy and poor! But a lovely character and, as a youngster, he was the only one of the seven children who dared rebel against the domineering Paternal.

Both sides of Véro's family are therefore artistic but her mum is not only artistic but deeply cultured since she has an interest in everything artistic. She reads a lot and helps with many artistic activities in Crémieu and in the neighbouring town of Morestel. I am rather in awe of her talents and knowledge. This is because, sadly, all the artistic talent possessed by my parents was snaffled in my mum's womb by my artistic older sister; I got left instead with the love of science and logic. But no real complaints from my side as Véro and I complement each pretty well.

Mic has been reading up about Rix – which is a strange name for a French village. She has read that our hamlet can lay claim to having inspired a very gifted artist called Adolphe Appian (his real name was Jacques Barthelemy Adolphe Appian). He was born in Lyon in 1819, studied at the Ecole des Beaux-Arts before undertaking a period of further study in Paris. There he became great chums with Corot and Daubigny and they both greatly influenced his work. In 1866 he exhibited in Paris and his fame was sealed when Napoleon III bought two of his works. The connection with Rix is that he spent many summer vacations here and developed some of his best-known works in and around the village with the most famous being called 'Environ de Rix'.

We decide to go to look for his old holiday home which we know must overlook the River Rhône where he painted many of his rural scenes. Mic has read the approximate emplacement of Appian's house and so it should be easy to find as there are only two that sit on the edge of the river. We place Mélanie gently into her pushchair, and go out onto the little lane that descends from our house to the old chapel. Stopping to post some letters home to the UK, we cross the rather quiet D19, waving to Gilles whom we had met at the Joly's house, over a glass of wine, for the first time only a few nights previously. Gilles owns the eponymous agricultural materials business that sits on the D19 and at which we turn down a small lane aptly called the chemin du Rhône. A sharp left at the bottom (otherwise you would fall in the river) and we turn on to a dirt track called locally 'Le Roule' which was in fact a towpath for hauling boats and barges against the powerful currents of the Rhône. One hundred metres along the Roule, we come across Appian's house that is set back some twenty metres from the river. During Appian's time there would have been a chain linking the bank on our side to that on the other bank in Isère – it must have been a couple of hundred metres long to traverse the river at this point – and we see the remains of the hefty concrete pillar in the garden of Appian's house to which the chain would have been attached. A small boat cum ferry, attached to the chain, crisscrossed the river on payment of a toll. Similar crossing points occurred every couple of kilometres along the Rhône and were only superseded when the bridges were built – the closest to us in Groslée was only opened in 1912. At our point on the riverbank there is a gently sloping slipway where the little ferry boat would have stopped, picked up and discharged customers. Today, as the sun shines on the flowing water, it is the feeding ground for a school of large grey fish that my father-in-law informs me are called *Hotu* in French.

    The view from Appian's house is lovely as it looks right across the Rhône to another large property opposite while, on the far bank, off to the right is the beautiful Chateau of Mérieu that always seems to be bathed in sunlight. Back on our bank and almost opposite the chateau is Gilles' house and this, too, has appeared in a few of Appian's paintings both on canvas and on dinner plates. We are pretty sure that Appian's *'Lever de Lune au déclin de Jour'* was painted from the river right outside his house although I have my doubts that the title has been slightly romanticised by Appian because while the painting shows the sun setting in the West, the moon is nowhere to be seen! But that does not matter, as my mother-in-law tells me; artistic licence.

We are now well into June and, on most days, our time is split in two: From around ten in the morning until about four in the afternoon, I go to Cordon and get cracking on work in our house while Véro spends the time in Rix with the baby and gets on with one or other of her hobbies, usually sewing or reading. She also manages to catch up on any lost sleep although Mélanie continues to be a gem of a child. I try to get back to Rix in the mid-afternoon and then we either go for a walk around the village, do shopping or, if the afternoon is too hot, we go for a swim. Because of our frequent walks around the village pushing the contented little lady in her buggy, we have got to know most of the Rix residents. People here are so friendly, dare I say, far more so than in Cordon? It is a rare walk that does not see one or other of the people we stop to chat with hand over a fresh lettuce, a bunch of parsley or some sun-ripened tomatoes. Leon invariably ticks me off, playfully of course, for not coming to his house more frequently to collect the wild strawberries. His ageing back and the sheer quantity of the tiny red berries prevent him from picking all himself.

The longer we stay in Rix, the more we appreciate the calm beauty of the village and the friendliness of the villagers. We confess to Marie-Rose that we would love to live in the village but since we have already bought in Cordon, there is nothing much we can do. She says that is unfortunate because there is a large, old house that will soon be for sale on the next road up. Although there is no way that we could buy it, we are sufficiently curious to put Mélanie into her pushchair and walk up to take a look. The house sits on the corner of two small lanes and looks like it has been fortified to withstand a siege. Curiously too, all the windows are of different sizes and at different levels too. This suggests that the rooms inside must be rather higgledy-piggledy. The front door is accessed by five stone steps, as is very typical in the Bugey where the houses often sit on sheetrock so they have to be raised above the ground to allow the wine cellar and other storage or livestock spaces to be constructed underneath. At ground level, to the side of the house, is a large double door standing open. This allows entry to an inside courtyard where chickens are running around unhindered by the little grey cat sleeping in a patch of sunlight. The courtyard is surrounded by various buildings of different ancestry, suggesting that previous owners, going back a couple of centuries, must have added buildings as time, space, needs and, of course, finances allowed.

Our curious looks are seen by a small, elderly lady wearing a dingy-coloured smock and a bright blue housecoat over the top.

She comes out from the courtyard to greet us *"bonjour les jeunes, bonjour ma belle"*, saying hello to the three of us, "I suppose that you have heard that the house will soon be for sale? Would you like to come and have a look around?"

We reply that we are not in a position to buy but would love to look around the courtyard. Véronique, in particular, is a very nosey character, so we are invited in. The courtyard is enclosed on almost all four sides. In front is a rather ramshackle barn that serves as the poultry house with a large run for the free-range chickens and ducks on the other side of the barn, facing away from the house. During other walks we have often stopped to give the poultry our old bread and the outer leaves of lettuces. To the left is a balcony that madam tells us is her summer kitchen where she entertains her family and friends. To the right is a large and very high wall that separates her property from the neighbours. Since this part of Rix is on a steep slope that basically starts at the top of the mountain above Lhuis and finishes in the Rhône, neighbouring houses, like here, can be at significantly different levels. After a quick chat we say our goodbyes with Mélanie receiving a little kiss from the nice old lady.

We explore the little lane up from her house, admiring the beautiful house of her neighbour with its blue shutters and deeply pointed roof covered with *'tuiles d'écailles'* as well as the large barn that runs at right angles to the house. We both express at the same time "if only" and burst out laughing. I could imagine sitting under the expansive lime tree that grows in the patch of garden below the house where two cars, with 69 (Lyon) number plates are parked while Véro has spotted an amazing swimming pool at the end of the garden. A small boy is chasing a squealing little girl around the pool while a distinguished lady is calling from her deckchair for a little peace so that she can concentrate on her book.

We follow the lane past the front gates and around the end of the barn that has a curious rounded wall, presumably built at the time (probably around 1750) to offer sufficient space for a horse and cart to pass; and I wonder, given its shape, if it was not formally a dovecot. To the left of the lane are two small cottages and in the front garden of the first is working a slim, handsome man with an imposing moustache. He greets us in the friendly fashion that we now realise is typical Rix and leans over his fence for a chat. He tells us that he and his wife are from Lyon and they have recently bought their house as a holiday home. They are high-class biscuit makers! Only in egalitarian France can there be high-class and low-class biscuits. We laugh and tell him that in UK biscuits are either covered in chocolate or not.

He warns us that we will not be able to walk much further up the lane with the pushchair as it is blocked by a barrier. Indeed, we can now see the blockage fifty metres or so further on with, on its other side, two lorries stacked high with stones and pieces of rafter. Our new informant tells us that the doctor who lives in the beautiful house with the pool is demolishing a line of old workers' cottages that ran from the back gate, down the slope, close to the swimming pool at the bottom where there use to be the ruins of an outdoor bread oven and at the top, a mill.

Most evenings we take our milk pitcher to Marie-Rose in the milking hall behind her house and she fills it up with a litre of the creamiest and freshest milk you will ever taste. Memories of trying to dissolve Nido milk powder into a jug of filtered water occasionally flash to mind but Nigeria seems a million miles away from this idyllic part of France. Marie-Rose is a model 'milk maid' in this part of France having a clean stable, always wearing fresh pink overalls and rubber gloves and having her hair tied in a bun and under a hat that resembles a shower cap. The modern milking machine means that she only touches the cow to clean and disinfect the udders before milking begins. Contrast this to Cordon where the local milk is drawn in a crumbling stable with the largest cobwebs I have ever seen trailing from the ceiling beams to the floor and completely black with captured medieval dust. The occasional straw floating in the milk bucket is probably the least of the hygiene worries.

For swimming, we have two favourite spots. The first is in the mountains above Lhuis, about fifteen kilometres away, in the Lac d'Ambléon. This spot is beautiful and secluded with very few other swimmers around and then only locals. The lake is crystal clear as one might expect from an ancient glacial lake. It is also pretty cold and reputed to be bottomless (at least very deep). At the lakeside, where we usually park our car, is a monument to the Maquis, the French Resistance, who were very active in the Second World War, especially in the mountainous areas of France. We are told by friendly residents of Rix that the lake is haunted at night because there are innumerable bodies of German soldiers, along with their weapons, residing at the bottom of the water.

The area around the lake is beautiful with thick ancient woodlands, mostly beech, climbing up from the lake into the hills that surround it. Further along the road is a belvedere at an altitude of over 700 metres and it provides a magnificent view right across to a chain of mountains in the distance that marks the Bauges Nature Reserve. On a clear day, we can even glimpse Mont Blanc in the background but this beautiful sight is in reality a harbinger of rain. Immediately below the belvedere is the little stone built village of Ambléon, fully three hundred metres below its lake, while looking East across the countryside we can spot Belley as well as the distinctively-shaped 'Dent du Chat' (Cat's tooth) mountain that serves to signal but hide the magnificent Lac de Bourget and the lovely town of Aix-les-Bains on the other side.

Our other swimming hole is the Lac de Pluvis which lies within our community of Brégnier-Cordon and on the other side of the Mont de Cordon from our house. This lake, too, has a reputation for being haunted but from a saga dating long before any world war. We are told by the assistant mayor of Brégnier-Cordon, himself a university lecturer, that where the lake stands was previously a thriving medieval village. Legend has it that a stranger, a tall, dark traveller, arrived in the village one cold winter's night when the ground was deep in snow. He knocked on each door in turn asking for shelter for the night but was refused by every single one of the good residents of the village. In desperation, and now very cold and hungry, he walked towards a soft glow in the distance and came across a cave in which lived, as legend tells, a crazy old woman. She accepted for him to have a place for the night beside her small fire and to share her meagre meal. During the night, the snow turned to heavy rain and, in the morning when the stranger stood up to take his leave, the village had totally disappeared and been replaced by our swimming Lake. All that remains of the community of Pluvis is the cave which is called locally '*La Grotte de la Bonne Femme*'.

The legend does not concern us as the lake has a small sandy cum muddy beach, is not too deep at the edges and is considerably warmer than Ambléon. The first time we go for a swim in the lake another bather tells us that our little lake is to disappear later in the year. The government is building canals across the major meanders of the Rhône and placing hydroelectric stations at the end of each canal to capture the force of the water as it drops several metres and pours back into the Rhône. The canal for Brégnier-Cordon is due to commence building in a few months' time and will pass right through the lake, signalling its demise.

In conclusion, when the lake is drained so that the bulldozers can pass through during the construction of the canal, local people witness the ruins of a small village standing exactly where the lake once was. Every myth worth its salt has its roots planted in grains of truth. With hindsight, it is likely that some natural phenomenon, perhaps an earthquake or a flash flood, caused the Rhône to change its bed and pass through the village of Pluvis, wiping it out and so giving rise to the legend. Indeed, the entire area around the Rhône bears witness to its capricious nature since there exist dozens of *lônes* (cut-off sections of the river) and oxbow lakes (cut-off meanders). Between Cordon and Rix lies an area of land called '*Le Saugey*' and this is the perfect example of the Rhône periodically changing its bed. While the department of Ain lies on the East side of the Rhône and Isère on the West, Le Saugey is on the East side – and so should be in Ain – but it belongs administratively to Isère. This is because, at the end of the seventeenth century, the Rhône moved westwards cutting off Le Saugey on the wrong side of the departmental divide.

In our Cordon home, I am busy trying to make the house a little more habitable for our vacation next year although we are both sufficiently savvy to know that we will have to camp in the house for the next few years. Following Poupette's suggestions, my priorities for this year – in no particular order – are mostly restricted to the ground floor and include getting the water and electrics functioning; knocking down two internal walls to free up space and improving the quality of light; removing the horrendous cardboard-like material that has been nailed to the ceiling, and to make a start on repairing considerable damage to the plasterwork of the walls. Another, rather major challenge that I have set myself is to install a toilet on the first floor which also means that I must install a septic tank and connect this both to the toilet and to the mains drainage. Which job I tackle, and on which day depends a lot on the weather. When the sun shines, I try to do the outside jobs but when it rains I have plenty of activities to keep me busy inside. The Franco brothers have already promised to fix our roof over the coming year and we have paid them a small deposit to seal the deal.

Before I leave you in awe of the jobs I tackle and the skills I surely must possess, it is worth mentioning that my building, electrical and plumbing qualifications go as far as fixing shelves (slightly wonky), changing lightbulbs and even a plug, but not much else. But, 'where there's a will there's a way' and 'where there's no spare cash, there's a sound motivation'. We quickly learn that either we learn to do it ourselves or nothing can get done.

I start off by ordering the septic tank, all two thousand litres of it, from a supplier who lives in the backwoods of Evieu, about seven kilometres away, and I need to pick it up in a couple of days. Before that arrives I must make a start on the water supply and the disposal of wastewater. I have worked out and made a list and drawings of the material I need to buy from the local do-it-yourself supermarket in Morestel. The list includes the length of copper pipe that I will need to install water in the house both for the future kitchen and the future bathroom upstairs. I also need to buy and install the toilet and the kitchen sink (donated by the in-laws who use the opportunity to palm off a lot of the clutter that they have accumulated in their barn, including a massive immersion heater). My list expands as I try to calculate how many 90-degree bends for the copper and plastic pipes plus the number of pipe connectors for the water, waste and toilet pipes. Then there are washers, taps, silicon sealant, plastic pipe glue, and so the list goes on. I also need a blowlamp, solder and a copper pipe-cutting tool plus a hacksaw for the plastic pipes. The only trouble is that while I know all the words in English, I have absolutely no idea what most are called in French. But that should not be a problem if I follow the example of my brother-in-law and great friend, John. Despite knowing one hundred times less French than me, he managed to buy a chicken in the butcher's shop simply by flapping his arms and clucking (*ils sont fous ces anglais*).

Luckily there are very few customers when I arrive at the store and so I can grab an elderly shop assistant to help me with my purchases. He chuckles as he tries to speak to me in English but can get no further than 'Hello sir' and 'God Save the Queen'.

Many of the items are laid out in separate containers and so I can just take what I need and place them in the shopping trolley. But I cannot, for the life of me find the right angle bends for the water pipes. I try to explain to the assistant by making the shape with two fingers and he responds *"les coudes, monsieur"* (elbows to you and me).

Six lengths of copper pipe are added to the trolley. We then move on to the toilet section and load up with a couple of four-metre long waste pipes, both 100 and 40 mm diameter versions, a toilet with a wooden seat (for winter comfort) and all the other gubbins on my list. One problem I have – and it seems insurmountable – is that I need an adapter to convert the outlet from the water meter – which for some unknown reason is Imperial – to the Metric connections that have been standard in France for rather a long time. My friendly shop assistant tells me that short of getting a plumber in to completely change the pipe leading from the water meter, all he can suggest is that I find a plumber who might just have such an adaptor in stock. Feeling a bit let down by this news that effectively blocks the work I had hoped to do, I pay for my purchases and load them into the car, propping open the boot to allow the overlong plastic and copper pipes to stick out the back by at least a metre. I tie a piece of Union Jack material on to the end of the pipes to warn French drivers not to get too close to this particular Englishman.

Back in Rix, I share a beer with Bruno and tell him of my problem with the adapter for the water pipe. Straightaway he suggests that I go and ask the old man who lives in the last house as one drives out of Lhuis, on the right-hand side. I am told that he was formerly a plumber but has long since retired but apparently has a cellar full of remnants from his working days.

I leave immediately and knock on the last door in the village. A genial, elderly gentleman opens the door and I explain the problem showing him the joint that I had unscrewed from the water meter. He takes me into his cellar and riffles through a box of oddments quickly finding the missing piece.

"There you are", he says, "I knew I had one." When I ask how much I owe him, he laughs and tells me '*cadeau*' (gift).

The next day we go to the post office and ring through to Alan Seddon who is now on vacation from Calabar and staying with his parents in the UK. He is coming to see us and will arrive at Satolas Airport in a week's time. One of the items on his list is to help me with the installation of the septic tank which I need to pick up from Evieu as well as confirm the hire of a mechanical digger and driver. Being very green in the field of septic tanks, I have absolutely no idea how large a two-thousand-litre tank is, nor how much it weighs but if I had thought carefully, I would have realised that it must be at least two cubic metres in volume since that is the space that two-thousand litres of water occupies plus other bits and pieces adding to the size. But no matter. I turn up with the Renault-6, complete with a roof rack, and the tank is pointed out to me.

"Ah, I didn't realise how large it is!" I exclaim to the salesman.

"No problem, we can fix it on your roof." He produces a ball of bailing twine and tells me to give him a hand in lifting the tank up. Ten minutes later I have a very small car with a very large tank sitting on top of it ready to leave.

"Drive carefully" he instructs me!

Luckily, I have only seven kilometres to drive but at 20 km per hour max, it does take me almost half an hour to cover that short distance. I receive some very funny looks from the curious indigenes as I drive through the tiny village of Glandieu which foolish politicians, in the dim distant past, had decided to carve into two separate communities. I slow down to look at the magnificent waterfall that forms the dividing line between the two administrative halves of the village and also take care as I drive past as the falling water often causes considerable gusts of wind; the last thing I need! Opposite the waterfall is the gastronomic restaurant, not surprisingly called 'La Cascade' that we like to visit, then the seedy hotel that never seems to have customers (cause or effect, I am unclear). From there, I dawdle into Brégnier, past the Mairie and its adjoining café and into the connected village of La Bruyère where the tramway once ran and the old station building is now the bakery. I notice a fisherman at the Lac de Pluvis trying to catch a few final catfish before the canal migrates all the fish into the Rhône. Finally, after driving around the Mont de Cordon, I enter my village turning left at the *lavoir* (originally the village wash house) and pull into our communal courtyard. Pépé Parcoret is standing outside his house, next door, deftly sharpening his long-handled scythe with a whetstone.

He comes over to shake my hand and asks how I will get the tank off the roof. I get a couple of planks of wood and place them at an angle from the roof rack to the ground. He then pulls out his *Opinel* pocket knife, cuts the bailing twine and gently starts to push and slide the tank from his side of the car towards me and the planks. Hey presto, the tank gently slides down the planks to the sandy ground.

While I await the dual arrivals of Alan from the UK and the digger from Saint-Benoît, I have a few urgent jobs to get on with, especially to break through the stone walls of the house so that I can pass the 100 mm toilet pipe and the 40 mm wastewater pipes through from the inside to the outside and then fix the toilet. Breaking through the wall is not as easy as it sounds since our walls are made of chunks of limestone – a very hard stone – and are 80 cm thick. All I have to make the holes are a club hammer and various shapes of cold chisel. No matter, by hammering away for an entire morning, I finally get the main hole for the upstairs' bathroom broken through and then cut the waste water pipe, for the future bathroom, and the toilet pipe to the right lengths and out through the hole. The toilet pipe is then fixed to the new toilet which is itself screwed provisionally to the old floorboards. Only the water to connect and we are almost there.

Do try to imagine our toilet as it sits all alone in fifty square metres of space on the first floor, a real throne room. I then turn to cut the smaller hole downstairs for the kitchen waste water where the 40 mm piping is to pass and this time the work is relative child's play.

A full day of rain then follows so I am able to take my club hammer to the two inside walls that Poupette has advised to demolish. They are made of ancient bricks covered with lime plaster and this, in turn, is covered with several layers of 1950s-style wallpaper. I rather enjoy this job as only four or five blows of the club hammer are needed to knock out a few bricks at shoulder height and then the rest of the wall comes down very easily. With the walls down, the room is now more than 30 metres square and very bright from the three windows it now contains.

In the evenings, when I get back to Rix, my first port of call, by necessity, is the shower. I notice that while all houses have dust, the dust in new houses seems to be grey but in old houses, it is black and sticks to the body like soot on a chimney sweep. Apart from my straight hair, I would have real problems convincing any passer-by that I hail from the UK! After the shower, I am allowed to cuddle and play with my baby while Véro invariably pours me a long glass of '33 Beer' to wash off the dust inside my throat. Today, as I tell her of the great breakthrough (of the walls for the pipes, that is) and the demolition job on the walls, she tells me that tomorrow she wants to come with me to help. I know it must be frustrating not to be involved now that Mélanie is no longer a newborn. There are really two jobs to get on with at the moment, so we can split them between us. The first is to start filling the many holes and cracks in the walls – also plastered with lime – with a modern plaster (later when all is repaired we can paint over them) and the second is to remove the compacted cardboard that is nailed as insulation to the ceilings. The first is a job Véro can handle while I will use the stepladder to begin removing the ceiling covering. We are both excited to know what lies behind this 'cache misère' as the French call building materials used to cover up potential defects.

The sun is shining when we arrive and Pépé Parcoret's middle-aged daughter comes around to chat and to give Mélanie a cuddle. As it's the morning, the sun is bright and hot on the south-facing, front of the house and the stone terrace – we call it the platform – that marks the typically raised entrance to houses in the Bugey. We take Mélanie inside, out of the sun, and get on with our respective jobs. Véro is more keen to see what lies beneath the cardboard than to fill holes with plaster, so she watches me as I climb the stepladder and carefully insert my 'pied de biche' (crowbar) between two adjoining pieces of insulation. A quick downward movement and one large piece of compressed cardboard snaps off from the ceiling, closely followed by several kilograms of walnut shells – all landing on my head and shoulders.

In my great distress and pain, I hear my lovely wife sobbing with laughter as the walnuts continue to dislodge from the ceiling space individually bonking off my head and on to the floor followed by a goodly amount of medieval dust. Most seems to go down the inside of my t-shirt but a solitary walnut sits resplendent on my (now) grey hair. We both look over at our little girl and I swear she is chuckling too (now what age does that wretched book by Pernoud say a child should start to chuckle?) while dust continues to shower down on to the pushchair's little parasol, thankfully sparing the baby beneath. Once the humour subsides, the teasing stops and the walnut shower ceases, we gather under the hole that served to create all the fun and see that our house also has what looks like a beautiful *'plafond à la française'*.

Realising that the removal of the ceiling will be a pretty quick but very dirty task, and I am concerned for Mélanie with all the dust – and not to forget potentially half-a-ton of walnut shells – I suggest to Véro that they take a stroll around the village while I finish the ceiling. By the time my two ladies return, I have pretty much completed the task and find that we really do have a complete *plafond à la française* with the exception of two missing beams over the remnants of the fireplace. I have also accumulated a large pile of walnut shells, as anticipated, and also a few kilograms of undamaged red kidney beans. To round off the list there are also two entire but deeply mummified rats who certainly died of overwork, at least a hundred years ago, getting all those walnuts and beans into their storage space in the ceiling. However, the less good news is now we have plenty of light, we can see the floorboards above very clearly. They are, as we suspected when we bought the house, in a really terrible state and cannot be saved. Add another job to the list; that of taking up all the floorboards and putting down new ones! Other tasks to add to that growing list are to lever-off all the round-headed tacks that had kept the insulation in place on our newly discovered beams – a sixty-minute job with a claw hammer – and then to clean the beams of an unknown number of paint layers; and that looks very hard work.

If I can elaborate on the beam cleaning? Here I am repeating what both Poupette and Mic have separately advised us. The first step is to determine if the paint is water or oil-based. If the former, then it is water-soluble and so can be (theoretically) washed off. However, if oil-based, it is a dog to remove and will need paint stripper and/or a hot-air blower – and, given its age, would be lead-based and so poisonous. Luckily, our beams turn out to have layers of water-based paint, some white, some yellow and some blue. These can be removed in two ways: sand-blasting or elbow grease. The former is sometimes erroneously used in old houses often with catastrophic effects, especially when the beams are made of softwood, such as pine. Most of our beams are indeed pine and sand-blasting would differentially eat away the softer parts of the wood from the harder parts leaving a dry and wrinkled effect – not what we want. So cleaning has to be by pure elbow grease. Poupette tells me that the best formula is to use the strong commercial dishwashing powder called *St Marc*, dissolved in boiling water, and the beams washed and rubbed with *scotch brite* (sponges with a green scratchy surface beloved by French households). Best to wear strong rubber gloves too!

In the last few days, before Alan arrives in France, I start experimenting with cleaning the beams in the kitchen. It is very slow and extremely arduous work. After washing and rubbing for a whole morning, I estimate that I can clean a two-metre beam per hour – and it must not be forgotten that a beam has three visible sides! Since the house is seven metres by seven metres, and there are a total of twenty-two beams composing the *plafond à la française* running across the ground floor, I calculate the effort needed to be in the region of 230 hours. To that must be added the time to be taken for cleaning the four large beams that run across the house and carry the weight of the ceiling beams and the floor above. And then let us not forget the need to use a paintbrush to paint on Xelophane against any lurking woodworm and then to nourish the cleaned wood with a mixture of turpentine and linseed oil.

The day arrives when I go off to the airport at Satolas to pick up Alan. He seems fine, relaxed, and happy to have his vacation travel paid by the university. However, on the trip back to Rix he tells me that he has some bad news for me. Two of the lecturers from our department have made a formal complaint against me to the Registrar for derogation of duty. This despite the fact that the Dean of Science intervened on my behalf with the two lecturers and then with the Registrar. The outcome is not as bad as I had feared. After discussing with the Dean and hearing the circumstances of my leaving and the fact that I had taught a double load in the first semester, the Registrar had agreed not to suspend or fire me but rather to stop my salary over a couple of the summer months. While this is the best outcome I could have hoped for, what hurts the most is that one of the complainants is supposedly a friend, and he had taken off the whole of the first semester because his wife had been sick. I fully supported him, covered a lot of his classes and marked all his exams while he continued to receive full pay. The hypocrite is all I can say to Alan. No matter because for nothing would I have missed out on the adventure that Véro and I have lived these past few months.

We leave early for Cordon, making a detour to the back of Saint-Benoît, where I have hired the digger and driver to help bury the septic tank. This is costing me 125 FF an hour and strictly cash, I am told. Therefore, I am hoping that the work does not take too long to complete.

Yesterday, I had stopped at the Mairie of Brégnier-Cordon to ask the *Maire* if I needed any special permission to bury the tank and his response, luckily, was negative. However, he did say that there are rumours that our house is built on the foundations of a Roman villa and if we come across any artefacts, we must stop work immediately and report to him. What a nuisance that would be but hardly surprising since the Romans developed large settlements all along the Rhône valley. In fact, just over the river at the next village called Aôste, there are so many buried artefacts – mostly carved stones – that every time gardeners in the village plant their potatoes, they are sure to dig up something interesting. Then they are supposed to call the archaeologists who then dig out the potatoes looking for more finds. Most villagers have learnt to keep quiet, fearing hordes of students from Lyon University descending to dig under their carrots and lettuces.

We start work in the small garden at the side of the house and the driver takes one scoop (only sand), a second scoop (sand again), a third and then a fourth (all sand). In five minutes the hole is dug and the driver says that the work was far, far easier than he had feared. As he turns off his engine, Lili (really Louis) comes out of his house from across the courtyard to inspect the work and to say hello to the driver; apparently they are old friends. Out come the beers from my fridge and a bottle of toxic, home-brewed white wine that Lili is carrying and we have an early aperitif.

All four of us take the septic tank and lower it in the hole; a perfect fit. I connect and seal the toilet pipe at the left end and then measure and cut another length of pipe to go on the other end. Meanwhile the driver gets back on his digger and makes a trench from the tank and across the garden to the communal drain cover that sits conveniently at the edge of my garden. A few whacks of my club hammer onto a pointed cold chisel and he drives a hole clean through the cement pipe of the drain and pushes the newly cut end of the outlet pipe from the septic tank through the hole. A bit of cement and the plastic pipe is sealed perfectly into the cement drain. The driver accepts the proffered cash, climbs back on his digger and waves goodbye to us all.

We now have two tasks to complete before going back to Rix that evening: the first is to fill in around the sides of the tank with the surplus sand that was dug out of the hole while at the same time filling the tank with water before screwing on the cap of the septic tank and filling the remainder of the hole with some of the remaining sand. The water acts as a support to the structure of the plastic tank while it is buried with the weight of the contained water pushing outwards against the surrounding soil. Obviously, therefore, important to fill in the gaps between the septic tank and the hole with as much of the surplus sand as possible. To show how important this exercise is and the strength generated by the water, the following day a careless *paysan* decided to park his enormous tractor slap bang on top of the newly installed septic tank. He receives the very sharp edge of my tongue and the few steamy words I have learnt in French (mostly from my naughty little brother-in-law, Nico); and he decides, there and then, that he will never be civil to me again (*tant pis*).

Back to the functioning of the septic tank because I am sure that the reader must be eager to find out how it will work! As toilet flush water enters from the left of the tank, the same quantity of water is pushed out through the right side and into the drain. The toilet waste is prevented from simply going in and straight out by a plastic separator.

Our second task is then to lay the wastewater pipes from an eventual upstairs bathroom and from the kitchen sink, now installed on the ground floor at the back of the house. Alan's chore is to dig a seventy-centimetre deep trench tight up against the wall of the house while I add and seal together the wastewater pipes as we proceed and then backfill the trench. As we work so we joke and chuckle about THAT infamous trench that was dug by the botanical garden staff to carry water from the student residence to the nature reserve back in Calabar.

We have almost finished being foolish and digging the trench itself, only having about two metres left to backfill, when the heavens open up with Calabar-style rainfall. Alan begins to panic when he sees the remaining section of the trench quickly cave in from both sides: from the garden side of the trench, not a problem, but also from the house side. This was the first inkling we had that our house is built directly onto a sand base and does not seem to have foundations that penetrate down to bedrock. We fill that last section of the trench five times faster than the other parts! But a good job well done.

The rain stops as quickly as it started and we think about packing up for the day and going back to Rix, and from there possibly on for a swim in Ambléon to wash off the sand and sweat.

As we start packing tools away into the house, an elderly couple arrives in the courtyard in their old Renault, closely followed by a large van. Without a word or a glance, they open the door to the cottage to the left of us and go in through the door. The driver of the van then starts to unload boxes, chairs, then a table and follows them in. These are the new owners of the old cottage across the courtyard from us. They are recently retired. We do not pay them much notice as they work together to empty the van but after half an hour of travail, monsieur comes across and asks us to lend a hand. Now, just as in Nigeria and I do not know how many other countries around the world, it is considered very bad manners in France to ask for help without, at least, saying a polite hello.

I reply "good afternoon, my name is Malcolm and this is my house. This is my friend Alan. How may I be of help?" Only then did he remember his manners, say hello and introduce himself and his wife.

"We have a real problem", he tells us, "our wardrobe is too big to go through the front door and is rather heavy. Do you have any idea what we can do?"

I can see that the aforementioned wardrobe is from the end of the nineteenth century and constructed in walnut, a very common and beautiful furniture wood in this part of France but it is almost as heavy as oak. We have recently purchased a wardrobe from a similar epoch and it was delivered by the antique dealer in parts and then reconstructed on the first floor. This type of furniture has no screws or nails but rather is held together by lengths of dowelling hammered into predrilled holes. My first idea is therefore to suggest that we drill out the dowelling, take it apart and then get a carpenter to rebuild it.

"What a silly idea" replies madam, looking at me with piercing eyes. I decide that it is best not to argue with our new neighbours, especially madam.

"OK, that's settled then! Would you rather that Alan and I take it up my ladder and pass it through the upstairs window into one of the bedrooms at the front of the house?"

"Yes, of course. That is why I sent my husband to bring you to help." I can see that this lady and I will get on really well in the future!

So to cut this story short (because Alan and I really are hot, damp, covered in sand, and frankly tired and needing that swim), the van driver and Alan go upstairs with a rope, I place the ladder at the bottom of the relevant window and monsieur and I then manoeuvre the wardrobe to the bottom of the ladder. Alan throws one end of the rope down to me, I tie it around the top of the wardrobe, and the two men upstairs pull the rope taut. I lift the wardrobe off the ground and they pull. Slowly it slides up the ladder with me pushing underneath and rung by rung we (the wardrobe and me, that is) move up the ladder until the wardrobe reaches level with the window. I am still underneath silently praying that the rope holds. Once it passes the sill, we begin to lever it through the window. At this point, being at the right height on the ladder, I notice that only Alan is pulling on the rope. No matter. I push, he pulls and the wardrobe is finally resting on the sill. A quick run down the ladder and up the stairs and together we bring it into the room and place it against a wall.

As we go back down the stairs, I ask Alan why the van driver had stopped helping him. He tells me that he did not understand what he was saying but he kept repeating 'aïe *mon dos, mon dos!*' (ouch my back). We say goodbye to our new neighbours, receiving absolutely no thanks for our efforts, and go off to collect Véro for the swim.

A couple of days later, Lili invites Véro and I into his house for an aperitif and his wife says that she had seen me lifting the wardrobe up the ladder for the new neighbours and asks how I had found them. Being new in the neighbourhood, I do not want to say too much but said that I found them a little rustic.

Lili's wife replies laughing, "do you mean rude?"

"Well a little. I was surprised that the lady spoke as though she expected us to help and when we had finished she did not even bother to say thank you. But that's not important."

"Did you know that I have already met her?" and she starts to giggle. "I took my daughter to the University of Lyon to start her studies and we could not find the right section for her to go. So, I asked the concierge for directions and *'elle m'a envoyé balader'* (basically told her to get lost!). It was her, it was our new neighbour." And she giggles again and we all join in with her.

~ 10 ~

CHAMPAGNE OR MÉTHODE CHAMPENOISE?

We are now well into July, Alan has gone back to the UK, and we are busy preparing for Mélanie's christening. Since our new commune is to be Brégnier-Cordon, we would like to have the christening at the church there. We phone to get an appointment to speak to the priest and today we are off to fix the details. Of course, as soon as we arrive he recognises my accent and asks about the UK and is surprised when we tell him that we actually live in Nigeria.

As a little aside at this point, the Anglophone reader should understand that the French find the English accent when speaking French as appealing as the English find a French accent speaking English. Indeed, Jane Burkin and Petula Clark have made their fortunes in France, not only due to their talent but also to their perceived sexy English accents. *Vice versa* is the handsome crooner Sacha Distel in the UK.

In my case, the priest is interested to know our story and how we came to wash up in Brégnier-Cordon. After a quick potted history, I ask him if there will be any issue for baptising our baby in his church given that I am a Protestant but that we were married in France.

He looks at me with a broad smile on his face and a twinkle in his eye and asks me "and are you a good man, *mon fils*?"

"Yes, I believe I am Father."

"Perfect then. Better one good Protestant in my church than fifty bad Catholics!"

We fix the date to allow for the arrival of my sister and her family from the UK. Sandra is to be Mélanie's Godmother while Véro's little brother, Nico, is to be the Godfather.

In the meantime, we have a few things to get organised in advance of the due date, especially the food and the booze for the party to follow the church service. The food can easily be taken care of by a trip to the supermarket in Morestel while I chat to Bruno, my neighbour and the captain of the Lhuis rugby team, about the drinks side. He advises me not to consider serving champagne for two reasons: first it is too expensive and of course we are on a tight budget and second because the local sparkling wine from the Bugey region is considered locally to be just as good as champagne. There are at least ten '*vignerons*' (winemakers) within a fifteen-minute drive of our house in Rix. The sparkling wine, in particular, is very good in Bugey. It is made by the same process as Champagne and so has marked on the label '*méthode champenoise*' although Champagne later mounts a legal challenge and enforces a change to the labels to '*méthode traditionnelle*', which to my mind is rather splitting hairs. Bruno recommends we go to the family business of the '*Domaine Trichon*'. They are based in another hamlet of Lhuis called '*Le Poulet*' (yes, you are right, it does mean the Chicken!) and we meet up there with Henri Trichon, a large man of around sixty, the head of the family, and soon to retire from the business. The wine cellar is right next to his house and so we drive into his courtyard and park conveniently close to the cellar. Henri comes across to greet us at the car as though we are old friends, despite this being our first visit. He is wearing dungarees, large size that is, and I do not believe that in future years I ever see him wearing anything else. We explain that we need to buy wine for the christening and he leads us into his cellar cum shop where he offers us several different wines to taste. He first pours us generous amounts of his sparkling white, called Crystal (in future years, Champagne has a go at this name too), and we both declare it perfect. At that moment, a younger, slimmer version of Henri along with a pretty young woman come into the cellar to say hello. We meet Jean, a real character, and his wife. They are about our age and, as simple as that, we make long-term friends. The next wine we are given to taste is a sparkling rosé that goes by the curious name of '*Cuisse Rose*'. '*Cuisse*' translates to thigh and the label on the bottle complete with a revealing garter leaves no one in any doubt! Henri tells us that Jean had chosen the name and the label; once I get to know Jean better, I can well believe it! We then try the white Chardonnay which has a pleasant bouquet and a strong flavour of fruit. Then finally a red. While the white is very drinkable, the red needs a little more work, in common to almost all Bugey reds at this time.

We load cases of crystal, cuisse and chardonnay into the boot of the car, say goodbye to our new friends and drive back down the hill to Rix.

My sister and her family arrive two days before the christening. John has purchased an old camping van and fitted it out for the five members of the family. First out of the van is chatterbox Alexandra, a cheeky and vibrant six-year-old and our Goddaughter. Next is a blond, curly-haired and beautiful little angel called Amber. She is only three and a half and looks so much like a very young version of my mum with her pale skin and curly hair. Poor little Amber is very ill and my sister and John have been trying to combine this trip with a visit to Lourdes. Amber is helped down by John who then turns back to help my sister descend the steps carrying their newest arrival, a little baby boy called Adam. Adam was born only ten days before his cousin Mélanie so they are now both around two months old.

The christening at Brégnier-Cordon goes well and Nico does not drop his niece, mostly because my sister keeps a firm hold on the baby. Now back at Rix, we are joined by the priest, the Joly, the Conand and Bruno for a celebratory drink of Bugey wine, courtesy of the Trichon. Also in attendance are several of Véro's family, including her grandmother, Minouche, and her youngest child, Canou (really Henriette), sister of my mother-in-law. Canou is now 40 years old and rather a character (but then again all the siblings are). She loves sports and will cheerfully set off on her bicycle to ride a hundred kilometres before lunch or travel to small aerodromes with a bunch of friends and jump out of small aircraft (with a parachute of course). Canou is only eleven or twelve years older than Véro and me and so we are close.

Of course, this is also the first opportunity for my sister and John to see our house in Cordon. I do not think that this is quite what they had in mind when we told them that we had purchased a holiday home and I am convinced that they did not really believe me when I had said, the previous year, that the house was a ruin. They believe me now!

John is five years older than me and I have always looked up to him for his calm, pleasant manner and helpfulness. He is also far more experienced at DIY than I am. Being an electrician, he is particularly interested in the 'deadly state' of the house electrics. Before they set off on the next part of their journey, he promises to do a few odds and ends to the electrics to make them a little safer while he tells me that if we invite them to stay next year, we can re-do the entire electrical system together. Deal.

Once the christening is passed, we get back to life as usual, especially working in Cordon. I manage to get a simple cold water supply set up in the kitchen and for the toilet and add extra pipes for an eventual shower and wash basin on the first floor. And there are not too many leaks when I turn on the water supply. I am getting a dab hand at soldering copper pipe although I do make the mistake of having the slope of the water pipes going in the wrong direction on the first floor. That coming winter Jack Frost points out my error in the obvious manner by popping all my carefully soldered joints! Luckily the water was switched off at the mains.

Belou has given me a very large immersion heater that he had taken from an old apartment in Lyon. Together we load it into the back of my Renault-6 and I take it to Cordon on my next trip. It is heavy ... but I manage to get it out of the car on my own, roll it up two planks on to the kitchen windowsill and then into the kitchen. The only issue now is how to get it up to the first floor (remember there is no hatch to get access from the inside). Well, if there is no hatch, the easiest thing to do is to make one. So I remove some of the old floorboards in the position where Poupette calculates the stairs should eventually go. Actually, when I say 'remove' I really mean 'break' since a well-placed crowbar levered upwards and the first board simply snaps in two with a puff of dust (and squeals of displeased woodworm). I soon make a hole of a couple of square metres, place the old wooden ladder in the gap and little by little push the immersion heater up, rung by rung. A last heave and it is on the first floor. I half push, half carry the water heater across the floor towards the far wall where it will eventually be lifted up and fixed – but for that I need more muscle power. Suddenly, a board gives way under my right foot and my leg goes down through a hole surrounded by jagged and dirty two-hundred-year-old wood. The result is a badly scraped calf and shin and a fear of infection. Luckily, Lili's wife is at home and she swabs the grazes with alcohol, laughing at my ouches, and declares me fit to return to work. She has seen far worse coming, as she does, from a farming family.

With the water and toilet in place, cleaning the beams rises back to the top of our list of priorities. However, the rotten nature of the floorboards on the first floor (fortune only knows how they are on the second floor) is a concern and, when I discuss with Véro that evening, she asks whether it would not be best simply to remove them and start to put a new floor down; after all, we know it must be done eventually.

"O-Kayyy, but first let's see how much fifty square metres of boarding will cost and whether we have enough money left for the remainder of the summer. And second, how does one lay floorboards?"

Since I have never laid floorboards, I ask around and it seems that it is not too difficult. I need to get a good quality handsaw to cut the required lengths of each board to give the desired pattern, select the type of wood (chestnut and oak are expensive, pine is cheaper), choose the width of the planks (the wider they are the more they cost) and purchase a few kilos of small-headed nails and a *'chasse clou'* or nail punch. Although my father-in-law never lends a hand in the house (we never learn why), he is a font of knowledge in all things do-it-yourself (called *'bricolage'* in French). He is also interested in what we are trying to achieve and so keeps an eye out for any bargains that he believes might be useful to us. He has discovered a DIY shop, close to Crémieu, where they currently have a sale (*'promotion'* as the French call them) of floorboards. I go straight over and buy the fifty square metres and then make three, thirty-kilometre roundtrips to get the heavy floorboards back to Cordon in the back of my little car. Long story short, in two weeks or so we have a new floor. The toilet can now be fitted to the water supply and bolted down properly, I give Véro the honour of the first flush while I check outside that the toilet downpipe does not leak and that water emerges successfully from the septic tank and into the drain.

An enchanting summer in Rix and a fairly exhausting but satisfying one in Cordon is coming to a close. We have a lovely and good-natured little girl, now four months old, and we have made some nice friends, particularly in Rix. Breaking the ice with the Cordon residents has been harder. Nonetheless, le Pépé Parcouret is a kind, elderly gentleman and his daughter is very sweet while her brother-in-law Lili and his wife, Yvette, are relaxed and friendly. We have noticed that on the other side of the Cordon road lives a couple of about our age. While we have been able to chat a few times with the lady, her husband, Gérard, appears a bit 'sauvage' (this means insular not savage, by the way!). We learn that he is a biology teacher, so he and I should have a few things in common. We agree that we will try a bit harder to get to know them next year when we spend the summer in Cordon.

We are delighted with the good progress we have made in our house which is now starting to look a little less of a ruin and starting to need some serious decorating instead. Providing the Francos keep their promise to repair the roof over the winter, we can move into Cordon the following summer, albeit in camping mode. The main jobs to complete on arrival next year will be to install the water heater, buy and install a shower and a hand basin, connect hot water to the kitchen as well as to the shower and hand basin and receive John and family to get on with the installation of the new electricity system. We have also placed an order with a local carpenter to construct and install a simple stairway to link the ground floor to the first floor as well as to fit a wooden framed window to our *fenêtre à meneaux*. Funds do not yet allow us to put in stairs to the second floor. My old wooden ladder will have to suffice for a while longer. We also decide to plant a few trees in the small piece of land that came with the house in Cordon. This land is just over three hundred square metres in area and lies eighty metres or so down a little lane that leads, just after our land, into a woodland. We plant three trees: an apple, a cherry and a walnut, in the same year as our little girl is born.

It is now mid-September and so our thoughts begin to wander unintentionally and too frequently to Calabar but first we are to make a trip to the UK to see my parents. Our flight dates are approaching when my sister tells me that her little daughter has gone from bad to worse. Just after we arrive at my parent's house, our lovely niece goes to join Jesus' angels. She was just short of her fourth birthday. Our hearts are broken; we can only imagine how her parents are coping with such a loss.

Just after this news hits us, I get a phone call at my parents' home from Klaus Voelger in Frankfurt. "Malcolm, the Cross River State draft report is finished, can you come over to Germany to edit it? It would be great if you can get this done before you go back to Calabar."

Obviously, the last thing on my mind is to go to Frankfurt so I explain to Klaus what has just happened and that our date to return to Calabar is in only two weeks. After many kind words of sympathy, Klaus persuades me that the work can be completed in five or six days and so he books me a flight from Heathrow in the evening, straight after the funeral. With a heavy heart I board the Thai Airways flight and arrive late in the evening to be met by Klaus at Frankfurt Airport.

My distress at losing my little niece is, in very small part, helped by the warm and sympathetic reception that I get on arrival from Klaus. On the drive back from the airport, he tells me that I am to stay with him, his wife, who is curator of a museum of African art, and his elderly mother rather than going to a hotel. He explains that the arrangement will allow us to work and eat together in the evenings and get to know each other better because he has an idea he wants to put to me; interesting.

My first morning in Frankfurt is spent reading through and making notes on the first section of the report on the vegetation types and agricultural products of Cross River State. I feel at home reading this section but note that the next section is dedicated to the geology of the state; less my field although I did take an introductory course at university.

In the evening, Klaus offers his excuses because he and his wife are hosting a museum dinner and so are obliged to attend. After dinner, would I mind spending the evening with his mother? The evening actually proves to be both interesting and entertaining. Frau Voelger, who must be at least 80, speaks not a word of English or French while I have only a comic book level of German! Nonetheless, we spend the whole evening chatting, as well as we possibly can in the circumstances, and I find her a very charming lady.

My days pass by quickly as I put in place a general routine of reading sections, making notes and writing out suggested improvements to the text in the morning and having interviews with the various authors in the afternoon. During these interviews we look at problem areas and agree on re-writes and corrections or the addition of extra information. This way of splitting the days in two works well for both sides: I can get up to speed with the text of individual sections before meeting the authors while they can use the morning to travel to Frankfurt on the highly efficient German rail network. Most of the authors live and work outside of Frankfurt.

Generally, their level of English is excellent but I am insisting that together we re-write complicated or muddled areas. My logic is clear. If I cannot understand what the author is trying to say, how can we expect civil servants in Cross River State to understand? Most of the German contributors work well with me, are prepared to listen and to provide further explanations while I sketch out the modified text. Only one person gives me grief, a university professor in Geology from Berlin. He stubbornly refuses to be contradicted and simply states that he knows geology better than me (true) and he can write English better too (dubious!). Finally, after three hours of heated debate with little progress, I suggest that we invite Klaus to our meeting. The professor agrees. Klaus enters our room and takes a seat. Immediately the professor harangues him for having the audacity to get a third party to check his text. Klaus remains very calm and simply asks:

"Who did I recruit to produce the Geology section?"

"Me, of course" spits the professor.

"Who did I recruit to edit the text?"

"This young person here, whoever he is" states the professor with a certain vitriol.

"Good. It is clear that you understand the two roles. Now, final question. Who leads and pays for this report?"

Our Berlin professor goes red, adjusts his glasses and replies sheepishly "you Herr Dr Voelger." Within an hour the Geology section is ready to go to press.

Most evenings Klaus takes me to a different restaurant in Frankfurt. By chance, Klaus tells me, I have arrived during the

Frankfurt '*Apfelweinfest*' (cider festival) and so the restaurants are full of very noisy and friendly diners or perhaps I should say friendly drinkers because I am unsure if they are having cider with their food or food with their cider. On our first evening together, the one after my evening with his mother, Klaus takes me to a vibrant restaurant that we access via concrete steps leading down from the street to a large, cavern-like room with a vaulted ceiling. He is known and expected as we are led to the only free table in the establishment. The buxom waitress hands each of us a menu, written exclusively in German, and Klaus asks me if I would like cider, beer or wine. Since we are in the cider festival, I of course ask for a glass of cider while Klaus orders a bottle of white wine. As I have no idea what the menu is offering, I ask Klaus if he would not mind ordering for me. He suggests the '*schweineschulter*' which I realise is something to do with pork (you see now how well my comic book German serves me?). Twenty minutes or so later, our buxom waitress comes back with a large oval serving dish held at shoulder level with her right hand, a large mug of cider, a delicate wine glass and a bottle of white wine all gripped in the left. She twirls the serving dish down to table level and places it next to me. The bottle of wine goes to the other side of Klaus, the wine glass in front of him and the mug of cider (is it a full litre?) in front of me.

I can now complete the translation of the order because what I have on the serving dish is a full shoulder of pork together with a mountain of sauerkraut and boiled potatoes. Our waitress leaves with a '*guten appetite*' and I ask Klaus where our plates are.

He corrects me by saying "your plate is there" pointing to the large dish.

"But this is for the two of us, no?" His laugh gives me the reply. So I ask "but what did you order?" and he pats the bottle of white.

We play out a similar scenario each evening although I try to be careful with the quantity of food ordered and the amount of alcohol consumed. Klaus, on the other hand, continues never to eat but he does drink significant amounts of wine while smoking innumerable cigarettes. I cannot help but think that he is not being very careful with his health.

On the last evening of my stay in Frankfurt, my work is finished and my suitcase is packed ready for the return to London early the next morning. Klaus asks me to come into the office he maintains in his home.

"Malcolm, I want to thank you for all the work you did in the field in Calabar on the salt concentrations in the river courses", he pats my consultancy report, "and also for editing the Cross River State report. I know some of my consultants were not easy to work with, especially the geologist, but you coped well with the work and managed to finish everything on time. Also my wife and I have really enjoyed having you stay with us here."

Well, of course, I am delighted to receive such praise and tell him so as well as the fact that I have really enjoyed working with him and learning from him.

Klaus looks at me with a serious air and says "I think you now realise that I have a very successful company and quite a number of staff working for me but I have no children nor anyone in the company that I believe has the correct attitude to take over the business from me when I retire in a couple of years. I appreciate that you are well installed in Nigeria, and you have chosen university lecturing as a profession, but would you be prepared to consider becoming a consultant and working with me here in Frankfurt? There would likely be lots of overseas travel. I believe that with a little more experience and some mentoring from me, you can take over the running of my business in a couple of years. What do you think?"

Well that came out of the blue! I knew that Klaus and Frau Voelger had no children but not in my wildest dreams did I ever imagine such a career opening.

"Wow Klaus, that was an unexpected but incredible offer. And yes, I am very, very interested in a future that involves working with you. Obviously, first I will need to talk this move through with Véronique but I am convinced that she will be as delighted as me. We both realise that we cannot stay in Calabar for too much longer and I only have one year left on my contract unless I wish to renew it yet again. Getting work in Europe or the States as a lecturer is almost impossible at the moment and I know that the consulting business offers new challenges with lots of opportunities. What then would be the next steps?"

Klaus looks at me with a big smile on his face "Well I am very happy that you like the offer. So please talk this over with Véronique and let me know her response. Why not bring her to Frankfurt to have a look around the next time you are in Europe? Assuming she says yes, go back to Calabar to finish out your contract and I will contact you via Kurt in the next month or so with the deal I propose. Oh, and before I forget", Klaus hands me an envelope, "here is a cheque for all your valuable work."

I feel that I should be on cloud nine as I make my way home to discuss this possible next turn in our lives but my gut refuses to stop telling me that there is another and much darker cloud on what should be a bright horizon.

How lovely it is to be back with Véro and little Mélanie. As I cuddle my daughter, I explain to Véro about the trip, the work, the stay with Klaus and then his surprising offer on our last evening together. As I had predicted, she is over the moon about the thought of coming back to Europe and, as she quite logically states, Frankfurt to Cordon is only about an eight-hour drive so we can spend lots of time in our new home. We both start to talk about making a new life in Germany. Of course we will have to learn German but what the heck? Véro now speaks pretty fluent English while my French is becoming quite passable but is not yet as fluent as her English. To learn another language does not worry us over much. As she becomes more excited about the opportunity – knowing that we are now setting a date for leaving Nigeria is adding to that excitement – I confess to her that I feel a dark cloud coming over my shoulder.

"Pourquoi mon chéri?" (why my love?) she asks.

"Klaus is a lovely guy, I felt really at home with him and he is so knowledgeable and sharp but I am concerned about his lack of eating – and despite that he is a little overweight. I feel that he is driving his health to the wall with cigarettes and drinking but not eating. Sorry, but I just do not feel confident for the future."

Nonetheless, we both realise that my gut feeling, just like reading tea leaves, does not necessarily foretell our future with accuracy. Sadly, in this case it does.

Our baby is now a little more than four months old and so we take her for her first vaccinations and also manage to get hold of her future vaccines so that we can take them back to Nigeria, wrapped in ice packs, for later injection. For obvious safety reasons, we had always said that we would not go back to Calabar before she has started her vaccination programme and so now we feel less worried about our return flight in little more than a week.

~ 11 ~

RAINSTORMS AND BANANA LEAVES

Our evening flight out of Heathrow is on time and the next morning we arrive in Lagos; now feeling like the seasoned travellers we are fast becoming. We arrive at passport control, with Mélanie sitting comfortably in the crook of my left arm while Véro pushes the pushchair filled with our discarded jackets and pullovers. I hand over the two passports, Mélanie is currently in mine, expecting to receive the usual polite request for dash. But not at all. The passport officer smiles at our new baby and asks me for her name.

When I reply Mélanie, he responds very seriously "oh, that is lovely, you have named her after us."

All I can think to reply is "yes, that's right."

After collecting our suitcases and taking yet another beaten-up yellow taxi to the Domestic Airport, we are waiting for our flight on the hard plastic chairs when Véro asks me "did you understand what the officer at passports meant by naming Mélanie after them?"

"No, not the faintest idea" I reply. We go back to reading our books when a light suddenly flickers in my brain.

"I've been thinking about Mélanie's name and you know the colour pigment in the skin is called melanin? I bet that is what he meant."

And indeed he did because Mélanie is the Norman version of Melania and that comes from the Greek for blackness and dark. We have just met a very scholarly passport officer.

Being back on Road-10 does not feel at all bad. We have had an extraordinarily long and near-perfect holiday and count our blessings that our little girl is such a happy soul. Rose returns after some well-earnt vacation and Peter has kindly moved back to the guesthouse. He will stay a little longer in Calabar but eventually resigns and leaves. I am sad to see him go. Although he is not a typical friend for me, if such an animal actually exists, he is a mature and calming influence from whom I have learnt a lot about teaching and consulting in just a few short months. A few other colleagues have left the university too, including the former trench digger.

As soon as Rose sees Mélanie she beams so widely that her face almost splits from ear to ear. Before we realise what is happening, she reaches down, takes our baby's right arm and hoists her up into her arms.

"Noooo", splutters Véro, "you must not pick her up like that. Please take her under her two arms."

"Why?" asks Rose with real curiosity; and it is true that I have always seen Calabar mothers hoick their babies up by an arm; and I have never seen any of their arms dislocated either!

Mélanie greets our concerns by looking at Rose and returning a loving smile to her new Nigerian friend. From that moment, right up until we finally leave the country, the two are practically inseparable. Indeed, Rose takes to doing the housework with a towel wrapped around her waist and Mélanie plonked in the back being carried around the house gurgling away or sleeping peacefully. She is such a happy child.

Things are not so easy for the little girl of about twelve living next door to us. On several occasions in the recent past I have heard a man screaming at her, usually followed by the child screeching or crying loudly. I do not know the guy or his family because they only moved in a few weeks ago, while we were away in Europe, but I assume that he is also from the university. However, today, I see the little girl run screaming out of their front door, down the three steps and towards my house while the man is running after her swiping at her with a cane-like stick. No way will I accept that. I drop my briefcase and scoot out the front door, run across to the man and grab his raised arm near the wrist.

He swirls around on me and says "do you want to be hit too?" and he tries to raise his arm, which I am still holding. One of the sports that I enjoyed at school and university was judo, not because I am a vicious character, far from it, but I am quite small and judo and self-defence have occasionally come in useful in the past. So, rather than simply letting go of his arm, I go with the movement of his attempt to raise it and then twist. There is a small crack and a louder ouch. Then I let go. He sinks to the grass and rubs his shoulder proclaiming that it is broken. It is not, but I know that it hurts and will continue to hurt for a few days more.

The little girl is standing near me sobbing and I can see welts on her exposed arms where the bully has hit her with that nasty little weapon. A lady then appears and shouts loudly at the man in a language I do not recognise. He stands and walks off up the road turning his head back to shout curses at us both.

The lady turns to me and I can see tears staining her face. Between sobs she manages to say "my name is Alice and I teach at the university. That man is from my village and, because of that, I have been obliged to let him stay but he is really nasty, does not help or pay and beats the poor girl for no good reason. When he left he said that he was going back to the village to tell everyone about you!"

I ask in response "but why do you allow him to beat your daughter like that?"

She replies "no, you misunderstand, she is not my daughter, she is my housemaid."

Here is a little pre-pubescent girl and she is already obliged to earn a living. How sad, and how lucky are our kids? In the time I knew that little girl, she never once went to school. Calabar does actually boast a good number of schools. There are many primary schools, several secondary ones both for day students and for boarders, and a few private schools at all levels. In the mornings, we always hear the chatter of the children as they go past the house on their way to class. When it rains we witness a spectacle that we could never forget – homemade umbrellas! Really. The children snap off banana leaves which have a natural downwards curve and carry them above their heads. Apart from the arm carrying the leaf, the rest of the body stays relatively dry.

One morning Véro calls me to witness a very cute scene. Why do we never have our camera when this type of event occurs? In the middle of a rainstorm, a lady stops outside our house to try to shelter from the teeming rain under a tall bush that grows at the end of the garden. She has a baby on her back, *à la Rose*, and the banana leaf is protecting the mum and the little baby boy from the worst of the downpour. The mum cannot see, but we can from the house, that there is a steady drip of water off the drip-tip of the leaf and it's falling towards the baby. In response, he has his mouth open and is happily drinking the drops as they fall into his mouth.

On my first morning back at the University, I go immediately to see the Registrar in his office; better to get this dilemma over with quickly. His secretary greets me, as always by my first name, and pokes her head around the Registrar's door to tell him that I am outside. I hear him tell her to bring two coffees and to invite me in. I feel a little less trepidation as I knock and walk in.

"Your Excellency" he greets me as always "congratulations on the birth of your baby. Do sit down and tell me your story."

So I begin to tell him about the need to be in France for the birth and the arrangement that I made with my fellow ecology lecturers to shuffle our teaching loads to allow me to do far less work in the second semester when I needed to leave for the birth.

He nods and takes a few notes and says very openly "that is the explanation that I heard from your Dean but not the one told me by two young lecturers in your department. They told me that you left without a word leaving everyone to cover for you. Of course I believed the Dean of Science over two juniors but, I think you understand, that I had to be seen to act, and that was the reason I stopped your salary for two months. I reinstated it for September and now I know the whole story, I will authorise the two back months too."

"Thank you for your kindness, sir, but I think I agree that you have to be seen to punish me so perhaps best to leave the two months unpaid."

"Tell me doctor, do you have issues with these two young lecturers?" he asks curiously.

"Not until now, sir. One is a near neighbour on the housing estate and the other I thought was a good friend, especially as I covered for him for several months when his wife was sick."

"Best not to trust them too much in the future then! This sounds more like departmental politics than anything else. Tell me, has your head of department spoken about the faculty's plans for you?"

"No, not yet but then I haven't yet reported back to the department. I only got back from vacation this weekend."

"OK, I will not steal his thunder but suffice to say that all the seniors in the department appreciate your work and attitude to staff and students and we have been discussing certain issues that you might appreciate. We believe that the trouble stirred by your, err, friends might be due to, err, let's call it, 'competition for space'."

I drop into the departmental office and ask the secretary to tell the Professor, when he arrives to the office, that I am back at the university. I then take a quick drive to the Botanical Gardens to greet all the staff after so many months of absence. Iyamba cheekily asks "what did you call your son, doctor."

"I have a daughter, Iyamba. Her name is Mélanie."

"Sorry-O" replies Iyamba turning away.

Frank comes over to shake my hand and puts his arm around my shoulder "take no notice, doc, he is a bushman and a fool. We all know you had a baby girl, Dr Seddon told us before he left for leave. This is just Iyamba being rude."

But in reality, many of the less educated workers at the university have the same attitude to the birth of a baby girl as Iyamba. In Calabar, boys are looked on as being the future for families, staying with parents, protecting and supporting them as they get older. Girls, on the other hand, will eventually leave, after the payment of a steep 'Bride Price' and go to live in the husband's extended family. Frankly, I am over the moon with my little daughter, so any such talk of boys versus girls is just so much rubbish to me.

As I am about to leave the gardens, a young Nigerian woman walks in and introduces herself as a new lecturer in the department. In fact, she had been an assistant lecturer at the university before my arrival in Calabar, had gone away for further study and now was back at the university to teach. She tells me very openly that she wants to be the Director of the Botanical Gardens. I need to think about this before replying.

I go back to my office which has been practically closed up tight since my departure at the start of May. There is a massive stack of mail on my desk that the messenger would have dropped off each day and a beautiful growth of green mould on my once white lab coat. The room has an overpoweringly musty stench and so I have to forego the air conditioner and leave the door wide open for the rest of the day. I wade through the mail, most of it being composed of requests hailing from across the world for reprints of my recent papers and parcels of the actual reprints too, sent by the journals. There is also a letter from my mum, dated February, snail-mail indeed and various other odds and ends.

Just as I start to drink a cup of instant coffee, the secretary pokes her head around the door and wants to talk about my new baby. I give her a cup of coffee too and pass the screw jar of sugar cubes that seems full of little red ants – as sugar cubes always are here in Calabar. She takes a handful, eight, nine or ten; really but I do not count, and stirs them well. How do Nigerians have such strong, healthy and white teeth? I will never know given their incredible powers to consume sugar.

After our chat of twenty minutes or so she gets up to leave and says "oh, Prof is waiting for you, I forgot to say earlier."

Welcome to laid-back Calabar!

The Indian professor is as shy and as friendly as always. He congratulates Véro and me on the birth, asks about our vacation, and whether I have yet been to speak to the Registrar. He pointedly avoids mentioning my apparent AWOL, and so do I.

As head of department he is feeling a little more comfortable now. I seem to remember that he has been at the university for around seven years, and I doubt he is in any hurry to leave now that he is a full professor. He tells me that he has three points he needs to speak to me about. First, if I would kindly join the Appointments and Promotions Committee (of course, with pleasure). Second, would I join the Procurement Committee that is to start planning for the new university (of course, and a surprise because I knew nothing about a new university campus). And third, and even more surprising, will I accept to renew my contract at the end of the current academic year because the department (read the Dean and he) want to fast track my promotion to Reader, bypassing the senior lecturer grade which should be my next step. Rather than blurting out that we will leave at the end of the year, I thank him and ask for time to reflect.

Véronique quickly gets back into the swing of things, and her pupils: the two young baker boys and George's young Lebanese wife start to come back for their lessons. The boys, in particular are pleased to return to an ordered life as their parents' bakery becomes more successful and so their available free time with the boys decreases even further.

Véro sees Jane (the lady who had helped us find cheap air tickets) very frequently, both at the house and at the pool, and Jane is besotted by our little girl. I offer a sharp warning to her husband that he needs to be careful because I think someone's hormones are rising!

He has new colleagues in his company who hail from Italy. Jane brings the wife over to meet Véro and Mélanie. Chat among the ladies often turns to food simply because it is so difficult to find a sufficiently good variety for sale in Calabar. While talking about noodles, as of course one does, the new Italian lady mentions that she has a pasta-making machine (all Italians seem to possess one) and she proposes that the girls get together to learn how to make homemade pasta. Well, the experiment seems to have gone well as the ladies now meet up one afternoon a week, theoretically to make fresh pasta. However, counting the number of dead Mateus Rose bottles, us husbands have serious doubts.

Most expatriates working for companies in Calabar do not own their own cars but rather have a company vehicle with a driver. The driver is employed more to deal with the hazards of African traffic than being essential to drive the car. This means that the ladies often have to wait for their husbands to finish work before collecting them from wherever they happen to have spent their afternoons. This then leads to an evening of socialising when all husbands turn up at the same time, from different directions. One late afternoon, I arrive at Jane's apartment to collect Véro and the baby. This has been another pasta-making afternoon and to show their efforts (and distract from the empty bottles), there are long bands of pasta hanging across the room, held off the ground by looping them over the backs of Jane's dining chairs.

"Hi everyone", I say as I walk into the room with the ladies all seated around the table taking turns to swing the pasta machine handle. I give Véro a kiss on her flour-spotted cheeks and ask "where's Mimi?"

"She's crawled under the table; I can feel her by my feet" replies my observant wife.

I go on my knees and peep under the table and find my little girl sitting up with a grin on her face and chomping on the soft pasta that the ladies are inadvertently dropping onto the floor. From that day to now, Mélanie is a dedicated pasta eater, be it soft or crunchy hard, she cannot resist eating it.

While the Italian lady's speciality is pasta, Véro has become a dab hand at cheese-making, and of course we expect nothing less from a French lady. I forgot to mention that it is almost impossible to buy cheese in Calabar. Who would imagine anything else? Rarely, some tinned processed cheese becomes available for a few days in the Children's shop when Margaret's husband manages to get some sent down from Lagos but forget a mature cheddar or a throbbing camembert; hence the need for us to make cheese if we want to eat any. The process is rather long and the results are, well, middling to say the most. It starts with making milk – you cannot buy fresh milk in Calabar and, if you could I would be too concerned about brucellosis and bovine tuberculosis, to drink it. The method for making milk is simple: take a bottle of filtered water, pour it into a jug, add the requisite number of spoons of Nido milk powder and stir. And stir. And stir ... because we never can get the wretched stuff to dissolve. Add some yoghurt culture kept in the fridge from the last batch that was made, put a tea towel over the top and wait. The next morning and, heh-presto, the milk in the jug has become yoghurt (well, a sort of yoghurt-like gung). The yoghurt is then put into a muslin bag and hung over the sink to drip off the excess fluid. The dryer it becomes, the harder is the eventual 'cheese' produced. Making a block of cheese invariably takes two days.

But seriously, I have already mentioned that getting a sufficient variety of food in Calabar is hard as is getting a reasonable quality of what actually does exist. One would imagine that in a lush vegetation zone like Calabar there would be fruit and vegetables aplenty. Not in the least. We know of one avocado tree in Calabar and that's the one that drops its fruit into the Calcemco swimming pool. There are many mango trees but they are not grafted and so their fruit is small, the pip is enormous and the little flesh they contain is full of fibre that gets stuck between the front teeth. We do have oranges but they are not orange, they are green, and contain more pips than pulp. Luckily, we can get a lot of local lemons and limes and this helps drive the popularity of gin and tonics. When I can threaten Iyamba sufficiently well, I do get to eat a delicious soursop from the gardens. There are bananas aplenty. Bassey, the Sunday evening vegetable seller from Jos, tries to fill the gap in fresh vegetables (while quickly becoming a multi-millionaire) but the quality is squashed, to say the least.

Now, I know, I can hear the reader (just as I regularly hear all my friends in our social circle in Calabar) say that someone who was able to write more than two hundred pages about wild lettuce and who runs the university botanical gardens must be able to come up with a few vegetables. Well, believe me, I tried. I brought back from UK various types of lettuce and tomato seeds (in hindsight, probably illegally I suppose) and germinated them in the shade house before planting them out into well-prepared plots in the gardens. Despite many efforts, I never harvested a single lettuce or tomato. The lettuces either bolted or were eaten by insects while the tomatoes were bashed down and broken by the first violent rainstorm and then went white with mildew.

Turning back to Mateus Rose. This Portuguese, slightly sparkling wine, sold in dumpy bottles, is the only one we can find in Calabar except when a hardy soul braves the terrors of Lagos and brings back a few bottles of something, I hesitate to say, more decent. But since we have Champion and gin and tonic, wine is not missed overmuch (I would struggle to say the same today!). Speaking of gin, and all other strong alcohols known to man, there is a thriving trade in smuggled and bootleg hooch all across Calabar. The police either turn a blind eye or, more likely, are at the origin of the trade, I know not which. Indeed, after leaving the university and just before arriving at the French Bakery there is an impressive line of young Nigerians, on both sides of the road, openly selling every imaginable brand of every form of strong alcohol, from whisky to brandy, from gin to vodka and from Cointreau to Baileys Irish Cream. (I promised Véro that I would not say any more about this easily quaffable liqueur, so sorry-O!). The prices are much, much lower than in Europe but there is a serious problem in buying from these guys: it is impossible to know which bottles contain the labelled alcohol and which contain something less interesting. Indeed, on one occasion when Andy came to visit – and knowing he adores vodka and tonic – I poured his glass before he arrived and handed it to him as he walked in the door. He took a sip and replied 'nice water'. Yes, the vodka bottle I had just purchased was filled with tap water. Whisky bottles invariably contain tea and so on. One entrepreneurial young man decided to meet his clients halfway by filling empty vodka bottles with Ky-Ky, a strong local alcohol made from distilled palm wine. Andy was one of his best customers until both Alan and I warned him of the dangers of drinking methylated spirits!

Having been sold a donkey on a couple of occasions, I quickly learn to tell the young salesmen at the side of the road that I will only pay for the purchase if I can taste it first. If my suggestion is refused, I simply move to the next stall. Eventually I manage to find an Honest Joe who now supplies all my alcohol needs without me having to take a long pull from a whisky bottle by the side of the road at 5 pm in the evening!

Work at the university slips back into its familiar routine with my time split about 40 per cent / 40 per cent between teaching and research and the remaining time for the botanical gardens and committee meetings. As last year, I am only teaching the specialist ecology and plant physiology students but 'kind of' miss the hordes of first-year students who made my life so much fun a few years back. That is not to say that my specialist groups are getting smaller, actually they seem to swell every year. My third-year ecology classes now number up to one hundred, and many of the students are from that original band of first-year students that started my lecturing days at Unical. They no longer moan about my accent either! The problem with having so many students attending these specialist classes is that the timetable committee – a job I have been spared – did not anticipate such large classes and so I was allocated small lecture theatres that cannot possibly accommodate the numbers that have signed up. The only way around the problem, and it is not perfect, is to open all the windows and doors have the overflow students sitting out on the balconies either side of the classroom. Then I must speak loudly so they can hear me and take notes. I am teased by friends that some of the members of the Theatre Arts Department, in the neighbouring building, hold up my ecology renditions to their drama students as the correct use of the pectorals and diaphragm in voice projection!

I have several new students wanting to carry out projects with me as their supervisor while Tony, now in the second year of his Masters has got on well with his research. So well, in fact, that with his first-year data added to mine, I am able to start sketching out a research paper; and this time from purely Calabar-based research. I actually have three articles on the go, each based on different groups or characteristics of weed species. The one with Tony explains the germination characteristics of fifteen tropical weed species and will eventually be published, after we both leave Calabar, in the very prestigious Weed Research Journal of the UK. The two others are from my own research and are much more focused on supporting improvements to the timing of weed control by synchronising traditional control methods with the periodicity of natural seedling emergence. Both have already been accepted and are to be published next year. The first is for a group of dicotyledonous weeds and will be produced again by Weed Research. The second looks at similar germination characteristics in some common monocotyledonous weeds (grasses and similar families) and this has been accepted by *Oecologica Applicata*, a French journal. I chose to go with a relatively lesser-known French publication in order to get 'my foot in the door' of French academia, so to speak. One never knows for the future. Add to these papers, the article by Callistus and myself on achene dimorphism and I feel quietly pleased with the progress of my research. As the cherry on the cake, Alan and I have now completed two years' worth of data collection on the interactions between the weed bush, *Chromolaena*, and the large grasshopper, *Zonocerus*. I make a mental note to try to find the time to write up the article. In fact, this fifth and final article that I produce in Nigeria from Calabar data, was accepted for publication by the Journal of African Science and appeared in print in 1985.

Being a member of different departmental committees begins to take more of my time as the departmental senior groom me for higher things. While I am less happy to lose a growing amount of time out of my research agenda, I am enjoying the extra involvement in helping to run the department and in planning for the future of the university.

My involvement in the Appointments and Promotions Committee is proving bittersweet. At the very first such meeting I attend along with another six staff members, our Chairman (the Dean of Science) makes it clear to all participants that the discussions and conclusions of the meetings are strictly confidential.

He warns "none of you should be tempted to leak decision points outside the meeting" and asks "does everyone understand? If you disagree, then kindly leave the meeting now." Everyone nods, no-one leaves the room.

The first item on the agenda is to discuss applicants for several vacancies that have arisen in the department since our two international and a couple of local lecturers have left. On paper, none of the candidates looks very exciting but we agree to call a couple of the Nigerian applicants for interviews. The second item is to decide on the possible promotions of a couple of more junior lecturers, one of whom is my 'friend' who had reported me to the Registrar. I realise that I must be scrupulously fair with anything I say openly and with my eventual decision. Also on the committee is his buddy who had also reported me to the Registrar. When the chairman asks for comments on the junior lecturer's efforts, publication history and suitability to move up to the grade of Lecturer II, his buddy reels off a list of superlatives that makes all of the other members in the room look at each other and at me with questioning expressions.

The Dean cuts the eloquent speech short by saying "I assume this means you support his promotion even though he does not teach or research in your field of biology?"

The way the Dean puts so much emphasis on the phrase 'field of biology' makes the rest of us chuckle unintentionally since we both know that the two guys are inveterate lady chasers. The chairman then turns to me and asks my opinion given that the lecturer is a plant physiologist and so teaches – or is supposed to teach – on a couple of my courses.

I riffle through the papers that we have been provided on each candidate for promotion and state quite honestly, "Can we start by looking at his efforts in research? I notice that he has only one publication to his name and that was from several years ago when he was a master's student and he is not the lead author either. Our promotion guidelines state clearly that candidates should have a minimum of two publications in refereed journals since appointment or since the last promotion. Does he match this criterion?"

The assembled committee, with a single exception, says 'no'.

"Nonetheless", I continue, "if he is an excellent teacher, I believe that lack of research should not be a hindrance. Since he does not seem currently to make the grade for research efforts, can we instead look at his teaching capacities?"

Dr Jahn, another lecturer in plant physiology, raises his hand to speak "in the first semester last year he was supposed to teach on my course for a total of ten hours but only turned up for the final hour. He then set two questions in my exam that were impossible for any of the students to answer, so none did. This put extra work on the other lecturers who ended up marking far more papers than the average. I am not impressed by his teaching capacity."

Trying to temper this harsh but truthful criticism, I state "but we should not forget that his wife was sick during the first semester as she lost the baby she was carrying. However, I do agree with what has just been said about the complexity of his exam questions. Also he told no-one that he would be away for so long so we missed the opportunity to cover for him in the classes until the students reported his absence."

"I knew you would gang up on him" states his buddy with some vitriol "you could all be more sympathetic."

The Dean then directs that we draw this particular debate to a close and asks our recommendation by a show of hands for or against promotion. "Those for?" One hand is raised; "Those against?" five hands, including mine, go up. "Any abstentions?" our solitary female committee member raises her hand. "Promotion rejected" states the Dean. "Now the next candidate to consider for promotion is ..."

The meeting runs to the end of its agenda and we all collect our papers and walk out chatting and discussing some of the tighter decisions. The buddy does not linger but disappears out the door first. Dr Jahn and I, having neighbouring offices near to the Theatre Arts Department, walk together towards our rooms and we both spot the buddy having a whispered conversation to his friend on the balcony of the floor above.

As we arrive at our doors, the rejected lecturer comes charging around the corner behind us, spitting out with real venom "you bastards. I know what you both said in the meeting. I am going to kill you."

So much for the confidentiality of our meeting! For the record, he did not kill either of us neither did he ever speak to us again. I sent a two-line letter to the chairman offering my resignation from the committee while Dr Jahn made a formal and verbal complaint of harassment. My resignation letter was sent back to me with a red rubber stamp across the middle reading 'rejected'. The buddy never attended another of the committee meetings.

The other committee I am now a member is the Procurement Committee to discuss the planning and equipping of the biology department in the new, still to be built, university. While the Dean and the Head of the Biology Department are joint chairs, one of my assigned roles is to pull together an itemised list of all equipment that will need to be purchased for the new laboratories. A complex process that means that I need inputs from all members of the biology staff as well as access to equipment catalogues and price lists. As a partial reward for accepting the job and I believe as a bribe to go with accelerated promotion, I am allocated a large, bright and well-equipped laboratory-style room complete with a brand new air conditioner. This is to be my research room and is also to be where Tony, my research student, can be based and do laboratory experiments. The Dean tells me that I can now empty my office of all the equipment and experiments and have it organised as a Reader-style office. The only drawback with the new research laboratory is that it is located in the Administration and Finance Department rather than in biology; but it is far more peaceful and I will be disturbed less frequently while trying to concentrate on research work and article writing.

Our three lab technicians help me to move my equipment and research papers from my office to the laboratory and, by Monday morning, my research is well installed in the new room.

One morning while counting germination levels of seeds sewn on damp Whatman's filter paper in petri dishes, I see arriving an Israeli friend who owns a company in Calabar that supplies and installs air conditioners. In fact, he is a direct competitor of another expat, the husband of the renowned Erma who had loped off the snake's head during that infamous Pro-Am Golf tournament. My friend sees me through the window and so comes into my new office and tells me that I can make him a cup of Nescafe because he is fifteen minutes early for an appointment with the head of finance. He is one of the Israelis that I had met at the Israeli village film nights that we regularly attended a couple of years previously. I see him often at the

Harbour Works swimming pool. I like him very much but know him to be a very sharp and successful businessman.

"Why do you need to see the finance guy?"

"I am making a bid to get the contract for the air conditioning systems in the new university. The contract is really big, the biggest I have ever bid on."

Mockingly I ask "then will you need to offer a lot of dash?"

He puts his finger to his lips in a 'hush' gesture and then turns the combinations on his attaché case, releasing the two catches with a click. He slowly opens the lid, lifts up a layer of business papers and reveals stack after stack of Naira notes. He tells me that this is the price simply to be able to bid on the contract and get on the shortlist. More must be paid when he, confidently, wins it.

By now I am only too aware of the depth of corruption that exists within the business environment. I know that I may not be able to claim much success from my stay in Nigeria but one thing I can claim is never to have paid or received dash.

During this time of rapid industrial and social expansion with oil dollars sloshing around the Nigerian economy, the amount of money that illicitly changes hands is mind-boggling – and the civilian politicians know exactly what is going on. Rumours go around at this time of large caches of banknotes held in secret places in Calabar by businessmen. One rumour that is currently being talked about is that a certain and very well-known Nigerian businessman (hint: he makes and sells plastic water pipes) has a disconnected metal water tank at the top of a scaffold and has filled it with banknotes waiting to be laundered through his many companies. Partial justice for these criminals arrives in the April following our eventual departure when the government of the time changes the colour of banknotes thus making the tank-load of currency worthless overnight.

The delivery of electricity to our homes in Calabar and to the university is steadily deteriorating with cuts becoming more and more frequent and much longer in duration as the weather warms up. There is talk at the university that the cuts are being driven by the national government who are targeting states that do not support the current President, Shehu Shagari. We are told around town that the drive for political representation by the Ibibio in our state and in neighbouring ones is worrying the ruling National Party and this is part of their revenge. Is this true? I do not know, but the electricity cuts are real and cause everyone severe discomfort. More worrying are the rumours of rumblings within the military; and these might well lead to an eventual move by the officers.

During our years in Calabar, Véro and I have gotten used to frequent electricity cuts but we notice that Mélanie is starting to get patches of prickly heat on her body where perspiration rests and the salt it contains irritates her delicate skin. The electricity cuts also mean that we have to be extra careful of food in our refrigerator, especially now that our little girl is starting to eat some solid foods. We chat and make the decision to buy a small petrol-powered generator. I have noticed a shop close to the main Calabar market that has a good array of machines and our friend George tells us that the shop is owned by one of his Lebanese relatives. He has promised to speak with his cousin and ensure that I get a good generator at the right price. The next day I come back with a little 1 KVA generator, sit it out on the balcony near the front door and chain and padlock it to the safety barrier that surrounds the balcony. If anyone wishes to steal it, they will have to work very hard with a hacksaw.

How does one run the electrics of a house with a generator? I do not have the faintest idea. My logic tells me that if I attach a plug to the outlet lead of the generator and plug this into a house plug socket, it should send electricity to all parts of the house. But best to try first in daylight. So I fill the tank with petrol and switch off at the mains. This is an important move because otherwise the poor generator tries to service the electricity demand for the entire city of Calabar. I only made the mistake once of forgetting to switch off at the mains and luckily the generator has a circuit breaker for just such an eventuality. The breaker did kick in but not before the poor generator had leapt three feet into the air!

The generator starts by a simple pull of a cord (theoretically speaking 'simple' that is), rather like starting an outboard engine on a boat. Once the generator is running, the flow of electrical power is enabled by a switch on its side and the electricity is ready to feed the house. By trial and error, we find that we can run rather a variety of equipment; providing they are switched on in the correct sequence. First to go on is the fridge and as the fridge motor kicks in, the little generator complains by emitting a lower and lower moan but then it starts to pick up its generating speed again. Next are the overhead fans either in the sitting room (if we are there) or in the bedrooms and these are then followed by the lights. We ran that little generator for almost a year with no major problems. The only drawback is that the built in petrol tank is small and only allows a running autonomy of about four hours and so when the electricity is off for longer periods, especially at night, I am obliged to set the alarm and get up to refill the tank at least once during the night.

Mélanie's prickly heat decreases with the use of the fan and prickly heat powder. However, one morning we notice that she is a little listless and has diarrhoea. We try different child medicines like calpol that we have brought with us from France and the UK but the diarrhoea does not seem to slow. After a few hours we are getting concerned since we know the seriousness of dehydration in young children. This is the first time she has been sick, and so we worry even more. We are fortunate to have made friends with an Egyptian Professor of Medicine who works at the new School of Medicine at the university and so I go around to his house for advice. He tells me that it is best if he comes to check out the baby and goes to another room to pick up his medical bag. He comes back with me to the house, exams Mélanie who gives him a one-tooth smile; a charmer even at six months old. He opens her mouth and runs his finger around her gum and jokingly says ouch. Feel here, he says to Véro and there we have the probable cause of the diarrhoea, two new teeth breaking through the gums. She recovers very quickly and we agree to keep a closer eye on her teething in the future.

The news I have been expecting has finally arrived in the form of a visit to the house by Kurt and Gerda. After Gerda has given Mélanie a cuddle – she would so love to have a baby herself – and they have accepted cold Champions, Kurt starts off with "sorry but I have some bad news for you."

I know word for word what he will tell me. He is trying to cushion the blow and so starts off with "I heard from Klaus that you had gone to Frankfurt and done excellent work for the company. Also that he has asked you to go to work for him when you finish here. I really am sorry then but I just heard from his wife that he passed away yesterday, likely of a heart attack."

I just knew it and had been preparing myself and Véronique for this sad news. And here it is. "Thanks Kurt. When you next speak to Frau Voelger please do tell her how very sad we are for her. Klaus was a lovely man and I really had hoped that working with him would be the next step in my career. Now I must start to look for something else because we will leave in July at the end of my contract."

Véro and I have already had the 'what if' conversation and we had decided that no matter what happens, we owe it to ourselves and to Mélanie to go back to Europe at the end of this contract; even if I have no job awaiting me. I know Véro feels for me, no words are needed, but after our German friends leave she perches on my lap, hugs me and tells me not to worry. I do appreciate her selflessness because I am convinced that this news has hit her far harder than it has me. But then that is at the base of her character and makes her the special person she is.

I consider myself a rather lucky individual, at least Madam Luck does seem to smile on me quite frequently. Or do we, in reality, set in motion the events that eventually create our own luck? I do not know but tend to think that the latter is more likely. Just as Kurt and Gerda leave our house, so Roger, the friend who works in the new Meridian Bank as a trainer, stops by for a Champion and tells me that he has been working with the bank staff on the process involved in transferring accounts from one bank to another. That is interesting because I had put in a request to transfer my own account from Standard to Meridian Bank. When I remind him that my account still needs transferring to his bank, he laughs and tells me that he used my account as the model of how transfers should be done ... and hands me over a new chequebook, transfer complete!

Both Véro and I are delighted. Now we have decided that we are going to leave at the end of the academic year, we have to follow a quite complex Nigerian process to close down our account and be allowed to transfer the funds from the closed account in Calabar back to the UK. Nigerian law theoretically allows three separate elements to be transferred. First, 50% of the final month or two of salary, as usual. Next, the 15% expatriate allowance on the university salary that is only paid out at the end of the final contract can be remitted in full. Even after only four years, this is for us, quite a reasonable amount. The expatriate allowance is in lieu of the university pension scheme that Nigerian staff contribute towards. Finally, any remaining funds in the account can be remitted, providing that one can show by formal receipts that the funds have accrued from selling items pre-departure. The remittance process is the same as for the usual monthly salary transfers but with one big difference – the person remitting will have left the country long before the paperwork is ever completed and the foreign currency cheques cut. This means that any blockages cannot be resolved and many expatriates leave behind and eventually lose large sums of money from their final remittances.

It was Roger who advised me to move bank during this final year so that he could help me do the necessary paperwork and, importantly, follow the remittance process for me once we are back in Europe. Knowing and working with the Managing Director of the bank is an added advantage just in case Roger encounters any problems with the process himself.

After thanking Roger for his kindness, I ask if I can do anything to reciprocate and he replies that I can do him the big favour of coming to dinner the following Saturday evening; bringing Mélanie too, of course. I laugh because as two couples of the same age, us with one girl and Roger with one little girl, a bit older than Mélanie, and a new baby girl, we see a lot of each other. I tell him that eating together is a pleasure not a favour and this causes him to laugh in return.

"Ah, but I did not tell you that you will be entertaining my visiting boss on Saturday. He is OK, much older than us and so a little bit hard to bring into the conversation. His field is training and agriculture and so I think you may be able to entertain him!"

Saturday arrives and we drive around to Roger's apartment and meet up with his two colleagues while Roger and his wife work away in the kitchen. Roger loves cooking and entertaining; a love that eventually leads him and his wife to open numerous tourist-oriented ventures around the world; not always very successfully.

The boss of Roger's company, ORT based in Geneva, then arrives. He must be in his late 50s, sports a razor haircut and comes across the room to me for a chat. The chat lasts throughout the aperitif, carries on at the dinner table and continues afterwards too. Few can get a word into our conversation and I fear that I am over-monopolising their boss but apparently not judging by the smiles and nods I am getting from Roger. His boss wants to know about everything related to my academic and professional life. Why ecology? Why teaching? What work I did for Klaus in Germany? What are my plans for the future? When do I plan to leave Calabar? What languages do I speak? What does Véronique think about this life? and on and on.

At the end of a copious meal, French Roger (my friend Roger's immediate boss in the training school) tries to hide a yawn and confesses to being tired and takes his leave, closely followed by Roger's other colleague and his wife who live in the apartment upstairs. Mélanie and Roger's two girls are all sound asleep in the next room and I can see Véro beginning to fidget and make a discrete 'time-out' sign to me. Time then to try to wrap up my conversation. As I rise and start to say goodnight, my conversation partner tells me that he is to leave Calabar in two days and before then I must give him a copy of my CV because his company often has work related to agriculture in different countries, especially Francophone ones. I make a mental note that the following morning I must sit down at the department's typewriter and type up my out-of-date CV for him. That one pleasant and chance evening encounter eventually leads to a change of career ... but not in the immediate future.

~ 12 ~

THE PRIESTS FIX OUR ROOF

Now that we have made the decision that this academic year is to be our last in Nigeria, we need to start putting in place our plans for returning to Europe. Our tentative idea is to leave Calabar a week or so after the end of the summer term around the start of July, go back for the summer to France and from there to the UK.

I hope that I can get work quickly when back in London but my old supervisor at QMC has told me already that I can always help with his practical classes while I look around for something more permanent. Our little apartment in Culford Road has been let throughout our time in Nigeria and the current contract is due to expire at the end of September. The tenants, both students, will move out at that time and we can have our old roof back over our heads.

I start to lay the foundations at the university for our eventual departure, now in around six months' time. My first port of call is to my fellow ecology and physiology lecturers: Alan, John, Barry, Jahn and a few others. We have become not only trusting colleagues but also firm friends and so there is sadness all around but an acknowledgement that 'we all have to leave sometime'. Apart from John, I have been at the University of Calabar longer than the others and they are also beginning to think about moving on in about eighteen months' time. Only John seems to see himself as a relatively permanent fixture at the university. I believe that in the outside world he feels like a square peg trying to fit a round hole but here in Calabar he can enjoy his isolation and love of animals like nowhere else in the world.

As far as an employment future is concerned, the biggest problem with being in Calabar is the wretched impossibility of communicating with the outside world that I described earlier. It is just impossible to get work outside the country while being based in Calabar. No matter how many copies of New Scientist, Nature, The Economist, Times Education and so on we receive, by the time they arrive, the closing dates for jobs have long passed and the jobs been filled. So for me, the only logical alternative is to go back to Europe, accept that there will certainly be a few months of unemployment and look for a job there. I will gladly do replacement teaching, labouring or work in a supermarket while I await a more relevant job suited better to my training and experience.

Next, I visit my head of department and fill him in with my plans. I do realise that my leaving creates a hole in his department not only for the teaching aspects but also for the many other responsibilities that I have now assumed. He tries, rather feebly I feel, to ask "and what if we go for a professorship?" but I do not think that such a promotion – equivalent to three steps above my current grade – is possible and, even if it could be swung, it would only put off the time of my leaving for a couple more years. I do tell him that I believe now might be the right time for me to stand down as Director of the Botanical Gardens. I recommend that he considers appointing the young Nigerian lady who had coveted the position a few months back and that I am happy to work with her to ensure a smooth handover.

But it is not just the problem of getting work that concerns me. We both realise that we have a serious responsibility to little Mélanie. To date, we have been extremely lucky that she has never been seriously ill, certainly no malaria or any other of the horrific tropical diseases. However, we do not want to ride our luck for too long. Indeed, neither Véro nor I have ever knowingly had malaria although I have, on several occasions, felt ill, nauseous and fevered for a few days that could have been the disease. Doctor friends tell me that malaria is often misdiagnosed since there are hundreds of unknown viruses doing the rounds in our area of Nigeria that could produce such symptoms. The only problem is that it usually takes longer to identify which virus is concerned than it takes for a relatively healthy patient to recover from it. With malaria, the best diagnosis is a blood analysis that seeks out the so-called signet ring in red blood cells that demonstrate the malarial parasite actively reproducing in the blood.

The worry is not only about our personal health because we are also getting increasingly concerned about the political health of the country. I have already mentioned about the declining quality of electricity supply in the town that is being blamed on the party in power and about the unhealthy levels of greed and corruption among many of the elite. As we move closer to the August general election, we can feel an undercurrent that does not give me confidence and certainly does not allay my fears. We still see our friendly Hausa traders who come by the house about once a month despite knowing that we rarely buy anything. They tell me that life is becoming harder for them in Calabar; and they fear a repeat of events from the Biafra War. They cannot put a finger on any single event that makes them feel uneasy. They just find Calabar citizens are no longer as friendly towards them as they were even a year ago and mention for example that they cannot now stay in the rooms they used to rent when in Calabar. Similarly, Bassey who supplies us with Jos vegetables, moans frequently that he feels tensions present when he makes his weekly trips to Jos to purchase fruits and vegetables. Farmers no longer treat him as a friend. They appear suspicious of him and have started to accuse him of not being ready to negotiate and not paying good prices when he buys from them, despite the fact that he pays market prices.

The final worry for me about the future health of Nigeria is generated by a letter that I receive from the British High Commissioner to Nigeria. He writes to me, as the Community Liaison Officer for Cross River State, just prior to finishing his four years as High Commissioner, based in Lagos. I know that his letter is written to try to instil confidence in the British population-based in Nigeria but his words have the reverse affect and make me feel increasingly worried. His letter runs to two full A4 pages – in itself unusual – and so I will not repeat it all here but the central theme that I must now pass on to the British contingent in and around Calabar is that all is safe in Nigeria. He stresses that he has never '... advised British families to consider leaving Nigeria ...' and has '... had to put the record straight several times with diplomatic colleagues who have quoted inaccurate .... reports that I had advised .... evacuation of British families ...'. This in itself concerns me because I have to wonder why should his colleagues have gotten the wrong end of the stick so frequently? But then in his letter he goes on to say that 'The next few months will be a period when particular vigilance will be required ...'.

What concerns me the most are a few words hidden near the end of his letter in which he says 'We ... constantly recommend that maximum attention be paid to personal security'. At least he does pay '... tribute to the spirit and guts of the British Community ...' as we try to continue to live and work in the country which he is just about to leave.

I meet up with a group of Brits based in Calabar and read the letter out to them. Not one single person feels more secure after we discuss the contents than they had before hearing it. The most common rejoinder from the invited Brits went along the lines of 'no one from the high commission has ever bothered to come to Calabar to see the situation for themselves so how can they possibly advise us?'

I do not mean to give the impression that life at the moment is full of doom and gloom nor that the British and other members of the expatriate communities are considering leaving *en masse*. However, we all agree that members of our embassies and high commissions – of whatever nationality – are rather like birds in gilded cages; everything is provided for them and they always live conveniently close to an international airport, just in case ...! They rarely, if ever, have to experience the concerns and dangers that the people they are paid to represent encounter on an almost daily basis. In my knowledge, no member of our high commission deigned to visit Calabar in the four years I was there.

In another life, I hear about the tantrums of a Royal, the 'special representative' who drove embassies crazy trying to fulfil all demands before the noble person arrived in country. These demands went down to the single type of toothpaste that could brush Royal fangs and the brand of toilet paper that ... well, you get the drift.

May 24th arrives and with it, our little girl is one-year-old. We celebrate by holding a party for a number of babies and toddlers, including Roger's two little girls. Mélanie celebrates by pulling herself up the sofa leg, into a standing position and stagger-walking across to her mum. She has a big beam on her face and I am still unclear whether this is to say 'look how clever I am' or if she means 'well in chapter fourteen of Pernoud's book it says that baby will walk around the first birthday, so I am!' No matter, everyone is thrilled and pleasant trouble begins now we have a toddler and not a crawler.

Sunday arrives and we have another invitation to the highly popular curry luncheon. The bank MD, or rather his chef, has excelled yet again. Not only are the curries, of several types, absolutely superb but so are the many accompaniments that he has produced to go with them: ginger, coconut, mango chutney, chili, and on and on. There is also always a goodly stock of wine that has mysteriously warped to Calabar from Lagos (and probably further afield); such is the benefit of being a Managing Director of a large bank. We are around a dozen who have received today's invitation along with Roger, his wife and the other members of their training team.

After the meal, one of the participants at the dinner asks me to come and sit in the garden with him. We each carry out a glass of wine, mine red and his white, and sit away from the other guests.

He does not beat around the bush but simply says "Three days ago I met a couple of new Irish priests who are looking to build a church in Calabar. They have sufficient Irish Punts, back in Ireland that they need to convert to Naira but they have decided to avoid transferring the funds formerly via the Central Bank because they have been asked already to pay bribes to get the money through the system. By preference they have decided to work with a few trusted expatriates who have money in Nigeria to exchange for Punts in Ireland, on a one-for-one basis. If you have any spare Naira, get it to me in cash before next weekend."

This rather surprises me, and I say so, since while the official, Central Bank controlled rate is indeed about one Naira for one Punt, there exists a thriving black market that will give around two Naira for a Punt and so the priests could double their money by going via the black market. This they neither want to risk nor take advantage of.

Since splashing out on the generator, I know that we have almost no excess Naira in our account so it looks like we might have to pass the chance of a remittance at such favourable rates. On the short drive back to Road-10 I tell Véro of my conversation and she asks why I do not speak to one or two of the older expats at the university. This is a sound idea because I know two or three seniors that moved from the older universities in Nigeria to Calabar and in doing so were reimbursed their accrued pension contributions, sometimes representing quite significant sums. On several occasions they have moaned to me that they will never be able to repatriate this money.

So the next evening I drop in to speak to a professor from another department and explain that I have the opportunity to transfer some Naira out of the country. Without prompting, he tells me that he has five thousand Naira that he would be delighted to get out of the country at the black market rate. When I tell him that I would make a profit on the transfer, he simply replies that he is happy with whatever I make as he is desperate to achieve the remittance. I then stop at a second friend who is close to retirement and tell the same story. He wants to remit three thousand Naira and is happy with the black market rate too. In total, I deliver eight thousand Naira to the priests and they transfer eight thousand punts to my UK account which translates to £7,600. I transfer to my friends their four thousand pounds and make a profit on the deal of £3,600. A nice evening's work, thank you very much! That will pay for the roof, the stairs and window in Cordon as well as covering our mortgage repayments for a few months.

Our leaving time gets closer and so does my 30th birthday. Steve and Jane, the Kiwis, suggest we have a party – any old excuse for a party works in Calabar – and the suggestion is overheard by a colleague of Steve. Apparently both his birthday and his wife's are on or close to the same day as me and so we agree to combine our celebrations. As we individually start to invite people, so the manager of the cement factory declares his birthday at the same time, followed by a Dutch guy who works at Harbour Works. In the end, we are five buddies who gather around the cake to receive the Happy Birthday songs of our friends. This last party and celebration is a fitting closing curtain on our stay in Calabar.

There remain basically three items to complete before we are ready to board the aeroplane home: finish off all my academic obligations; sort through all our personal items - sell those that we will not take back to Europe with us – and pack and ship those we will, and finally sort out tax details for our final remittance.

My remaining academic obligations are few and for the most part involve completing my lecture courses, setting and marking the relevant exams. Now at the end of my fourth year as a lecturer, I find this work enjoyable and simple to complete. Harder for me is to complete activities with my ecology students. I just hope that I have been a good enough teacher, mentor and friend to have had a positive influence on their lives and future careers. Writing these words, I cannot help reflecting back on my own student days and the massive influence that several of my old lecturers and professors had on the way my life and career subsequently unfolded. But the saddest moment for me is to say goodbye to my three student cavaliers: Tony, Callistus and Emmanuel. Just before leaving Calabar, I hear that Tony is to be awarded a Masters of Ecology (the first ever awarded by the university), Emmanuel receives a 2:1 Hons in Ecology and Callistus will get the same honours the following year. Sadly, I will never see any of them again.

I put a list of items that I have for sale on the department notice board: air conditioner, small generator, fishing equipment, clothes iron, pair of binoculars, pots and pans, and so on. Five minutes after it is posted, my colleague Dr Jahn, walks in holding the list and peels off the exact amount of money from a bundle of Naira that he holds in his hand and buys the lot. I get him to sign purchase forms, needed for the bank to allow me to remit the funds to the UK. That was quick.

I also tape a 'For Sale' notice on the rear windscreen of my Passat. I am asking fifteen hundred Naira but am prepared to negotiate down to a thousand if necessary. Apart from the generally good state of the car, it is also Nigerianised (import tax was already paid by the previous owner) and so can be purchased by anyone without needing to pay any additional taxes. Within a day I receive a visit from the senior laboratory technician of the Physics Department. He offers me twelve hundred and fifty Naira which I accept but with two conditions. First that the car remains with me until the day before we board the plane from Calabar and second that I am paid the full amount three days before leaving. On the second condition he hesitates and so I knock another fifty Naira off the price and then we shake hands on the deal. The following day he hands me five hundred Naira and says that he is getting a bank loan for the other seven hundred. This involves a visit from a mechanic appointed by the bank. We go for a test drive and the mechanic checks that the universal joints are not click-clicking when he makes tight turns nor that the brakes fail when he makes an emergency stop. The car passes the checks and the remaining cash is handed over to me a couple of days later with a signed purchase form.

I take the cash that I have accumulated from the different sales together with the necessary tax forms, purchase forms and other paperwork around to Roger's apartment. He has kindly offered to get all the remittance processes started for me and then to follow them through to conclusion. I know that this will be a difficult and time-consuming process and so I really appreciate his kind gesture.

Meanwhile we have been busy packing the items we wish to send by freight. The duffel bags are stuffed and padlocked while our infamous travel trunk is filled and locked. I take everything to the freight handling office of Calabar Airport, sign the relevant forms, hand over the miscellaneous charge orders that the university has provided me, and wish the luggage *bon voyage*. We will hopefully pick it all up in a couple of weeks from Satolas Airport in Lyon.

To complete the car story, at 4 pm on my last day, both in the university and in Calabar, I hand over the keys to my car and wish the new owner happy motoring. Alan gives me a lift home and has kindly offered to drive the three of us and our suitcases to the airport the next morning.

We wake up early and are excited to be going home. Alan is to arrive at 10 am to take us to the airport but before he arrives, a car containing two of my departmental colleagues pulls up in front of the house. I go out to greet them; assuming that they have come to say goodbye again.

"Oh thank God", says Maurice while another Nigerian colleague comes across to hug me, "we thought you had been seriously hurt."

"What do you mean?" I ask. "I'm fine, what's happening?" and they tell me that when they arrived at the university entrance first thing this morning, they found my car had managed to leap across the cement culvert and was wrapped around a *Casuarina* tree. The whole car was badly damaged, the windscreen was shattered and there looked like blood on the bonnet. It seems that the new owner had not possessed the car for more than a couple of hours before crashing and writing it off. Alan then arrives and confirms the details of my crashed car and also says that he heard that the driver had no driving licence nor insurance. I never heard how badly he had been injured.

We have plenty of time before the flight and so Alan drives us at a leisurely pace to the airport. He drives slowly along the dusty tracks leading out of the housing estate and on to the tarmac that takes us past the bakery, with its usual queue of sugar-craving Nigerian clients, past the empty tables where later today the young men will be laying out their bottles of hooch, of cold tea, and perhaps a few bottles of genuine whisky and gin. We turn left and drive past the police station and visa office and then proceed past our old guesthouse on the right and see the end of the runway on the left. Old memories continually resurface from our arrival four short years ago. We remember the surprisingly loud noise that vultures make when they land on the guesthouse tin roof. Then Véro points out the tables lining the road where the ubiquitous sardine cans are still for sale, the piles of bitter manioc that must be cooked to become edible, unlike its sweet, northern variety that is delicious chewed raw with a taste of chestnut. We pass the stands of Awolowo weed that line the access road to the airport, pass through the gates receiving a wave from the two guards who have got to know us by now, over the culvert that permanently drains water from the airport and up to the small terminal building. A last big hug with Alan that leaves me with tears in my eyes to be saying goodbye to such a sweet and kind friend. With a final kiss for Mélanie and a call of bon voyage and see you soon, we watch as Alan climbs back into his car and drives off waving out the window as he goes.

The Calabar to Lagos flight takes off on time and the hostess gives us sardine rolls, little tetra-packs of fake fruit juice and then ignores all the passengers waiting to receive their culinary delicacies by picking Mélanie from her seat and giving her a hug. Anything is possible in Nigeria.

~ 13 ~

EPILOGUE CRACKING WALNUTS

Close to forty years have sped by since our adventures in Calabar. Despite long- and short-term work in some twenty-odd African nations, I never managed to return to Calabar to see the new university that was eventually built. I did once get back to Nigeria but only to sit on the airport apron in Lagos on an Air Afrique flight that was supposed to take me and a group of Batswana that I was leading directly from Abidjan to Dakar. Geographically, it can be seen that we managed a very strange detour; but that was Air Afrique; it was not long before it went out of business.

The work I did for Klaus sat lonely on my CV for a few years but Roger's boss from ORT did eventually come good on his word and provided me with some consultancy work in Chad. The call asking me to go to the desert region of this magnificent and proud nation came through in the evening of July 2nd when we were celebrating our 10th wedding anniversary in the UK. Without the extra courage furnished by the then empty bottle of champagne, I wonder if I would have had the confidence to say yes. Thank the Lord that I did because this opening led to more and more opportunities in Africa and then in Asia.

I said previously that I wonder if luck finds us or whether our activities lead us to good fortune. I tend to believe more and more in the latter. Certainly this work in Chad and other early work opportunities led to chance encounters and those chance encounters slowly but very surely slanted my career away from teaching to consulting. However, I never strayed too far away from my love of ecology and desire to help people to help themselves.

My fears of a coup d'état in Nigeria came true; rather more rapidly than I had imagined. President Shehu Shagari did manage to win a hotly contested election in August 1983 but on 31st December of the same year, while most people were preparing for New Year celebrations, the military drove their tanks out of the barracks and took control. For a good while they had sat back and watched the level of corruption steadily increasing but enough was considered enough and Nigeria's four, short years of democracy came to an end via the gun barrel. The following April, the military ordered a reprinting of banknotes in new colours while allowing only 100 Naira of old bills to be exchanged at banks. Many of the corrupt saw their hidden stocks of Naira made worthless overnight. Good for them.

My old friends John (of the dented beetle) and Alan left Calabar in the couple of years that followed the military takeover. Alan was to become Professor Seddon and have a successful career at Kingston University. John finally left Calabar and I understand first moved just up the road to the Oban Hills working for the WWF in setting up a national park when, as I had always thought, they discovered a population of Mountain Gorillas living there. By coincidence, I caught a flight out of Johannesburg Airport in 2000 and sitting next to me was the WWF recruiter who had hired John for the Oban Hills. The news she told me of my old friend was so sad and left me feeling shattered. It seems, but I have never been able to verify, that he was killed during a burglary gone wrong, not in Nigeria but back home in Brixton, London.

Marian, that lovely, vivacious and caring lady went with Andy and their two girls to live in Australia and took up a post as a mathematician at the University of Melbourne. Sadly, she was taken from this world by breast cancer. The Lobbs, our Kiwi friends, went back to New Zealand where Steve runs a successful building company. They wander over to the Old World from time to time, never forgetting to look in on their old friends.

Roger and his family continued to live an expatriate life moving from country to country as one training contract led to the next. Roger never gave up his desire to run people-facing hospitality businesses as a side-line (luckily) because he never seemed to get much better at it, despite how many times he tried. We lost count of the number of new ventures he began: a camping site in Deal on the south coast of England, a bar in the Czech Republic, another bar in Singapore, a Thai guesthouse, bar, and restaurants ... His ever-patient wife followed and supported him to the end. But sadly, this dearest of my friends passed away a few years back and his ashes are mingled with my tears in the Garden of Remembrance in our native Kent.

Mélanie got a little brother when she was four and the pair of them became great friends from the moment our little girl held her new brother in her arms. To say that they were, and still are, chalk and cheese would be to under-exaggerate their sibling differences!

We continued to work on our house in Cordon during every possible vacation with the kids joining in as soon as they could hold a paintbrush or plaster spatula. The Franco Brothers have stayed with us through the years opening new windows, adding roof-lights, converting the second-floor loft to two extra bedrooms and building a wall around the property. As our finances strengthened, we brought in skilled tradesmen to do other jobs like adding double glazing and fitting stairs to the attic. We continued to use that house as our holiday home and bolt-hole when between contracts until, in 2008, we both admitted to seeing retirement on the not-too-distant horizon. Then we started to look around for a larger property and garden, somewhere that we could start a small Bed and Breakfast (*chambres d'hôtes* as we say here).

By chance, a large sprinkling of magic and our inevitable good luck, the perfect property came up and – would you believe it? – in the little village of Rix. We signed contracts on the very house that we had admired so many years ago while walking the newborn Mélanie around the village. The house with the pool and the enormous Lime tree where, many years before, we had seen the barrier blocking the road and lorries taking away rubble.

We call our house and our B&B business '*Cœur de Rose*'. While there is really no straight translation for the name we chose, suffice to say that it is a place where we both feel happy and at home. Our heart (*cœur*) is here in Rix, it has been since the year we rented that little house from M. and Mme Conand for the birth of Mélanie, and dear Bruno knocked on the door to get me to play *boules* and rugby. Our garden is full of flowers, none more imposing than some of the beautiful roses that Véro has planted and tended and, as all my French friends know only too well, there is no more fervent supporter of the English rugby team (*le Quinze de la Rose*, as the French call us) than me.

By one of those strange coincidences that seem to have followed us throughout our life together, we signed contracts for the house on 2nd July 2010 – our 33rd Wedding Anniversary.

Mystically, the number 33 represents the energies of compassion, blessings, inspiration, honesty, discipline, bravery and courage – and we hope that we bring all of those features to our friends that have and do share our lives.

We have come a long way together since I discovered Véro in *La Poubelle!*

Sadly, Marie-Rose left us in 2013 and her funeral was on the same afternoon that we had invited her and André and many more friends to my 60th birthday party in our garden in Rix.

Time has not left us totally without scars although both Véro and I are doing pretty well as we start to enjoy retirement. Mélanie and her husband Alexis have gifted us two beautiful grandchildren that make every day as welcome as the last. Sadly, we have lost three of our parents with only my mum, now into her 90s (bless her) still with us. While her mobility is severely limited, her mischievous wit still sparkles, but perhaps less frequently than before. The last of our parents to leave us was Mic, just a year ago, and we both miss her incredibly. Her passing means that there remains only her younger sister Canou, now eighty years old, from the original five children of grandmother Minouche. Canou has had a tough last few years with illness and is now a resident of the Retirement Home at Crémieu. Véro looks after her with a lot of love and some considerable patience (mostly directed at the staff of the retirement home). When Covid-19 confinement allows, Canou is a frequent guest at our home. She loves to chat to us about her memories and hear our own from so many years on the road.

We often say, here in France, that the first thing to do when you move to a new home is to plant trees. Do this even before you start to paint or to wallpaper because the longer you delay planting, the longer it will take for the trees to provide their harvest, be it shade, fruit or nuts. As soon as the ink was dry on our purchase contract for our new home in Rix, we drove to a tree nursery and bought fig, apple, pear, bitter and sweet cherry and plum trees and planted them in the best spots in the garden. But more importantly, I went back to our old home in Cordon and dug out the walnut tree that I had planted so many years before. This poor creature had hardly grown an inch since planting because it was overtopped by tall poplar trees on a neighbouring piece of land. It survived but did not thrive; that is until I planted it into an open and well-watered spot on the lower lawn at *Cœur de Rose*. Within two years it had (to quote Boris) got its Mojo back and started to produce kilos of the largest walnuts you can find on the market. In 2019, I collected ten apple boxes full of walnuts and stored them for at least six months in the wine cellar so they would dry and be ready to eat.

In June 2020 the French government allows life to open up slightly after the long three-month period of confinement stimulated by the first wave of Covid-19. Canou has come to stay with us for three days.

I am sitting at a garden table in the shade of our large cherry tree and I have a box of walnuts with nutcrackers at the ready. Canou joins me at the table and asks if she can help. Knowing that her elderly hands are not up to using the nutcrackers, I propose that I crack the nuts and she sorts the kernel from the shells. I warn her that getting through the boxful of nuts will take the whole afternoon.

"No matter", she says, "it's a lovely afternoon and I've always wanted to ask you to tell me about how you and Véro met and your early life together in Africa." The afternoon progresses well; as we chat she asks questions and I reply. When the last walnut is cracked and the kernel extracted, she tells me "you should write all that down."

So I did!

Milton Keynes UK
Ingram Content Group UK Ltd.
UKHW022006011223
433620UK00014B/782